The Ptolemaic Kingdom

A Brief Guide to Egypt's Last Pharaonic Dynasty

B.R. Egginton

Copyright © Ben Egginton 2023

The Ptolemies

Ptolemy I Soter and Berenice I 305-282 BC

Ptolemy II Philadelphus 282-246 BC (ruling with Arsinoe I until c. 273 BC and Arsinoe II c. 273-270/268 BC)

Ptolemy III Euergetes and Berenice II 246-222 BC

Ptolemy IV Philopator 222-204 BC (ruling with Arsinoe III from c. 220 BC)

Ptolemy V Epiphanes 204-180 BC (ruling with Cleopatra I from 194/193 BC)

Ptolemy VI Philometor and Cleopatra I 180-176 BC

Ptolemy VI Philometor and Cleopatra II 176-170 BC

Ptolemy VI Philometor, Ptolemy VIII Euergetes II, and Cleopatra II 170-164 BC

Ptolemy VIII Euergetes II 164-163 BC

Ptolemy VI Philometor and Cleopatra II 163-145 BC

Ptolemy VII Neos Philopator 145-144 BC (reign debated)

Ptolemy VIII Euergetes II and Cleopatra II 145-142 BC

Ptolemy VIII Euergetes II, Cleopatra II and Cleopatra III 142-132 BC

Civil war (Ptolemy VIII Euergetes II and Cleopatra III vs. Cleopatra II) 132-127 BC

Ptolemy VIII Euergetes II and Cleopatra III 127-124 BC

Ptolemy VIII Euergetes II, Cleopatra II and Cleopatra III 124-116 BC

Cleopatra III and Ptolemy IX Soter II 116-107 BC

Cleopatra III and Ptolemy X Alexander I 107-101 BC

Ptolemy X Alexander I and Berenice III 101-88 BC

Ptolemy IX Soter II 88-80 BC

Berenice III and Ptolemy XI Alexander II 80 BC

Ptolemy XII Auletes 80-58 BC (ruling with Cleopatra V 79-69 BC)

Cleopatra V (or Cleopatra VI) and Berenice IV 58-57 BC

Berenice IV 57-55 BC

Ptolemy XII Auletes 55-51 BC (restored)

Cleopatra VII Philopator and Ptolemy XIII 51-47 BC

Cleopatra VII Philopator and Ptolemy XIV 47-44 BC

Cleopatra VII Philopator and Ptolemy XV (Caesarion) 44-30 BC

Contents

Preface	6
Ptolemy I: The Founder	11
Ptolemy II: The 'Sibling-lover'	34
Ptolemy III: The Benefactor	54
Ptolemy IV: The Fratricidal King	65
Ptolemy V: The Boy King	80
Ptolemy VI and Ptolemy VIII: The Warring Siblings	98
Ptolemy IX and Ptolemy X: The Warring Siblings Part 2	130
Berenice III, Ptolemy XI, and Ptolemy XII: Continued Decline	143
Cleopatra VII: Depraved Seductress or Masterful Politician?	158
Epilogue	206

Preface

The House of Ptolemy presided over the final and longest-lasting dynasty of ancient Egypt. It ruled over Egypt for nearly three centuries – from the death of Alexander the Great in 323 BC until the suicide of Cleopatra VII in 30 BC – and had two very different faces. On the one hand, the Ptolemies were infamous for their tendency for murder, intrigue and inbreeding, which makes their story a thrilling and dramatic one. On the other hand, they were generous sponsors of the arts and scholarship. In this capacity, they oversaw the construction of the greatest centre of learning in antiquity and one of the Seven Wonders of the Ancient World, and although both of these are now lost, their contributions to academia are still felt today.

The declining power of pharaonic Egypt over the last millennia of its existence is reflected in it being conquered and ruled by various foreign powers during this time, and the Ptolemaic dynasty was one of these foreign dynasties.[1]

In 332 BC, Alexander the Great conquered Persian-controlled Egypt as part of his campaigns against the Achaemenid Empire. His premature death nine years later at just 32 years of age, with an unborn son and mentally disabled brother as his heirs, caused his vast empire to unravel as quickly as it had been assembled. Initially, Alexander's generals (known as the *Diadochi* or 'Successors') divided the empire between themselves, but were still technically subordinate to the Macedonian crown. However, the weakness of the Macedonian monarchy and the ambition of the generals soon led to many decades of war between Alexander's successors known as the Wars of the Diadochi.

During this conflict some of the *Diadochi* declared themselves to be rulers in their own right. This included the Satrap of Egypt, Ptolemy, and resulted in Alexander's empire being carved up into a number of independent Hellenistic kingdoms. The three most powerful kingdoms that emerged from this were Macedonia, the Seleucid Empire and – you guessed it – the Ptolemaic Kingdom.

Therefore, the Ptolemies were of Macedonian Greek, not Egyptian, origin. Their rule resulted in the blending of Egyptian and Greek cultures and ushered in the last period of Egyptian greatness.

---

[1] The last native ruler of the entirety of Egypt was Nectanebo II, who reigned between 358 and 340 BC. He was defeated by the Persian king Artaxerxes III.

The 'golden age' of Ptolemaic Egypt spanned the reigns of its first three rulers – Ptolemy I, Ptolemy II and Ptolemy III. During this period, the Ptolemies turned Egypt from a Macedonian satrapy into an independent kingdom once more and gained overseas territories that made their kingdom the dominant power in the eastern Mediterranean. This included Cyprus, as well as parts of Libya, Asia Minor and the Levant; and they also used their naval strength (*thalassocracy*) to bring the Aegean into their sphere of influence.

From the late third century BC onwards the Ptolemaic Kingdom went into a long-term – and, as it turned out, *terminal* – decline. This can be attributed to a range of factors, with the most significant ones being domestic unrest, territorial losses to foreign enemies, the emergence of Rome as the preeminent force in the Mediterranean, and infighting within the royal family itself.

In the mid-third century BC, Rome was asked to intervene in the disputes between Ptolemy VI and his brother Ptolemy VIII, and continued to do so thereafter. By seeking to appease the Romans rather than attempting to challenge their growing authority, the Ptolemies managed to cling onto power for many generations to come and outlived the other major Hellenistic kingdoms that had succeeded Alexander's empire. Nevertheless, they were only delaying the inevitable. Over time, the Ptolemaic Kingdom's autonomy was gradually whittled away by the Romans, who sought to exploit Egypt's wealth and resources, until the situation finally came to a head during the reign of the last (and most famous) Ptolemaic ruler – Cleopatra VII.

While Cleopatra's attempts to gain the favour of leading Roman aristocrats – first Julius Caesar, and after his death, Mark Antony – initially made it possible for her to rebuild her ancestors' empire in the eastern Mediterranean, this high-risk strategy had fatal consequences in the long-term. Her love affair with Mark Antony caused Egypt to become entangled in a civil war between Antony and his arch rival, Octavian, and when they came out on the losing side everything went up in flames. Cleopatra took her own life, the Ptolemaic dynasty came to an end, and Egypt was turned into a Roman province.

On the upside, the romantic and tragic legends that blossomed after her death turned Cleopatra into an icon. While most people on the street couldn't name any of her Ptolemaic predecessors, Cleopatra is arguably the most famous woman in ancient history. She remains a household name to this day, and has inspired books, plays, poems, artwork and Hollywood blockbusters through the ages.

*

The challenge of distinguishing one member of the Ptolemaic dynasty from another isn't helped by their names. Every Ptolemaic king was called Ptolemy and the dynasty's queens were confined to three names: Berenice, Arsinoe and Cleopatra. Most ancient sources used the epithets or nicknames of Ptolemaic rulers (such as 'Soter' for Ptolemy I) to make it clear which member of the dynasty they were referring to. More recently, modern academics have given the Ptolemies regnal numbers, as they have done with the monarchs of other Hellenistic dynasties.

The number assigned to each of the Ptolemies is based on the order in which their names appear in the Ptolemaic dynastic cult, although co-regents who never became sole or senior monarchs (such as Ptolemy Epigonos and Ptolemy Eupator) are generally excluded. One possible exception to this is Ptolemy VII, whose identity is unknown. If he was the youngest son of Ptolemy VI, then he may have ruled briefly after his father's death, before his uncle, Ptolemy VIII, took the throne. However, if he was in fact Ptolemy Memphites (a son of Ptolemy VIII), then he never became pharaoh but was posthumously incorporated into the Ptolemaic cult.

In any event, the lack of variation in their names fails to reflect the diversity of their kingdom.

By far the largest group in Ptolemaic society were native Egyptian peasant farmers. They were particularly predominant in rural areas and served as the backbone of the workforce. In return for their toil, they were ruthlessly exploited: having few rights and being expected to pay crippling taxes to fund foreign wars and the extravagance of the Ptolemaic court.

Admittedly, the Egyptian priesthood remained incredibly important, as the Ptolemies relied on their support to legitimise their rule, and from the time of Ptolemy VIII onwards some Egyptians were granted senior posts in government. However, this privileged native Egyptian elite remained relatively small.

Due to the Macedonian origin of the Ptolemies, political, economic and military life in their kingdom was dominated by Greek merchants, generals and officials.

Even before the arrival of Alexander the Great and the Ptolemies there had been a Greek presence in Egypt. Partly as a result of the demise of the Assyrian Empire in the seventh century BC, the Saite dynasty (664-525 BC) had paid increasing attention to the Mediterranean and Greek world.[2] The pharaoh Amasis II (570-526 BC) was friendly towards the Greeks and granted the legal status of polis to the Greek trading post of Naucratis (in the Nile Delta). This close relationship with the Greeks naturally resulted in an influx of Greek soldiers, merchants and tradespeople, which in turn increased Egypt's exposure to Greek culture.

From the reign of Ptolemy I onwards, Macedonians and other Greeks were granted lands for their military service, which encouraged Greek merchants and soldiers to settle in Egypt with their families in far larger numbers than before. In contrast to the native Egyptians, they tended to live in a select few urban areas, such as the capital (Alexandria) and the Greek trading post of Naucratis in Lower Egypt, and the Ptolemaic city of Ptolemais Hermiou in Upper Egypt. Rather than assimilating, they retained their Greek culture, including their language, education, religion and customs. They were citizens of Greek cities and were even tried in Greek courts in accordance with Greek law. None of the Ptolemies bothered to learn the Egyptian language (with the exception of the dynasty's last ruler, Cleopatra VII) and the primary purpose of the complex government bureaucracy they established was to exploit Egypt's seemingly boundless resources for the benefit of the monarch and the Greek ruling class.

While Egyptians and Greeks were the two most prominent ethnic groups in Ptolemaic Egypt, it was also home to many minority groups, of varying importance. These were particularly prominent in urban areas such as Alexandria and included Jews, Syrians, Carians, Nubians and Phoenicians, as well as Germanic and Celtic peoples. Like the Greek population, there was a significant increase in Jewish immigration to Egypt during the Ptolemaic period. They were given their own neighbourhood in the capital and many Jews played an important role in the Ptolemaic military.

Because the Ptolemies were foreigners who had taken control of Egypt by force, they were constantly threatened by the prospect of native rebellions and went to great lengths to legitimise their claim to the Egyptian throne. In artwork they presented themselves to their native Egyptian subjects as traditional pharaohs and reinforced this image by deifying themselves. They also carried out traditional pharaonic duties, such as presiding over Egyptian religious rituals, and they secured the support of the powerful priestly elite by granting them special privileges and sponsoring cults and temples throughout Egypt. By far the most controversial measure they took, however, was their adoption of the ancient pharaonic practice of sibling marriage, which does

---

[2] The Saite dynasty was of Libyan origin and based in Sais.

not seem to have caused any genetic issues but certainly created a very confusing family tree.

As time would tell, such gestures were not sufficient to prevent social unrest and native uprisings from becoming a common occurrence, especially when Ptolemaic power started to decline from the late third century BC onwards. By exploiting Egypt's extensive natural resources and taking full advantage of its strategic geographical position to promote commercial activity, their kingdom became fabulously wealthy. But this wealth and power was concentrated in the hands of the Greek ruling class, leaving native Egyptian peasant farmers as second-class citizens in their own land. They had vanquished their unpopular Parthian overlords, only to end up with a new oppressor in the form of the Ptolemies. And when the Ptolemies fell in turn, the poor fortune of the Egyptian people was extended for many centuries to come – courtesy of the Roman Empire.

For someone who didn't have to live under the yoke of the Ptolemies though, it is a wonder to look back on. The Ptolemaic dynasty deserves to be recognised as one of the most important periods in human history. The foundations of many academic disciplines we take for granted in the present day were laid in Ptolemaic Alexandria. The demise of the Ptolemaic Kingdom brought 3,000 years of Egyptian pharaonic tradition to an end and ushered in the equally momentous age of the Roman emperors. Some of the most noticeable names in human history lived at the time – Alexander the Great, Herod, Pompey, Cicero, Julius Caesar, Mark Antony, Augustus, and Cleopatra to name just a few. And then there are the stories: tales of treachery, betrayal, intrigue, romance, bloodshed and tragedy. All of these things await you in the chapters that follow. So put on your seatbelt and get ready to enter the glamorous, dramatic and downright nasty lives of the Ptolemies.

Ptolemy I: The Founder

The founder, namesake and first ruler of Ptolemaic Egypt – Ptolemy I Soter – was not descended from the pharaohs or even an Egyptian. Born in Macedonia (in northern Greece) in about 367 BC, Ptolemy made a name for himself as a trusted companion and general of Alexander the Great. During his long and eventful life of over 80 years, he participated in Alexander's epic Asian campaigns, contributed to the dismantlement of the vast intercontinental empire this created after the death of his king, gained control of Egypt, established a dynasty that would endure for three centuries – and somehow managed to die peacefully!

Ptolemy was the son of a Macedonian noblewoman named Arsinoe of Macedon and a Macedonian courtier from Eordaea called Lagus, who came from a relatively undistinguished family. Some sources claim that Ptolemy's father was really the Macedonian king Philip II, on the basis that Arsinoe had been one of his concubines prior to her marriage to Lagus. If this is true, then Ptolemy would have been a half-brother of Alexander the Great, but it is likely that this version of events is little more than a myth that was fabricated to glorify and legitimise the Ptolemaic dynasty. Nevertheless, it is believed that Ptolemy at least had links to Macedonia's ruling house (the Argead dynasty) through Arsinoe, who is said to have been a descendant of the fifth century BC Macedonian ruler Alexander I (and in turn the Greek hero Heracles).

Ptolemy was probably raised and educated as a page at the Macedonian royal court. Here he became a close friend of King Philip II's son (and eventual successor), Alexander the Great, despite being over a decade older than him.

Because of the significant age difference, he may have served as some sort of advisor to the royal prince. According to one anecdote, Ptolemy advised Alexander to intervene in a marriage alliance Philip II had arranged between his son Arrhidaeus (the future Philip III of Macedon) and the daughter of Pixodarus (the Persian satrap of Caria).

The marriage was arranged after the Macedonian victory against a coalition of Greek city-states (led by Athens and Thebes) at the Battle of Chaeronea (in 338 BC). Until this point Alexander had been regarded as being next in line to the throne, on the basis that Arrhidaeus (his elder half-brother) had learning difficulties. However, this latest development made Alexander feel insecure. He interpreted it as a sign that his father intended to name Arrhidaeus as his heir and had arranged the marriage so his eldest son could produce heirs first.

Alexander responded to this perceived threat to his inheritance by sending an eminent actor named Thessalus to persuade Pixodarus to offer his daughter's hand in marriage to him instead.

When Philip learned of his son's intervention, he was furious. He called off the marriage negotiations and scolded Alexander, saying he wanted him to have a far more high profile bride than the one he had been arranging for Arrhidaeus. Philip then exiled Ptolemy, along with various other friends of Alexander (including Harpalus, Nearchus, Erigyius and Laomedon) for the role they had played in his son's intrigues.[3]

Soon after Ptolemy's banishment, in 337 BC, Alexander went into a self-imposed exile. This followed Philip's decision to marry Cleopatra Eurydice (the niece of his general Attalus), who it was hoped would bear him a fully Macedonian heir, as opposed to Alexander who was only half Macedonian.[4] However, given that Alexander was full-grown and trained in the arts of politics and war, there is every reason to believe Philip never intended to disown him, and within about six months Alexander had been persuaded to return to Macedonia.

Shortly after his return, in the summer of 336 BC, Philip II was assassinated by one of his bodyguards, Pausanias of Orestis. Immediately after this, Alexander had himself declared king and wasted no time eliminating any potential threats to his rule. The victims included his cousin Amyntas IV, the general Attalus, and possibly his half-brother Caranus, although he spared his mentally disabled half-brother Arrhidaeus.

Alexander spent virtually his entire 13-year-long reign fighting military campaigns that would take him as far as India. However, before he was able to embark on the grand conquests for which he became famous, his attention was required closer to home. Between 336 and 335 BC the new Macedonian king was kept busy suppressing revolts in various Greek states to the south of Macedonia and numerous Thracian tribes to the north, which had broken out when they received news of Philip's death. As a close confidant of Alexander, Ptolemy took part in these campaigns, although he did not become one of Alexander's leading generals until his conquests had reached Afghanistan and India many years later.

---

[3] Ptolemy did not return to Macedonia until Alexander became king in 336 BC.
[4] Alexander's mother, Olympias, came from Epirus.

Once the revolts had been taken care of and Alexander was secure at home, he was free to set out on his renowned Asian expedition. This began with the Macedonian conquest of the Greek world's most formidable foe – the Achaemenid (Persian) Empire.

Over the past century and a half the Greeks and Persians had fought for supremacy in the Aegean and Anatolia. At first the Greek resistance had been led by the Greek world's two most powerful city-states, Athens and Sparta, but by the time of Alexander the Great's birth Macedonia had become the pre-eminent power in Greece and inherited the responsibility of countering the Persian threat.

Before his death, Philip II had been planning a campaign against Persia: to free various Greek cities from Persian rule, address sundry grievances, and avenge Xerxes I's invasion of Greece (480-479 BC). Alexander shared his father's ambition and was now determined to follow through with these plans.

While he suppressed the Greek revolts against his authority, Alexander secured recognition throughout Greece as the leader of the League of Corinth. The League had been formed by his father as a means of unifying Greek military forces under Macedonian hegemony for his anticipated conquest of Persia – and now it would fulfil its purpose.

In the spring of 334 BC Alexander sailed across the Hellespont and landed in Anatolia. Marching south through Persian territory with his army, he confronted Persian forces at the Battle of the Granicus. Fought in May in north-west Asia Minor, the Macedonians prevailed in the battle and continued their campaigning in Anatolia throughout 334 and 333 BC. During this period, in the summer and autumn of 334 BC, Ptolemy is believed to have taken part in Alexander's siege of Halicarnassus (in south-west Asia Minor), where the besieged forces were being commanded by a Greek mercenary-commander in the service of Persia called Memnon of Rhodes. After the siege reached a successful conclusion, Alexander is said to have left Ptolemy with 3,000 troops to secure the city while the Macedonian king marched on to Gordion.[5]

---

[5] Gordion is best known for being home to a knot that was supposedly impossible to untangle. According to Ancient Greek legend, an oracle declared that whoever managed to untie the Gordian Knot would become the ruler of the entirety of Asia. When Alexander arrived in the city in 333 BC, he is said to have solved the riddle by cutting through the knot with his sword.

Alexander's campaigning in Anatolia culminated in a second pitched battle between the Macedonian and Persian armies at Issus (in November 333 BC), during which Ptolemy served on the left wing under the command of Alexander's chief general, Parmenion.[6]

Unlike the Battle of the Granicus, Alexander found himself facing a Persian army that was led by its king, Darius III. However, Darius' presence did not prevent his forces from suffering another major defeat that marked the beginning of the end for the Achaemenid Empire.

While the Persian king himself managed to escape the battlefield, many prominent members of the royal family were captured as a result of the debacle at Issus. This included his wife, Stateira I, his daughters, Stateira II and Drypetis, and his mother, Sisygambis, and dealt a severe blow to his prestige.

Alexander spent the majority of 332 BC besieging and capturing the cities of Tyre and Gaza, before marching his army into Persian-controlled Egypt late that year. He installed a garrison at the key border fortress of Pelusium without any issues and encountered little resistance from the Persian occupiers as he advanced into Egypt. The satrap of Egypt had departed his province with a large force to take part in the Battle of Issus and had died in the fighting. Consequently, the Persians did not have enough troops left in Egypt to challenge Alexander's invasion and the newly-appointed satrap, Mazaces, surrendered. Nor was Alexander opposed by the Egyptian population, who lacked a native hero to rid themselves of their despised Persian overlords and regarded Alexander as the lesser of two evils.[7]

With the exception of his nationality, Alexander possessed the right traits to be an effective pharaoh: a ruthless tyrant and proven winner, who was worthy of both fear and respect. The Egyptian people looked back on their country's long-lost glory days with nostalgia, and if anyone could provide them with the victory they were yearning for, it was Alexander.

Upon arriving in the Egyptian capital, Memphis, Alexander appeased the local population by paying his respects to the sacred Apis bull. By honouring Egypt's

---

[6] Parmenion had previously served in a similar role for Philip II.
[7] Egypt had been conquered by the Persian king Cambyses II in 525 BC. Although the Persian occupation was ended in 404 BC when a native Egyptian named Amyrtaeus seized the throne, Egypt was reconquered by the Persians in about 340 BC.

ancient customs and religious practices, he hoped to give the impression that he was a liberator rather than yet another conqueror, as well as to present himself as a traditional Egyptian pharaoh and in turn legitimise his rule. This contrasted with the actions of the Persian king Cambyses II, who some sources claim committed acts of sacrilege by defiling royal tombs, looting temples, mocking local Egyptian gods, and even killing the Apis bull.

Now Egypt was under Alexander's control, he did something rather surprising. Instead of heading east to continue his war against Darius without delay, he travelled west – embarking on a 300 mile trek through the Sahara Desert to visit the famed oracle of Zeus-Ammon in the Siwa Oasis.[8] Ptolemy accompanied his king on this famous excursion, and when they finally arrived at the Siwa Oasis the oracle is said to have proclaimed Alexander a son of Zeus (Ammon). This helped to legitimise his rule in Egypt given that the pharaohs were regarded as being divine representatives of the gods on Earth.

In the spring of 331 BC, Alexander departed Egypt. Before he did so, he founded a city on Egypt's Mediterranean coast near the existing settlement of Rhacotis. Named Alexandria, it was one of many new cities he would name after himself, although with the benefit of hindsight this Alexandria was destined to outshine all the others. Alexander is said to have personally drawn up the initial plans, which set the city out on a grid system and determined the location of the market square and various temples. Of course he wouldn't have had the time to oversee such an extensive project himself, so the majority of the urban planning was delegated to a Greek architect named Dinocrates of Rhodes.

Ptolemy remained with Alexander after his departure from Egypt and took part in the Macedonian king's decisive victory against the Persians at the Battle of Gaugamela. Fought in October 331 BC, near Erbil (in present-day Iraq), it dealt the final blow to Darius III and opened the floodgates for the complete conquest of the Achaemenid Empire. This was symbolised in 330 BC when the ceremonial capital of the Achaemenid Empire, Persepolis, was captured and burned by Alexander's forces.

---

[8] During this journey, Alexander stopped at Paraitónion (present-day Marsa Matruh) on Egypt's Mediterranean coast. Here he received an envoy from the Greek city of Cyrene (in Libya), which brought gifts and formed an alliance with the Macedonian king that guaranteed their city's status as a free and independent polis.

Plutarch asserts in his *Life of Alexander* that an Athenian *hetaira* named Thaïs convinced Alexander to reduce his fallen enemy's palace to ashes after giving a speech during a party: *'As the drinking went on, Thaïs delivered a speech which was intended partly as a graceful compliment to Alexander and partly to amuse him. What she said was typical of the spirit of Athens, but hardly in keeping with her own situation. She declared that all the hardships she had endured in wandering about Asia had been amply repaid on that day, when she found herself revelling luxuriously in the splendid palace of the Persians, but that it would be an even sweeter pleasure to end the party by going out and setting fire to the palace of Xerxes, who had laid Athens in ashes. She wanted to put a torch to the building herself in full view of Alexander, so that posterity should know that the women who followed Alexander had taken a more terrible revenge for the wrongs of Greece than all the famous commanders of earlier times by land or sea. Her speech was greeted with wild applause and the king's companions excitedly urged him on until at last he allowed himself to be persuaded, leaped to his feet, and with a garland on his head and a torch in his hand led the way.'*

This anecdote cemented Thaïs' place in history, and she is also well-known for being Ptolemy's lover. The couple had three children together – Lagus, Leontiscus and Eirene – and may have even married, although it has been suggested that she might have had romantic relations with Alexander too.

Ptolemy married at least three times during his life. His first confirmed marriage was to the Persian noblewoman Artakama. This took place in 324 BC when Alexander arranged a mass wedding in the Persian city of Susa (appropriately referred to as the 'Susa weddings'), during which the Macedonian king and his officers took Persian wives as part of an attempt to unite the Greek conquerors and the subjugated Persians.[9] This policy was not popular amongst the Macedonian nobility, most of whom divorced their wives after Alexander's death. Ptolemy is not known to have fathered any children by Artakama and there is no mention of her after Alexander died, which suggests Ptolemy quietly disposed of his wife before he set out from Babylon to take control of Egypt.

Ptolemy's second confirmed marriage was to Eurydice (a daughter of the Macedonian regent Antipater) with whom he had four known children – Ptolemy Ceraunus,

---

[9] At the same time as the Susa weddings, Ptolemy was appointed *edeatros* ('taster') of the royal food, which was presumably a prestigious title used in the Persian royal court.

Meleager, Ptolemais and Lysandra – and perhaps a fifth as well. They are believed to have been married at some point between 322 and 319 BC, and their two eldest children (Ptolemy Ceraunus and Meleager) went on to briefly serve as kings of Macedonia.

Ptolemy is believed to have dissolved his marriage to Eurydice at some point before he married his final wife, Berenice I, although the assertion that Ptolemy practiced polygamy and had a relationship with Eurydice and Berenice I concurrently cannot be ruled out.

Berenice I was Eurydice's second cousin and lady-in-waiting, and had already been in a romantic relationship with Ptolemy before their wedding in 317 BC. She had three children by her previous marriage to a Macedonian nobleman named Philip (Magas, Antigone and Theoxena) and also bore Ptolemy three children (Arsinoe II, Philotera and Ptolemy II Philadelphus), the youngest of whom eventually succeeded his father as king of Egypt.

*

Near the end of 330 BC Ptolemy was appointed as one of Alexander's seven *somatophylakes* (bodyguards), following an alleged conspiracy against the Macedonian king. By now he was clearly a rising star and secured his first independent command soon thereafter when Alexander sent him to apprehend the satrap and self-proclaimed Persian king, Bessus.

Bessus had murdered Darius III and attempted to hold the eastern part of the Achaemenid Empire against the Macedonians, but this all ended in tears when he was arrested by his own officers and surrendered into Ptolemy's custody. Ptolemy in turn handed Bessus over to Alexander in a particularly humiliating fashion – bound in chains and completely naked except for a dog collar – although the worst part was yet to come. In no mood for mercy, Alexander had Bessus publicly flogged and his ears and nose chopped off (a common Persian practice) before sending him off for execution at some point in 329 BC.

The following year, Ptolemy further distinguished himself by helping to crush an uprising by the Sogdians, and in early 327 BC he took part in Alexander's successful siege of the Sogdian Rock (a fortress in Sogdiana, or present-day Tajikistan).[10] As one

---

[10] The Sogdians were led by the warlord Spitamenes, who had played an instrumental role in

of Alexander's bodyguards, he was also involved in the discovery of a conspiracy among Alexander's pages to murder their king. This had been provoked by Alexander's decision to punish one of his pages, Hermolaus, for killing a wild boar during a hunt without allowing him to deliver the first blow. With the encouragement of his intimate friend and *eromenos* Sostratus, Hermolaus formed a scheme with various other pages to murder Alexander while he slept (as it was the duty of the pages to guard the king's bedchamber). Before the plan could be put into action though, they were exposed and those implicated in the plot were stoned to death.

In the years that followed, Ptolemy became an increasingly prominent figure. He held important commands during Alexander's Cophen campaign (327-326 BC) in present-day Pakistan, which aimed to secure their lines of communication before they launched an invasion of India proper. As part of this, he commanded the advance guard during Alexander's successful siege of Aornos (in April 326 BC).

In the winter of 326/325 BC, Ptolemy was involved in Alexander's campaign against the Mallians (in Punjab), during which the region was successfully pacified but Alexander was seriously injured and Ptolemy had a brush with death in a separate encounter. According to an anecdote (of doubtful truth) recorded by Diodorus of Sicily, Ptolemy was wounded by a poisoned arrow along the southern Indus while fighting the Brahmins. The wound was feared to be fatal, until he was miraculously healed by none other than Alexander the Great, who made an antidote using various native herbs after dreaming of a snake that showed him a plant that could be used to counter its venom. This story is generally regarded as a piece of propaganda aimed at emphasising the close friendship between the Macedonian king and the founder of the Ptolemaic dynasty.

At some point during Alexander's campaigns in Pakistan and India, Ptolemy became friends with an Indian gymnosophist named Kalanos. 'Gymnosophist' was a term used by the Greeks to refer to Indian philosophers who practiced a form of asceticism that was so extreme they even considered food and clothing to be detrimental to purity of thought. Kalanos also became close to Alexander, who persuaded him to accompany him and his men to Persis (Persia) upon their departure from India. A few years later (at Susa in 323 BC) Kalanos had grown increasingly weak from his travels and old age, and famously decided to take his own life by self-immolation. Although Alexander tried to persuade him not to follow through with this, Kalanos insisted he

---

Bessus' removal from power.

wanted to die and Ptolemy was assigned the grim task of building the pyre on which Kalanos was burned.

Shortly after this, Ptolemy served as Alexander's second-in-command in what turned out to be the last campaign of the Macedonian conqueror's eventful life. This was fought against a nomadic tribe called the Cossaeans (from what is now Lorestan province in Iran).

By the time of Alexander the Great's sudden and unexpected death – aged just 32 years old, at Babylon in June 323 BC – he had established an empire that stretched from Greece all the way to India. However, while his name would live on for posterity, his life's work started to fall apart almost from the moment he stopped breathing.

Without a strong and imposing adult male heir to succeed him, Alexander's senior generals started carving up the empire between themselves in a series of agreements. The first of these conferences took place immediately after Alexander's death and is known as the Partition of Babylon. This resulted in Alexander's feeble-minded half-brother (Philip III) and his unborn child with Roxana (if it turned out to be a male) being proclaimed joint kings of Macedonia, while Alexander's cavalry commander and *chiliarch* (vizier) Perdiccas was appointed as their regent.[11][12] The rest of the empire was divided into satrapies, many of which were given to Alexander's senior officers to govern. Ptolemy became satrap of Egypt, as he had wanted, and the previous satrap (a Greek man named Cleomenes) remained as his deputy.[13]

Ptolemy might have earned his reputation as a reliable and cautious military commander, but in the years and decades that followed he also revealed himself to be a master of politics and diplomacy. From the moment of Alexander's death, Ptolemy was convinced that it would be impossible to maintain the empire as a single unified entity, and was a leading advocate of the empire's division between the generals. He was well aware from his visit to Egypt with Alexander that it was the wealthiest part of the empire, as well as the easiest to defend, which were ideal foundations on which to build a powerful and independent kingdom.

---

[11] Alexander the Great's wife, Roxana, gave birth to a son named Alexander IV in late 323 BC or early 322 BC.

[12] It was necessary for a regent to be appointed due to the fact that Philip III was mentally ill and Alexander IV was an infant.

[13] Cleomenes was from the Greek trading post of Naucratis (in the western Nile Delta, Egypt).

These separatist ambitions conflicted with the interests of Perdiccas, who had received the king's signet ring on his deathbed and wanted to keep the empire intact, under the overall rule of his regency government.

Under the terms of the Partition of Babylon, Ptolemy and the other satraps technically answered to Philip III and Alexander IV (and in turn their regent Perdiccas), but that did not discourage Ptolemy from annexing Cyrenaica (eastern Libya) without authorisation in 322 BC. Prior to the annexation, Ptolemy had received a request for assistance off Cyrene's oligarchs, who had been forced into exile. Sensing an opportunity to expand his power and influence, Ptolemy agreed to support them and intervened in the civil war by dispatching his general Ophellas to retake the city. The defenders were allied with a Spartan mercenary commander named Thibron, who ultimately failed to prevent Cyrene from falling to Ophellas' forces. Thibron managed to escape but did not remain at large for long and was captured and executed in the Cyrenian city of Taucheira. Meanwhile, the exiled oligarchs returned to Cyrene and Ophellas captured the rest of Cyrenaica. He probably secured his position by establishing garrisons in the territory and spent the next decade and a half serving as the governor of Cyrenaica on Ptolemy's behalf.[14] This territorial acquisition removed any doubt that Ptolemy would not allow his ambitions to be kept in check by the Macedonian monarchy's overlordship. Nor did it deter him from giving orders for Alexander the Great's body to be seized in Damascus.

The remains of the great conqueror had been embalmed at Babylon after his death, but it had taken two years to make the funeral carriage and the royal corpse had only recently started the long journey to its final resting place.

Ptolemy had no intention of allowing the funeral cortège to continue to its intended destination of Aigai (in Macedonia), where Perdiccas planned to have Alexander entombed alongside his predecessors. Instead, he gave orders for it to be seized and diverted to Egypt.

Given that Alexander had asked to be interred in the temple of Zeus-Ammon at the Siwa Oasis shortly before his death, Ptolemy had some justification for this action.

---

[14] Ptolemy is reported to have visited Cyrene in 321 or 320 BC to negotiate a settlement aimed at ending the continued resistance against the Ptolemaic occupation of Cyrenaica. Under the new constitutional arrangement that was agreed, Cyrene lost its status as a free city and Ptolemy exerted supreme authority over the territory, but the Egyptian satrap appeased the oligarchs he had assisted in the civil war by allowing them to regain their local authority.

However, it was clearly self-interest that prompted him to do this, because instead of abiding by the late king's wishes he gave orders for him to be laid to rest in Memphis (the traditional capital of the pharaohs) instead.

Possession of Alexander's remains allowed Ptolemy to brand himself as Alexander's true successor and to legitimise his rule in Egypt. Unfortunately, everyone else wanted to get their hands on the great conqueror's body for the same reason, and Perdiccas retaliated by launching an invasion of Egypt in 321 BC.

While Perdiccas hoped to assert his authority as the dominant figure in the empire, the campaign had the opposite outcome. When his forces reached the Nile, they were prevented from crossing the river by Ptolemy's army and lost approximately 2,000 troops in the process. Soon after this setback, a mutiny broke out in Perdiccas' camp and he was murdered by his own officers. These officers then offered to make Ptolemy the new Regent of Macedonia, but he prudently declined the offer – deciding it would be wiser to focus on securing his power base in Egypt rather than risking everything to inherit Alexander's empire.

As part of this policy, Ptolemy accused Cleomenes of spying for Perdiccas and had him executed. However, this decision probably had more to do with Ptolemy's desire to dispose of the main check on his authority in Egypt and to take possession of Cleomenes' vast wealth.

To say the least, Cleomenes would not have been missed by the Egyptian people, who despised the former satrap. During his time in office he had abused his position in every way possible: amassing vast quantities of wealth by manipulating the country's lucrative grain trade, and extorting money from merchants, priests and government officials. Alexander the Great had turned a blind eye to the complaints made about Cleomenes' conduct, but there was no one to protect him now and he paid for his greed with his life.

*

For the next four decades Alexander's empire was plagued by a series of conflicts between his former generals, known as the Wars of the Diadochi (or 'Successors'). As has already been indicated, Ptolemy's primary concern during this struggle for supremacy was to secure Egypt by improving domestic administration and winning over the native population, as well as to strengthen Egypt's frontiers by gaining control of the territories around it – namely Cyrenaica, Cyprus and Syria.

The death of Perdiccas left a void at the head of the empire's government and prompted Alexander's successors (*Diadochi*) to meet at Triparadisus (in present-day Lebanon) to negotiate a new power sharing agreement. Under the terms of this settlement the veteran general Antipater was appointed as the new Regent of Macedonia and the division of the empire's satrapies between the *Diadochi* was revised. This included Perdiccas' former deputy (and one of his assassins) Seleucus receiving Babylon and the veteran general Antigonus being named satrap of Greater Phrygia and *strategos* of Asia (as well as being tasked with defeating Perdiccas' ally Eumenes, who was condemned to death).[15] Meanwhile, Ptolemy's possession of Egypt and Cyrenaica was confirmed, which legitimised his annexation of the latter territory, and sometime after this he further strengthened his position by marrying Eurydice (a daughter of Antipater).

Antipater was about 80 years old when he became regent and died a short while afterwards in the autumn of 319 BC, which set the stage for yet more conflict. While on his deathbed, he decided to leave the regency to his friend and lieutenant Polyperchon rather than his son Cassander, triggering a prolonged power struggle over the regency. This came to a head in 317 BC when Philip III and his domineering wife Eurydice (both allies of Cassander) were captured by Olympias (Alexander the Great's mother and an ally of Polyperchon), who had Philip III executed and forced Eurydice to commit suicide. Olympias was then able to install herself as Alexander IV's regent, but had a taste of her own medicine soon thereafter when she was deposed and executed by Cassander in 316 or early 315 BC. This enabled Cassander to take her place as regent, and he strengthened his hold on the kingdom by having Alexander IV and his mother Roxanna imprisoned in the citadel of Amphipolis.

While Macedonia was being torn apart by civil war, Ptolemy was busy consolidating his power.

In 318 BC Ptolemy capitalised on the death of Antipater by occupying Syria and Phoenicia, and establishing a protectorate over the rulers of Cyprus. This was part of his policy of creating a buffer zone around Egypt to protect his satrapy, although he would have to fight long and hard to maintain control of these territorial acquisitions in the years that followed.

---

[15] Antigonus' campaign against Eumenes was a lengthy one. While the Partition of Triparadisus took place in 321 BC, it was not until the winter of 316/315 BC that Eumenes was captured and executed.

When Antigonus finally succeeded in defeating and executing Eumenes in the winter of 316/315 BC he was able to redirect his resources to expand his power in the East. As part of these efforts, he travelled to Babylon (in the summer of 315 BC), where he demanded that its satrap, Seleucus, hand over his province's income. Seleucus refused but became so scared that his defiance would cost him his life that he fled to Alexandria. Here, he received a warm welcome from the Egyptian ruler and formed a coalition against Antigonus with Ptolemy, Cassander and Lysimachus, who all regarded Antigonus' actions as an attempt to bring Alexander's empire under his overall control.

Upon the outbreak of war, Ptolemy evacuated Syria and had to fight against various Cypriot city-kingdoms that sought to oppose Ptolemaic domination on their island by allying themselves with Antigonus. Thanks to the combined efforts of Seleucus, Menelaus (Ptolemy's brother) and Nicocreon (the king of Salamis), Antigonus' supporters on Cyprus were neutralised in 313 BC. As a long-term ally of the Egyptian satrap, Nicocreon was rewarded by Ptolemy for his contribution by being made *strategos* of the entire island and awarded personal command of the Cypriot cities of Citium, Lapithos, Keryneia and Marion.[16]

In the same year as Cyprus was conquered, a revolt broke out in Cyrenaica against Ptolemaic rule. During this period of unrest the rebels besieged the garrison on the citadel, but Ptolemy dispatched an army and fleet that succeeded in restoring order in the summer of 312 BC.

By this time, Ptolemy was finally able to switch from defence to offence, and launched a joint invasion of Syria with Seleucus aimed at regaining lost territory. This culminated in the Battle of Gaza (in the autumn of 312 BC), during which Ptolemy and Seleucus defeated Antigonus' son Demetrius I.

Off the back of this victory, Seleucus departed to reclaim his province of Babylonia, while Ptolemy reoccupied Syria. Unfortunately for Ptolemy, he only held onto Syria for a few months and was forced to evacuate the territory once again when Antigonus responded to Demetrius' pleas for assistance by arriving with a large army.

Meanwhile, Seleucus was ultimately successful in regaining control of his territories from Antigonus and Demetrius in the Babylonian War (311-309 BC), which marked

---

[16] Menelaus was appointed *strategos* of Cyprus after Nicocreon's death in 311 or 310 BC.

the birth of the Seleucid Empire and effectively ended the possibility of Alexander the Great's empire being reunified.

Shortly after peace was agreed between the two sides (allowing Antigonus to consolidate his power in the West and Seleucus to secure his position in the East), Macedonia's 13-year-old king, Alexander IV, was murdered along with his mother Roxana. This was carried out on the orders of Cassander, who had no intention of giving up his powers as regent when the king turned 14. Most importantly of all though, the death of the Macedonian king meant Ptolemy was now his own master.

The fragile peace agreed in 309 BC soon fell apart when Ptolemy and Cassander renewed hostilities against Antigonus on the pretext that Antigonus had installed garrisons in some free Greek cities. Later that year, Ptolemy led a fleet that seized towns along the coast of Lycia and Caria from Antigonus, which he branded as a campaign of 'liberation' but was really an attempt to gain influence and territory in Asia Minor. He then sailed to Greece, where he established garrisons in the city-states of Corinth, Sicyon and Megara in 308 BC (which contradicted his policy of 'liberation'). But offence can go two ways and Antigonus sent his son Demetrius to invade Cyprus with a large fleet in 306 BC. The island was being used by Ptolemy as a base for launching raids against Antigonus along the coasts of Asia Minor and the Levant, and the Antigonid ruler intended to neutralise this threat.

Demetrius' invasion culminated in the Battle of Salamis. During this engagement Ptolemy's brother Menelaus (who had been charged with defending Cyprus and ended up being besieged in Salamis) was compelled to surrender, while Ptolemy's rescue expedition was routed. Much of Ptolemy's army and fleet was destroyed or captured, and the rest fled back to Egypt, allowing the Antigonids to capture Cyprus.

As if this wasn't bad enough, Ptolemy also temporarily lost control of Cyrenaica at around this time, and was unable to maintain possession of Corinth, Sicyon and Megara.

*

Shortly after his son's victory on Cyprus, Antigonus gave both himself and Demetrius the title of 'king', which essentially meant he was declaring himself to be the rightful successor to Alexander's empire. He was able to do this as the Macedonian throne had been vacant since Alexander IV's murder, and his rivals – Ptolemy (Egypt), Cassander (Macedonia), Lysimachus (Thrace) and Seleucus (Seleucid Empire) – responded by forming an alliance against Antigonus and proclaiming themselves kings of their respective domains too. Ptolemy became pharaoh in approximately 305 BC (although his coronation feast is believed to have taken place in 304 BC) and moved Egypt's capital from Memphis to the newly-built city of Alexandria on the country's Mediterranean coast. One of his first acts as pharaoh was to order the construction of a lavish new tomb for Alexander the Great in Alexandria, where his body was reinterred in a golden coffin and served as the focal point for Alexander's cult.

Unfortunately, such grand gestures would not keep Ptolemy safe from his enemies. Between late October and November 306 BC Antigonus attempted to build on his son's victory in Cyprus by launching an invasion of Egypt. During this campaign Demetrius was placed in command of an invasion fleet, while Antigonus led an army from Gaza and into the Nile Delta. The plan was to launch a direct attack on Alexandria, but Ptolemy prevented Demetrius from landing and Antigonus' forces failed to penetrate Egypt's defences. Because of this, the campaign came to nothing and was swiftly abandoned, but Antigonus inflicted heavy losses on the Ptolemaic army and succeeded in deterring Ptolemy from leading any further overseas expeditions against him.

Nevertheless, Ptolemy continued to indirectly oppose Antigonid power, such as by offering significant assistance to Rhodes when it was besieged by Demetrius in 305-304 BC. As a mercantile republic and major commercial centre, Rhodes tried to remain neutral to protect its trade interests, but had a close relationship with Ptolemaic Egypt. With this in mind, Demetrius may have feared that the Rhodians would provide Ptolemy with ships or allow him to use their island as a military base. By conquering Rhodes, he would also cause significant disruption to the Egyptian economy, given that the island was one of the main trading centres for Egyptian grain and shipped a wide variety of goods to Egypt.

However, things did not turn out the way he hoped. The siege was ultimately lifted and the thankful Rhodians bestowed the nickname Soter ('Savior') upon Ptolemy and established a cult in his honour to show their gratitude for the support he had given them. They also erected a statue of Helios (the Greek sun god) at the entrance to the harbour between 292 and 280 BC to commemorate the successful defence of Rhodes. Known as the Colossus of Rhodes, it was the tallest statue in the ancient world (at approximately 108 feet high) and was one of the Seven Wonders of the Ancient World.[17]

*

The coalition against Antigonus was reformed in 302 BC at the request of Cassander, who had been driven from central Greece by Demetrius and was now at risk of losing Macedonia too. Lysimachus launched an invasion of Antigonus' power base in Asia Minor from Thrace, with assistance from Cassander's general Prepelaus, prompting Antigonus to recall Demetrius from Greece. Meanwhile, Seleucus marched with an army through Mesopotamia and Cappadocia to join forces with his allies.

While Antigonus was preoccupied dealing with Lysimachus in Asia Minor, Ptolemy lunged at the opportunity to invade the southern part of Syria once again in 302 BC. Ptolemy did withdraw from the territory when he received a report that Antigonus had won a decisive victory, but soon reoccupied southern Syria when he learned Antigonus had been defeated and killed by the combined forces of Lysimachus, Seleucus, Prepalaus and Pleistarchus (Cassander's brother) at the Battle of Ipsus in 301 BC. Any hope of Alexander the Great's empire being reformed died with Antigonus. The allied rulers accepted their domains were separate kingdoms, independent of each other, and most of Antigonus' territories ended up being taken over by Lysimachus and Seleucus.[18]

The three main successor states to Alexander's empire were the Ptolemaic Kingdom (Egypt, Cyrenaica and Cyprus), the Seleucid Empire (southern Anatolia, the Near East, Mesopotamia and Persia), and Macedonia itself.

During their attempt to define the boundaries of their respective domains, a dispute broke out between Ptolemy and Seleucus over southern Syria. The other members of the alliance against Antigonus had assigned the entirety of Syria to Seleucus (in response to what they regarded as Ptolemy's desertion during their final campaign against Antigonus), but the southern part of the territory had been occupied by Ptolemaic forces.[19] Eager to avoid a costly war and in recognition of his friendship with Ptolemy, Seleucus did not take any military action to reclaim the part of Syria

---

[17] The Colossus of Rhodes was constructed by the Greek sculptor Chares of Lindos. Much of the material used in its construction came from weapons Demetrius' army had left behind. The statue didn't remain standing for long as it was toppled by an earthquake in 226 BC. According to the Ancient Greek scholar Strabo, Ptolemy III offered to fund its reconstruction, but the offer was turned down after an oracle warned the people of Rhodes not to rebuild it.
[18] Demetrius survived the Battle of Ipsus and ended up seizing control of Macedonia in 294 BC.
[19] In addition to Coele-Syria, Ptolemy also occupied Pamphylia, Lycia, and part of Pisidia (in southern Asia Minor).

Ptolemy's forces were occupying and a compromise was negotiated, although he never surrendered his kingdom's rights to the region and the issue continued to simmer. Consequently, after Ptolemy and Seleucus had died possession of southern Syria would cause recurring warfare between the Seleucid Empire and Ptolemaic Kingdom for over a century (known collectively as the Syrian Wars).

Ptolemaic Syria was officially known as the province of 'Syria and Phoenicia', but is more commonly referred to as 'Coele-Syria' in the present day. It was the second largest foreign possession of the Ptolemaic Kingdom (with Cyrenaica being the largest) and served as a buffer zone to protect Egypt. Additionally, possession of this region gave the Ptolemies access to valuable natural resources (namely Lebanon's cedar trees) and agricultural products such as grain, oil and wine, as well as the ability to control the caravan routes from Saudi Arabia, which terminated at the ports of Coele-Syria.

In about 300 BC, Ptolemy appointed his stepson Magas as the governor of Cyrenaica, following a series of rebellions in the territory that had finally been subdued. The previous governor, Ophellas, had been killed in the autumn of 308 BC after being betrayed by his 'ally' Agathocles of Syracuse. Agathocles had persuaded Ophellas to support him in his war against Carthage by saying he could keep any territory that was conquered in North Africa. Eager to establish a North African empire at the expense of the Carthaginians, Ophellas had gathered a powerful army and embarked on a long and perilous march into Carthaginian territory, where he had joined forces with Agathocles. Initially, Agathocles had given his ally a warm greeting, but showed his true colours within a few days when he treacherously attacked the Cyrenaean camp and had Ophellas executed. By removing Ophellas, Agathocles was able to persuade the large (and now leaderless) Cyrenaean army to defect to his cause. Even more significantly for Ptolemy, the death of Ophellas left Cyrenaica without a ruler and plunged the territory into chaos.[20]

Outside his domains, Ptolemy tried to avoid getting entangled in the rivalries in Greece and Asia Minor once Antigonus had been defeated, but did reconquer Cyprus in 295-294 BC and gained control over the Phoenician port cities of Tyre and Sidon at around the same time – all of which had been in Demetrius' possession.[21] The

---

[20] Magas ended up declaring independence from the Ptolemaic Kingdom during the reign of Ptolemy I's successor, Ptolemy II, and had himself proclaimed king in 276 BC.
[21] The Sidonian king Philocles served as a leading Ptolemaic military commander and admiral under Ptolemy I and in the early stages of Ptolemy II's reign. He has been credited as one of the

absorption of Cyprus into the Ptolemaic Empire had been one of Ptolemy's key objectives for many years. Situated in the eastern Mediterranean, to the north of Egypt, the south of Asia Minor and the west of the Levant, Cyprus was strategically important, and the island was also rich in both metals and agricultural products.

Rather than relying on military action, Ptolemy spent most of the last decade and a half of his reign consolidating and expanding his empire through marriage and alliances. As part of an alliance with Lysimachus of Thrace in 300 BC, the Thracian king married Ptolemy's daughter Arsinoe II in 299 or 298 BC. At around this time, Ptolemy also married his stepdaughter Theoxena to the tyrant of Syracuse (Agathocles) and another of his step-daughters, Antigone, to Pyrrhus of Epirus. Pyrrhus was Demetrius' brother-in-law and was being held hostage at the Ptolemaic court at the time, and Ptolemy even made peace with Demetrius himself (in about 296 BC), which was sealed when Ptolemy arranged a marriage between Demetrius and his daughter Ptolemais.

*

The last coalition war Ptolemy participated in took place between 288 and 286 BC and pitted Ptolemy, Seleucus, Lysimachus and Pyrrhus against Demetrius.

Demetrius had seized control of the Macedonian throne in 294 BC by murdering Cassander's son Alexander V, but been threatened in his new position ever since by Pyrrhus and many of his own disaffected subjects. He was finally forced to flee Macedonia in 288 BC when Lysimachus and Pyrrhus launched a joint attack, and subsequently besieged Athens when the city revolted against him.

The arrival of Ptolemy's fleet played a key role in lifting the siege of Athens and liberating it from Macedonian occupation. This intervention enabled Ptolemy to become the leader of an alliance of Greek islands in the Aegean Sea known as the League of the Islanders, which gave the Ptolemaic Kingdom maritime supremacy in the Mediterranean and hegemony over the Cyclades for decades to come.[22]

Meanwhile, Demetrius continued his fruitless campaign by attacking some of Lysimachus' territories in Asia. His army was decimated by famine and pestilence,

---

principal architects of Ptolemaic imperialism in the Aegean Sea and along the coast of Asia Minor.
[22] Ironically, the League of the Islanders had originally been founded by Antigonus in c. 314/313 BC.

and when hostilities also broke out with Seleucus, his troops abandoned him and he was forced to surrender to the Seleucid king in 285 BC.[23]

In the same year Ptolemy promoted Ptolemy II (his son by his current wife Berenice I) to the rank of co-regent in order to prepare him for rule and ensure there was a smooth transition of power when he died. In other words, he had chosen his youngest son as his heir rather than either of his sons by his previous marriage to Eurydice (Ptolemy Ceraunus and Meleager).

Just a few years later, in late 283 or early 282 BC, Ptolemy died. Aged about 84 years old at the time, he was presumably laid to rest in a tomb in Alexandria's royal quarter and was succeeded by Ptolemy II in accordance with his will.[24]

Ptolemy left a compact and well-ordered realm behind for his son to inherit, which had gone from being a satrapy of the Macedonian crown to an independent kingdom. During his time as satrap and then king of Egypt he had laid the foundations for a dynasty that would rule Egypt and play a leading role in the Mediterranean for three centuries – longer than any of the other major successor states of Alexander's empire. By sticking to a cautious and defensive foreign policy, rather than taking excessive risks and allowing his actions to be guided by temptation, he navigated both himself and his kingdom safely through the perilous post-Alexandrian world of never-ending war and shifting alliances – keeping rival powers at bay; gaining possession of key territories around Egypt (namely Cyrenaica, Cyprus and Coele-Syria) to serve as a protective buffer; and promoting domestic stability by reforming his kingdom's internal organisation.

Given that the majority of his subjects were Egyptians, not Macedonians, Ptolemy took a number of measures to keep the native population content, present himself as a traditional Egyptian pharaoh, and to fuse Greek and Egyptian culture in his kingdom. This included respecting Egyptian religious traditions by making offerings to their gods, participating in rituals and honouring animal cults; serving as a patron of the Egyptian priesthood and nobility; restoring Egyptian temples which had been destroyed during the Persian occupation and commissioning new ones; deifying Alexander the Great (along with a cult, presided over by a high priest) to give his dynasty legitimacy; and establishing a new deity named Serapis, who had a blend of

---

[23] Demetrius died in Seleucus' custody in 283 BC.
[24] After his death, Ptolemy and his wife Berenice I were deified by their son Ptolemy II.

Greek and Egyptian attributes and was endorsed by the early Ptolemies as the patron god of both Alexandria and the Ptolemaic dynasty.[25][26]

Even though the religious construction work overseen by Ptolemy was eclipsed by far grander projects undertaken during the reigns of the later Ptolemies, he founded many sanctuaries throughout Egypt. Some notable examples include the temple of Hathor in Terenuthis, the temple of Amun-Ra in Naucratis, the temple of Soknebtunis in Tebtunis, and a Ptolemaic temple in Sharuna.

Nevertheless, these efforts did not change the fact that the native Egyptian population were second-class citizens in Ptolemy's Egypt and remained so throughout Ptolemaic rule. Most senior officials in the Ptolemaic state were Greek and Ptolemy also made the *nomarchs* (the Egyptian governor of each of the country's nomes) subservient to his Greek generals (*stategoi*) in local administration. The Ptolemaic army was primarily recruited from Macedonia and elsewhere in Greece, while the majority of Egypt's traditional military class was relegated to domestic policing duties. Greek was established as the language of government business and the only Ptolemaic monarch who bothered to learn the native Egyptian tongue was its last – Cleopatra VII. Egypt's fabled wealth was siphoned into the royal coffers by Ptolemy, who introduced coinage to regulate the economy and controlled the revenue generated by the temples. In Upper Egypt, he established a new city called Ptolemais Hermiou to challenge the domination of Thebes in the region, which had a tendency for native uprisings. And most strikingly of all, he moved the country's capital from Memphis to the newly built port city of Alexandria.

Doing this had a range of benefits. Alexandria was at the crossroads between three continents (Africa, Asia and Europe) and had access to both the Mediterranean Sea and the River Nile, as well as possessing a large natural harbour, which meant it was ideally situated for commerce. It had better connections to Ptolemy's Greek homeland than Memphis (which was inland) and would help to restrict the influence of the priests and officials in the former capital. In addition to these practical considerations,

---

[25] Ptolemy showed particular reverence for the cult of the Apis bull in Memphis, which had existed since the First Dynasty.

[26] Serapis was an attempt at uniting the religious traditions of Ptolemy's Greek and Egyptian subjects. The god was associated with Osiris and Apis on the one hand and Zeus, Hades and Dionysus on the other. However, even though the cult of Serapis spread across the Greek world it ultimately failed to win over the Egyptian people, who knew a traditional deity when they saw one and regarded Serapis as representing a Greek hero-god.

it had symbolic importance due to it being founded by Alexander the Great during his brief stay in Egypt in 332-331 BC.

Ptolemy continued to develop Alexandria on a grid system, as per Alexander's original plan, and oversaw the construction of much of the city, including its walls and the royal quarter (where the Ptolemies' palaces and tombs were situated, as well as the final resting place of Alexander). Alexandria's two main avenues were approximately 100 feet wide and intersected each other at right angles. The first of these roads was the Canopic Way (which ran east-west) and the second was the Soma (which ran north-south).

Once complete, the new capital of Egypt contained all the facilities a city in the ancient world could hope to possess: wharfs, warehouses, shipyards and an emporium for the facilitation of trade; temples for the worship of both Greek and Egyptian deities; a gymnasium for physical training and staging grand spectacles; a market square for procuring goods; and law courts and other public buildings for the administration of the state.

Most famously of all, Ptolemy founded the Musaeum of Alexandria in the city's royal quarter, which became the greatest research facility in the ancient world and enabled Alexandria to supplant Athens as the most important intellectual centre in the Mediterranean. The Musaeum got its name from the Muses (goddesses of science, literature and the arts), which it was dedicated to, and was presided over by a priest of the Muses, who was appointed by the king.[27] By offering generous salaries and academic freedom, Ptolemy and his successors attracted the best and brightest scholars from all over the Greek world, and the Musaeum's library was home to more manuscripts than any other.[28]

According to some accounts, the Library was originally organised by the Athenian statesman and peripatetic philosopher Demetrius of Phalerum. His enemies in Athens had sent him into exile in 307 BC and he settled in Alexandria in 297 BC. Demetrius was warmly received by Ptolemy and was appointed as a royal counsellor in cultural affairs.[29]

---

[27] The Musaeum was inspired by the Peripatetic school (a philosophical school in Athens that had been founded by Aristotle in approximately 335 BC).
[28] The first director of the Library of Alexandria was the Homeric scholar Zenodotus of Ephesus, who also served as a tutor to the royal children at the Ptolemaic court.
[29] Demetrius fell out of royal favour when Ptolemy II became pharaoh, allegedly because he had

Countless academic feats were accomplished in the Musaeum under Ptolemaic rule, such as the composition of a history of Egypt by the Egyptian priest Manetho, the invention of a water pump by Archimedes of Syracuse, the development of the first heliocentric model of the solar system by Aristarchus of Samos, and a remarkably accurate calculation of the Earth's circumference by Eratosthenes of Cyrene. Counted amongst the many Greek scholars who came to work in Egypt during Ptolemy I's reign were the historian Hecataeus of Abdera (one of several Greek scholars who wrote Egyptian histories during this period), the peripatetic philosopher Strato of Lampsacus (who served as a tutor to the future Ptolemy II), and the Cyrenaic philosopher Theodorus the Atheist (who was renowned for his alleged atheism). The physician Praxagoras of Cos introduced Alexandria to the Hippocratic tradition in the late fourth century BC, and in the first half of the third century BC his student, Herophilos of Chalcedon, became the most prominent doctor in the Egyptian capital: making scientific dissections of human corpses routine and playing an important role in the development of medical terminology.

Like Alexander the Great, Ptolemy was a patron of the arts and sciences, as well as being something of a scholar himself. He sponsored the work of the Greek mathematician Euclid and composed a first-hand account of Alexander's campaigns. This work has long since been lost, although it would have certainly emphasised Ptolemy's achievements and much of it lives on through Arrian's history of Alexander the Great's campaigns – *Anabasis* – which used Ptolemy's history as one of its main sources.

Ptolemy's determination to turn his capital city into an intellectual powerhouse set a precedent for his successors. Many of the Ptolemaic rulers who followed shared his passion for academia and continued to build on the sturdy foundations he had laid.

Just in case this wasn't a clear enough sign of the wealth and ambition of Egypt's new ruling dynasty, work on one of the Seven Wonders of the Ancient World was also started during Ptolemy's reign. This was a lighthouse on the small island of Pharos, which was connected to the mainland by a causeway that divided Alexandria's harbour in two. Possibly designed by the architect Sostratus of Cnidus, the lighthouse was completed during the reign of his son and successor, Ptolemy II, and ended up being a massive structure. Built from giant blocks of stone, it was composed of three

---

supported Ptolemy Ceraunus' claim to the throne. He was exiled from Alexandria to Upper Egypt and is reported to have died soon thereafter, as a result of being bitten by a venomous snake.

tiers (the first square, the second octagonal and the third cylindrical) and surmounted by a statue of Zeus. A beacon was kept burning around the clock and was magnified by mirrors to make it visible for many miles out to sea. This remarkable feat of engineering not only allowed ships to enter Alexandria's harbours safely, but also served as a very visible reminder of the Ptolemaic dynasty's wealth and power.

After hundreds of years of decline, the final period of Egyptian greatness had begun in style.

Ptolemy II: The 'Sibling-lover'

The second Ptolemaic monarch to rule over Egypt, Ptolemy II Philadelphus, was born in about 309 BC on the Greek island of Kos and acceded to the throne after his father's death in the winter of 383/282 BC. He was the youngest child from Ptolemy I's final marriage (to Berenice I) and had two older sisters (Arsinoe II and Philotera) as well as a whole host of half-siblings from his parent's previous marriages. One of these siblings was his elder half-brother Ptolemy Ceraunus, who was Ptolemy I's heir presumptive at the time of Ptolemy II's birth.[30]

Shortly before Ptolemy II was born, his father had captured Kos from Antigonus as part of a struggle for supremacy in the Aegean. Like many of his Ptolemaic successors, he benefitted from a first-class education and received tuition off some of the finest scholars of the age, which allegedly included the poet Philitas of Cos and the philosopher Strato of Lampsacus.[31]

As Ptolemy II grew into a man, he became embroiled in a power struggle over the succession with his half-brother Ptolemy Ceraunus. This ultimately resulted in Ptolemy Ceraunus leaving Egypt in about 287 BC and settling at the court of Lysimachus, who was the king of Thrace and Macedonia, as well as ruling over parts of Asia Minor. Meanwhile, Ptolemy I appointed Ptolemy II as his co-regent in December 285 BC or January 284 BC, and this arrangement remained in place until Ptolemy I's death a few years later.

After the death of his father, Ptolemy II assumed sole command of the kingdom and was probably crowned pharaoh on 7 January 282 BC. Upon his accession to the throne, he set a precedent by having Ptolemy I deified, and did the same for his mother (Berenice I) when she died in the 270s or early 260s BC. The late royal couple were worshipped in tandem – as the *Theoi Soteres* ('Saviour Gods') – and this marked the beginning of the Ptolemaic dynastic cult. As part of this, a festival was held every four years in Ptolemy I's honour. Called the 'Ptolemaia', it was inaugurated in the winter of 279/278 BC and included an elaborate procession, banquets, sacrifices and athletic competitions. This was used by Ptolemy to put his kingdom's wealth and power on public display, as well as to serve as a rival to the Olympic Games.

---

[30] Ptolemy Ceraunus was the eldest son of Ptolemy I and his ex-wife Eurydice.
[31] Strato had attended Aristotle's famous school in Athens (the Lyceum).

Moving forward, the rites of deified Ptolemaic rulers were presided over by the priest of Alexander the Great's cult, whose full title included the name of every Ptolemaic monarch. They also shared Alexander's temple, although the rituals and sacrifices that took place there continued to be made primarily to Alexander in recognition of their subordination to the great Macedonian conqueror.[32]

Even though Ptolemy II succeeded his father peacefully, the dispute over the succession continued to linger. This was particularly the case at Lysimachus' court, where there had been disagreement over whose claim to support ever since Ptolemy Ceraunus had gone into exile there. The situation was complicated by the fact that Lysimachus was married to Ptolemy II's sister Arsinoe II, while his heir Agathocles was married to Ptolemy Ceraunus' sister Lysandra.

At some point between 284 and 282 BC, Lysimachus had Agathocles executed for treason. While some accounts claim Agathocles had been conspiring against his father, other sources assert his downfall was orchestrated by Lysimachus' ambitious wife Arsinoe II, who sought to replace him with her own son (Ptolemy Epigonos) as Lysimachus' successor.

In any case, now Agathocles was out of the picture Lysimachus decided to support Ptolemy II's claim over his half-brother's. He sealed this by arranging a marriage between Arsinoe I (one of his daughters from his first marriage) and Ptolemy II at some point between 284 and 281 BC, which also secured an alliance between Lysimachus and the Ptolemaic Kingdom against the Seleucid king Seleucus I.[33]

Unfortunately for Lysimachus, his decision to execute Agathocles angered many of his subjects. This was exploited by Seleucus I, who launched an invasion of Lysimachus' territories in 281 BC. The campaign came to a successful conclusion at

---

[32] Ptolemy II established cults for a number of other family members after their deaths, including his sister Philotera and his sister-wife Arisinoe II. He also deified his mistress Bilistiche, with whom he is said to have had one son (Ptolemy Andromachon) and who famously won the *synoris* (two-horse) and *tethrippon* (four-horse) races in the 264 BC Olympic Games.
Although Bilistiche was probably the most influential of Ptolemy's mistresses, he is known to have had several other concubines throughout his life, which is hardly surprising considering his marriages were primarily political in nature.

[33] Arsinoe I went on to have three children with Ptolemy II – his successor, Ptolemy III Euergetes, as well as Lysimachus of Egypt and Berenice.

the Battle of Corupedium (near Sardis, in Asia Minor), which resulted in Lysimachus being slain and his domains absorbed into the Seleucid Empire.

After the battle, Seleucus brought Ptolemy Ceraunus into his inner circle, perhaps in the hope of using him to destabilise the Ptolemaic Kingdom (his last major rival). However, this backfired when Ptolemy Ceraunus had Seleucus murdered in September 281 BC while he was preparing to invade Macedonia.

With Seleucus out the way, Ptolemy Ceraunus was able to claim the Macedonian throne for himself, although his reign came to a bloody end less than 18 months later (in January or February 279 BC) when he was captured and executed by an invading Gaulish army under the command of Bolgios. He was briefly succeeded as king of Macedonia by his younger brother, Meleager, but he was deposed by his troops a few months later in favour of a nephew of Cassander, Antipater Etesias.[34] Therefore, within three years of succeeding his father as Egypt's pharaoh, Ptolemy II no longer needed to worry about any threats to his rule from his two half-brothers.

In the aftermath of Seleucus' assassination, his son and successor Antiochus I was preoccupied trying to regain control of the Seleucid Empire. This turmoil was exploited by Ptolemy, who enlarged his realm with the acquisition of Samos, Miletus, Caria, Lycia, Pamphylia, and perhaps Cilicia.

In about 279 BC, Ptolemy's sister Arsinoe II returned to Egypt. Following the death of her husband Lysimachus, she had married her half-brother Ptolemy Ceraunus for political reasons, as they both sought to claim the Macedonian and Thracian thrones. This had ended up being a brief and disastrous union that fell apart when Ptolemy Ceraunus discovered his new wife was conspiring against him with her sons. He reacted by having Arsinoe's two youngest sons (Lysimachus and Philip) killed, while Arsinoe and her eldest son (Ptolemy Epigonos) were forced to flee for their lives.

Arsinoe II was an attractive and determined individual, and plotted against her sister-in-law Arsinoe I in the hope of making herself queen. Within a few years of her arrival in Alexandria she successfully accused Arsinoe I of instigating a conspiracy to assassinate her husband, which resulted in Ptolemy divorcing his wife and banishing her to Coptos (present-day Qift) in Upper Egypt sometime after 275 BC. Arsinoe I

---

[34] Antipater Etesias was in turn deposed by the Macedonian general Sosthenes after less than two months in power. It was not until 277 BC that Macedonia found a long-term leader when a son of Demetrius I, Antigonus II, seized control of the kingdom.

spent the rest of her life in exile, but also in considerable comfort given that she was able to take advantage of the benefits of her status as a former queen.

Shortly after Arsinoe I's banishment, in about 273 or 272 BC, Ptolemy replaced her as his queen with his older sister Arsinoe II.[35] When the siblings got married they both received the epithet 'Philadephus' ('Sibling-lovers') and were elevated to divine status as the *Theoi Adelphoi* ('Sibling Gods'). Like the pharaohs that had preceded him, Ptolemy was frequently depicted with divine attributes in works of art, such as an elephant headdress (associated with Alexander the Great since his Indian campaigns) and the club of Heracles (who Alexander the Great was allegedly descended from). While these both reflected his Greek heritage, he also followed in his father's footsteps by making an effort to present himself as a traditional Egyptian pharaoh: visiting important religious sanctuaries, playing a central role in Egyptian religious rituals, and funding extensive temple building and restoration projects. This included enlarging the Temple of Min and Isis at Coptos and the temple of the cobra goddess Renenutet at Medinet Madi; constructing a temple dedicated to Horus at Tanis, to Arsinoe II at Pithom and to Isis at Philae; restoring the temple of Min at Akhmim; conducting decorative work on the temples of Mut and Opet at Karnak, the temple of Isis at Behbeit el-Hagar and the temple of Anhur-Shu at Sebennytos; expanding the birth house in the Dendera Temple complex; constructing a burial chamber for an Apis bull in the Serapeum of Saqqara; and building a gate between the temples of Isis and Imhotep at Philae. As an added bonus, Ptolemy granted the tax revenues from the Dodekaschoinos to the temple of Isis at Philae, which was reconfirmed on numerous occasions until Egypt came under Roman rule.[36] Doing these things helped Ptolemy to maintain support for his rule amongst the powerful Egyptian priesthood, although in private many of the priests (particularly in Upper Egypt) continued to regard the Ptolemies as foreign occupiers who should be removed from power when the time was ripe. This wasn't helped by the fact that the Ptolemies were determined to tap into the wealth of the temples, which were not only spiritual centres but also major landowners and places of significant economic activity. They did this by forcing the temples to accept the authority of trusted officials of the crown, who were sent to the temple estates to protect the central government's economic interests there.

---

[35] Although later Ptolemaic brother-sister marriages were undoubtedly consummated, the fact that Ptolemy II's marriage to Arsinoe II produced no children leaves it open to question whether their relationship was sexual or not.

[36] This donation upset the priests of Khnum in Elephantine, who had traditionally been the dominant religious authority in the border region to the south of Egypt.

Ptolemy's marriage to his sister set a precedent for the Ptolemies who succeeded him, many of whom married immediate relatives. Such incestuous relationships were unacceptable in the Greek world but had been practiced by the Egyptian pharaohs for millennia (to maintain their divine bloodline) and therefore helped to cement the Ptolemaic dynasty's legitimacy to rule in the eyes of their native subjects, as well as removing the potential threats caused by pesky in-laws. While some Greeks did defend the marriage by linking it to Greek mythology (such as a poet from Syracuse named Theocritus, who compared it to Zeus' marriage to his sister Hera), those Greeks who openly expressed their disgust at the marriage did so at their peril.[37] One such individual was the poet Sotades, who mocked the marriage between Ptolemy II and Arsinoe II in a lampoon, which included the famous line: 'You're sticking your prick in an unholy hole'. For his crude honesty, Sotades was imprisoned in Alexandria. Later, he managed to escape, but was tracked down by the Ptolemaic admiral Patroclus, who had him locked in a leaden chest and thrown into the sea.

When Ptolemy married Arsinoe II, he removed his children with Arsinoe I from the line of succession (including the future Ptolemy III) and named his new wife's son by Lysimachus (Ptolemy Epigonos) as his heir. For this and other reasons, Arsinoe II has often been presented as exercising considerable influence over her brother-husband. However, it is likely that this interpretation is an exaggeration considering the countless occasions that Ptolemy proved himself to be a forceful ruler.

When Arisnoe II died (probably at some point between 270 and 268 BC), Ptolemy deified his late wife and established a cult in her honour, whose rites are recorded on the Great Mendes Stela. Her son, Ptolemy Epigonos, was promoted to co-regent in 267 BC, but was stripped of his position and forced to renounce his claim to the Egyptian throne after taking part in a rebellion against Ptolemy II (along with the tyrant of Miletus, Timarchus) in Asia Minor in 259-258 BC. Consequently, Ptolemy II's children by Arsinoe I were restored to the line of succession.

It is unclear why Ptolemy Epigonos chose to rebel against his step-father, but it is possible that it was sparked by Ptolemy II seeking to take over his command in Asia Minor. In any event, Ptolemy Epigonos got off lightly for his defiance when the Ptolemaic king granted him Telmessus (in Lycia, Asia Minor). This had previously been part of his late father's (Lysimachus) kingdom, and he ruled over this city as a client monarch from 258 BC until his death in 240 BC.

---

[37] Similarly, in Egyptian mythology the god Osiris had been married to his sister Isis.

*

In about 275 BC, Ptolemy launched an invasion of the Kingdom of Kush to gain control over an area of Lower Nubia known as the Triakontaschoinos ('thirty-mile land'). This territory was situated between the First and Second Cataract of the Nile and may have been used as a base by the Nubians for launching raids into southern Egypt. Other motives for the invasion included restricting the Kingdom of Kush's steadily growing power, securing Ptolemaic rule in Upper Egypt (whose native population had a tendency for rebellion and may have sought Kushite support), obtaining access to the rich gold mines at Wadi Allaqi (which became a major contributor to Ptolemaic prosperity), and gaining control of African war elephants (which could help counteract the Indian elephants used in battle by the Seleucids).[38]

Ptolemy's Kushite campaign was a success and resulted in the northernmost twelve miles of the Triakontaschoinos being annexed by the Ptolemaic Kingdom, which was henceforth known as the Dodekaschoinos ('twelve-mile land'). He also established a new gold-processing city in Wadi Allaqi, which he named Berenice Panchrysos ('all-gold Berenice') in honour of his mother. Therefore, the campaign was not just an attempt to secure the Ptolemaic Kingdom's southern border, but also to further its economic and military interests.

Unfortunately for Ptolemy, he wasn't the only ruler with expansionist ambitions. By the end of 275 BC, Antiochus I's rule in the Seleucid Empire was secure enough for him to turn his attention to avenging the territorial losses he had suffered to Ptolemy at the beginning of his reign. At about this time, Antiochus married his daughter Apama II to Ptolemy's half-brother Magas, who had been appointed governor of Cyrenaica by Ptolemy I in about 300 BC but had proclaimed himself 'king of Cyrene' (and therefore independent of the Ptolemaic Kingdom) sometime after Ptolemy II's accession to the throne. Soon after this alliance was formed, in 274 BC, Magas launched an invasion of Egypt. He captured the Egyptian coastal city of Paraitónion (present-day Marsa Matruh) and advanced rapidly on Alexandria with the intention of deposing his half-brother, but was forced to return to Cyrenaica when he learned Libyan nomads had taken advantage of his absence by revolting. Nevertheless, despite the failure of his invasion, Magas succeeded in the more important goals of crushing

---

[38] These war elephants could be found near Meroë (in an area south of the Fifth Cataract of the Nile) and on the southern shores of the Red Sea. Numerous expeditions were launched by Ptolemy II, Ptolemy III and Ptolemy IV to capture them.

the Libyan rebellion and maintaining his self-proclaimed independence from Ptolemaic Egypt, until his death in 250 BC.

During Magas' failed invasion, Ptolemy also had to deal with some internal trouble of his own creation when the 4,000 Galatian mercenaries he had hired to help defend Egypt mutinied soon after their arrival. Ptolemy responded by marooning them on an uninhabited island in the River Nile, where they are reported to have 'perished at one another's hands or by famine.'

Because various other Hellenistic monarchs had fought major wars to repel Gaulish invasions in Greece and Asia Minor at around this time, Ptolemy was able to overplay the scale of his victory and ordered grand celebrations to be held. It is possible that the massive triumphal procession described by Callixenus of Rhodes – which went down in history as one of the most magnificent pageants held in the ancient world – took place at this time.[39] Intended to boast the material wealth and military prowess of the Ptolemaic dynasty, the parade had numerous elements. Statues of the Ptolemaic dynasty's patron deities – Dionysus, Zeus, Alexander the Great, Ptolemy I and Berenice I – were included and there were also figures representing the 'free' Greek cities, in an attempt at presenting Ptolemy as a champion of Panhellenic freedom. The overriding theme, however, was Dionysus returning from his mythical conquest of the East, which took him as far as India and weighed him down with treasure. A vast military continent of approximately 80,000 troops took part in the procession, and it was embellished by tribute from Africa, Arabia and India (which included elephants, antelopes, ostriches, wild asses, leopards, giraffe, rhinos, zebras and camels) and from Nubia (which consisted of women, cattle and dogs).

Despite these celebrations, Magas' ally Antiochus I still posed a serious threat to the Ptolemaic Kingdom. Perhaps in retaliation to the Seleucid king's alliance with Magas, Ptolemy sparked the so-called First Syrian War (274-271 BC) by invading Seleucid Syria. The Ptolemaic army had some initial successes, before being compelled to retreat back to Egypt when Antiochus advanced with an army to counter the invasion. This forced Ptolemy onto the defensive and left Egypt at risk of attack. The situation was so serious, in fact, that Ptolemy and his wife Arsinoe travelled in person to the eastern Nile Delta (in the winter of 274/273 BC), where they directly oversaw the organisation and reinforcement of Egypt's border defences.

---

[39] The date of Ptolemy II's great procession is uncertain and continues to be debated by historians.

Fortunately these defences never had to be put to the test. The Seleucid army was suffering from both an outbreak of plague and financial problems, which prompted Antiochus to abandon his plans to invade Egypt and assert his dynasty's claim to southern Syria (Coele-Syria). Instead, he agreed to a peace treaty with Ptolemy in 271 BC that essentially resulted in a return to the *status quo antebellum*.

*

Being an effective pharaoh wasn't all about waging war, and Ptolemy II was well aware of that. Egypt's wealth and prosperity was ultimately derived from its fertile land and trading links, and the country became a major trading hub once again under Ptolemaic rule.

Many previous Egyptian rulers had attempted to improve access to the Red Sea for the purpose of boosting trade. These efforts were revived by Ptolemy II, who sponsored the restoration of a forerunner of the modern Suez Canal that had been dug during the sixth century BC when the Persian ruler Darius the Great had been pharaoh.[40] The canal ran from the eastern Nile Delta (near the Egyptian city of Bubastis) to the Gulf of Suez (at the northern end of the Red Sea) but had been obstructed by silt by the time Ptolemy II came to the throne. The restoration work was completed and the canal operational by 270 or 269 BC, and this was made possible by the work of Ptolemy's engineers, who solved the issue of varying heights in the terrain by building canal locks.

Near the eastern terminus of the canal, Ptolemy established a city named Arsinoe (after his wife Arsinoe II). From here, he dispatched two expeditions along the Red Sea's east and west coasts that resulted in the establishment of a chain of coastal towns. This helped to boost Egypt's economy by strengthen its trade links, and some of these towns grew into important commercial centres. The Egyptian Red Sea ports of Philotera (founded between 282 and 268 BC and named in honour of Ptolemy II's late sister), Myos Hormos (founded at some point during the third century BC) and Berenice Troglodytica (founded in 275 BC and named after Ptolemy II's mother Berenice I) went on to play an important role in Indian trade and also served as termini of caravan routes that passed through the Egyptian desert. Another Red Sea settlement established during Ptolemy II's reign was Ptolemais Theron, which was used as both a military colony and a base for elephant hunters (who killed the adult

---

[40] The canal project had originally been initiated by Necho II, who was a member of the Twenty-Sixth Dynasty and served as pharaoh in the late seventh and early sixth centuries BC.

elephants for their ivory and captured younger elephants to be trained for use in war). Ptolemy II founded various other bases along Africa's Red Sea coast for the purpose of capturing war elephants, one of which was Adulis (in present-day Eritrea), and Ptolemaic fortifications were also established in the region such as Berenice epi Deirès (in present-day Djibouti). Meanwhile, on the Red Sea's east coast, the ports of Berenice (present-day Aqaba, Jordan) and Ampelone (north of present-day Jeddah, Saudi Arabia) gave Ptolemaic rulers access to the western end of the incense trade's caravan routes, which was controlled by a nomadic Arab people called the Nabataeans. Today, the Nabataeans are best-known for the city of Petra (in Jordan), which was a major trading hub at its zenith and is an archaeological wonder in the present day. They appear throughout the story of the Ptolemies and came into increasing conflict with the Ptolemaic dynasty from the reign of Ptolemy VIII onwards, when Egypt's rulers attempted to bypass the Arab middlemen and conduct direct trade with India.

*

Between 267 and 261 BC, Ptolemy allied himself with a coalition of Greek city-states against Antigonid-controlled Macedonia in the Chremonidean War.

In the early part of his reign, Ptolemy had benefitted from the turmoil in Macedonia, which was consumed by civil war. This had enabled the Ptolemaic Kingdom to remain the dominant naval force in the eastern Mediterranean, with its sphere of influence in the Aegean Sea extending from the Cyclades in the south all the way to Samothrace in the north. Ptolemaic authority in the region was partly based on the Ptolemaic monarch's protectorate of the League of the Islanders (an alliance of city-states encompassing the Cyclades islands). However, Ptolemaic hegemony in the region came under threat when the grandson of Antigonus, Antigonus II, firmly established himself as king of Macedonia (after the death of his rival Pyrrhus of Epirus in 272 BC) and proceeded to extend his power into mainland Greece: occupying large swathes of territory and installing tyrants loyal to the Macedonian monarchy in other areas.

The message Antigonus was sending was clear: Both the Peloponnese and the Aegean Islands had been in Macedonia's sphere of influence since the time of Philip II and now they were determined to get them back.

To make matters worse, Antigonus had good relations with the Ptolemaic Kingdom's other main rival, the Seleucid Empire, which threatened Egypt with the possibility of a war on two fronts.

Ptolemy responded to the resurgent Macedonians by forming alliances with Greece's most powerful city-states – Athens and Sparta – in 268 BC and presenting himself as a protector of Greek freedom against Macedonian aggression. Even though Athens and Sparta had traditionally been mortal enemies, they both resented Antigonus' domination in their own backyard and so put their differences aside.

Near the end of 268 BC the Athenian statesman Chremonides (with Ptolemy's encouragement) successfully persuaded his people to declare war on Antigonus II.[41] Antigonus retaliated by imposing a blockade on Athens and ravaging Attica with his army. Meanwhile, a Ptolemaic fleet under the command of the admiral Patroclus entered the Aegean Sea in 267 BC and set up a base on the Greek island of Keos (present-day Kea). Patroclus then sailed on to Attica (in 266 BC), where he established a fortified naval base on a small uninhabited island called Gaidouronisi.[42] It is likely that he planned to join forces with the Spartan army and use their combined strength to evict Antigonus' garrisons at Sounion and Piraeus (in Attica), which were keeping Athens in check and essentially amounted to a permanent siege of the city. This plan fell apart though when the Spartans failed to force their way through into Attica, because Patroclus did not have sufficient manpower to dislodge the garrisons by himself.

Throughout the war, the Spartan and Athenian armies were seriously outmatched on land by their Macedonian opponent. Sparta made a second attempt to come to the assistance of Athens in 265-264 BC, but this proved to be even more disastrous than the first and resulted in the death of the Spartan king Areus I in a battle near Corinth (in 265 BC). The situation was made worse for the Athenians by Ptolemy's reluctance to make any largescale military commitments to the war in Greece. He refrained from committing the full resources of his empire and only went as far as was in his political interests. No expeditionary force was sent, which confined Patroclus' operations to his sea bases and compelled him to avoid confrontations on land. Instead, Ptolemaic support – particularly in the latter part of the conflict – was restricted to naval assistance by Patroclus and financial aid for the Greek city-states in the alliance. One

---

[41] Chremonides was the namesake of the Chremonidean War.
[42] As a consequence of Patroclus establishing a camp on Gaidouronisi, the island became known as Patroklos' Island and is called Patroklos in the present-day.

possible reason for this was Ptolemy's desire to prioritise his military campaigns in the eastern Aegean, where his nephew, stepson and co-regent Ptolemy Epigonos seized control of Ephesus and possibly Lesbos in 262 BC.

Back in Greece, the capitulation of Sparta and the lack of commitment from Ptolemy eventually won the war for the Macedonians. By early 261 BC the siege of Athens had finally taken its toll and compelled the Athenians to surrender, while the main instigators of the war (Chremonides and his brother Glaucon) fled to Ptolemy's court at Alexandria, where they sought asylum.

The Macedonian victory in the Chremonidean War signified the end of the Ptolemaic Kingdom's naval supremacy in the Aegean Sea. It also contributed to the dissolution of the League of the Islanders at some point during the mid-third century BC. Nevertheless, Ptolemaic rulers continued to maintain a presence in the Aegean through various military bases in the region, many of which had been established during the war. The Ptolemaic Kingdom maintained a military and administrative presence on the island of Keos (present-day Kea) until the late third century BC, and their naval bases at Methana (on the Peloponnese), Itanus (on the island of Crete) and the island of Thera helped to project Egyptian power in the region until 145 BC.

Soon after the conclusion of the Chremonidean War, a conflict broke out between Ptolemy and the new Seleucid ruler, Antiochus II, in what is known as the Second Syrian War (260-253 BC). The war began when Antiochus II formed an alliance with the Macedonian king Antigonus II (who was eager to kick Ptolemy out of the Aegean) and launched an attack on Ptolemaic territories in western Asia Minor (namely Ephesus and Miletus) which the Ptolemies and Seleucids held competing claims to. Antiochus was no doubt encouraged to take this action by the chaos Ptolemy Epigonos' rebellion against Ptolemy II (259-258 BC) caused in the region.

Very little information has survived concerning the events of the Second Syrian War. It is unknown what happened in Syria itself, other than that Ptolemy campaigned there in the spring and summer of 257 BC. Probably in 261 BC (but potentially as late as 255 BC), Ptolemaic naval power was severely diminished when the Ptolemaic fleet (led by the admiral Patroclus) suffered a major defeat at the hands of Antigonus II at the Battle of Cos. Meanwhile, in Asia Minor the Seleucid king Antiochus II seized territory from Ptolemy in Cilicia, Pamphylia and Ionia (including Ephesus and Miletus) between 259 and 253 BC. Rather surprisingly, the Seleucids received assistance off the island of Rhodes during the war, despite the importance of its commercial relations with the Ptolemaic Kingdom and it being surrounded by Ptolemaic harbours. The most notable action the Rhodians took against the Ptolemaic Kingdom was the defeat they inflicted on a Ptolemaic fleet under the command of the Athenian admiral Chremonides at the Battle of Ephesus (which is generally believed to have taken place in c. 258 BC, although the date is open to dispute due to a lack of evidence). Therefore, despite all the ambiguity about the Second Syrian War, it clearly resulted in a Seleucid victory and reversed many of the gains Ptolemy had made during the First Syrian War. The war came to an end in 253 BC when Ptolemy completed a peace agreement with the Seleucid Empire by conceding his large territorial losses in Asia Minor and marrying his daughter Berenice Syra to Antiochus the following year. The marriage was accompanied by a hefty dowry, although Antiochus was required to divorce his current wife Laodice I, which resulted in the Seleucid king having to grant his ex-wife various pieces of land in Asia Minor as part of the settlement.

While the terms of the peace treaty might appear to be harsh on paper, the outcome could have been far worse and it highlights Ptolemy's knack for diplomacy. By luring the Macedonian king Antigonus II into concluding a separate peace in 255 BC, he was able to mitigate the damage caused by the war and to persuade Antiochus to make peace too.

As soon as peace had been secured, Ptolemy travelled to Memphis in the summer of 253 BC. Here, he rewarded his discharged veterans with grants of land that had been reclaimed from Lake Moeris in the Fayum Oasis as part of a broader effort to increase the amount of arable land in Egypt.[43] The land that was granted was contained within the newly-established nome of Arsinoite, which Ptolemy had named in honour of his deceased wife Arsinoe II.

In the aftermath of the Second Syrian War, Ptolemy's focus returned to mainland Greece and the Aegean Sea, where he continued his anti-Macedonian policy by agreeing to give financial support to the Achaean League (a coalition of Greek city-states in the north-western Peloponnese). He did this after he was visited by Aratus of

---

[43] An artificial lake was created in the southern Fayum during Ptolemy II's reign. It held enough water to irrigate 150 square kilometres of arable and made it possible to establish between 30 and 40 large settlements in previously uninhabitable areas. Because this land had previously been useless, it did not belong to anyone and was therefore incredibly lucrative for the Ptolemaic crown.

Sicyon, who came to Alexandria in the winter of 250/249 BC to secure Ptolemaic subsidies on the League's behalf.[44]

The League started out as a relatively small confederation of minor city-states but expanded over the next four decades to cover the majority of the Peloponnese. Therefore, this became a significant check to Antigonus' expansionist ambitions in mainland Greece, which Ptolemy dealt an additional blow to when the Ptolemaic navy won a battle against the Macedonians in about 250 BC. Ptolemy also compensated for his loss of political control in the Cyclades by continuing to influence the islands through cultural and financial means, such as by establishing a new festival on the island of Delos in 249 BC in honour of the Delian gods (which is regarded as a second Ptolemaia).[45]

Closer to home, Ptolemy also spent the late 250s BC trying to reach a peace agreement with his rebellious half-brother Magas, who continued to stubbornly maintain Cyrenaica's independence. This resulted in Ptolemy betrothing his son and heir Ptolemy III to Magas' daughter Berenice II in the hope that it would lead to the reunification of Egypt and Cyrenaica after Magas' death, although when Magas died in about 250 BC the bride's mother (Apama II) called off the wedding.

As a daughter of the late Seleucid king, Antiochus I, Apama's father had married her to Magas to form an anti-Ptolemaic alliance with Cyrenaica and bring it into the Seleucid Empire's sphere of influence. Therefore, her opposition was understandable, because the proposed union between her daughter and the heir to the Ptolemaic throne threatened to undo this.

Eager not to allow Cyrenaica to be reabsorbed into the Ptolemaic Kingdom, Apama arranged for her uncle Demetrius the Fair to marry Berenice instead and become the new king of Cyrene. Demetrius was a son of Demetrius I and a brother of the current Macedonian monarch, Antigonus II. Given that the Macedonians had friendly relations with the Seleucids at this time, the match made sense. The union marked a significant threat to the Ptolemaic Kingdom, not just because its attempt to reassert its

---

[44] Members of the Achaean League shared a common federal citizenship and foreign policy, but each of the member states retained independence in their internal governance.
[45] This was equivalent to the Ptolemaia already celebrated in Alexandria.
During the course of the third century BC various places in the Greek world established their own Ptolemaia festivals. This is a testament to the power and influence of the Ptolemaic dynasty.

authority over Cyrenaica had been thwarted but because it now had an Antigonid ruler on its western border. If it was any consolation though, the threat did not last long. Shortly after the marriage between Demetrius the Fair and Berenice II, Apama started an affair with her daughter's new husband. This made Berenice so jealous that she orchestrated a coup against Demetrius and had him assassinated in 249 BC. Berenice then travelled to Egypt, where she married her original groom, Ptolemy III, either shortly before or upon his accession to the throne (in 246 BC).[46] As Ptolemy II had hoped, the marriage spelt the end of Cyrenaica's independence and led to its reincorporation into the Ptolemaic Kingdom.[47]

*

Throughout his reign, Ptolemy II was one of the wealthiest and most powerful rulers in the Mediterranean, which meant he was kept busy managing relations with both neighbouring and distant rulers.

In the western Mediterranean, Ptolemy had a close relationship with the tyrant of Syracuse, Hiero II, which is reflected in the exchange of goods and ideas that occurred between their respective domains. One example of this is Hiero's tax system – the *Lex Hieronica* – which had similarities to the system used in Ptolemy's kingdom and therefore may have been influenced by it.

Ptolemy also had a more amicable relationship with Carthage than his father had, who appears to have fought at least one war against them. One of the primary reasons for this shift in attitude was probably Ptolemy's desire to isolate his separatist half-brother, Magas of Cyrene, whose territory shared a border with Carthage. Given the city's status as a major commercial power, maintaining friendly relations with Carthage also had obvious economic benefits, and the Ptolemaic naval commander Timosthenes of Rhodes was permitted to carry out an expedition through Punic waters, which took him all the way to the edge of the western Mediterranean.

With the benefit of hindsight though, the Ptolemaic Kingdom's most significant long-term relationship in the West was with the expansionist Roman Republic. According to Roman legend, the city of Rome was established on the banks of the River Tiber by

---

[46] In the four years between Berenice II's departure from Cyrene and her marriage to Ptolemy III, Cyrene was administered by a republican government that was controlled by two Cyrenaeans named Ecdelus and Demophanes.

[47] Two new port cities were established in Cyrenaica when it was brought back under Ptolemaic rule – Ptolemais and Berenice (present-day Tolmeita and Benghazi respectively).

Romulus in 753 BC.[48] For the first two and a half centuries of the city's existence, Rome is said to have been ruled by seven legendary kings (starting with Romulus). This continued until approximately 509 BC, when the seventh and final king, Lucius Tarquinius Superbus, was overthrown and a Republic established. The Roman Republic steadily increased its boundaries through conquest and by 264 BC had brought the entire Italian peninsula under its control. In other words, Rome was a rising star whose best days clearly lay ahead. This did not go unnoticed by Ptolemy II, who became the first Ptolemaic ruler to establish formal diplomatic relations with the Roman Republic when an Egyptian envoy visited Rome in 273 BC. As a result of the friendly relations between Alexandria and Rome, Ptolemy remained neutral during the First Punic War (264-241 BC). He was clearly eager to avoid falling out with either side, although in order to maintain his neutrality he had to reject a request from the Carthaginians for a loan of 2,000 talents.

While Roman-Egyptian relations were new, products such as ivory, spices and incense had long be acquired from the interior of Africa and the southern part of the Arabian peninsula, and far away in the east Ptolemy maintained Egypt's longstanding trading links with India by dispatching an ambassador named Dionysius to the royal court of the Mauryan Empire. The visit probably took place during the reign of the emperor Ashoka on the basis that Ptolemy is referred to in the Edicts of Ashoka, although there is still a possibility that it occurred during the reign of his predecessor Bindusara.

The Roman author Pliny the Elder mentioned Ptolemy's Indian embassy in his *Natural History* when he wrote: 'But [India] has been treated of by several other Greek writers who resided at the courts of Indian kings, such, for instance, as Megasthenes, and by Dionysius, who was sent thither by [Ptolemy II] Philadelphus, expressly for the purpose: all of whom have enlarged upon the power and vast resources of these nations.'

The fact that Ptolemy sent embassies to opposite sides of the world – one to Rome and one to India – reflects the wide range of his kingdom's commercial and political interests. But Egypt didn't just thrive diplomatically, militarily and economically under Ptolemy II: it was a powerhouse of arts, culture and academia too.

Ptolemy II took after his father as a major patron of scholarship. He oversaw the expansion of the Musaeum and Library of Alexandria and encouraged famous

---

[48] Romulus is said to have killed his twin brother Remus after arguing with him over which hill to build the city on (Remus favoured the Aventine Hill and Romulus favoured the Palatine Hill).

scholars to settle in his capital by offering generous grants and salaries. The learning that took place in the Musaeum was wide-ranging and included literature, philosophy, the natural sciences and mathematics. Academics were in abundance at Ptolemy's court, including the eminent mathematician Euclid (who is often referred to as the 'father of geometry') and the astronomer Aristarchus of Samos (who was renowned for developing the first known heliocentric model, with the Earth rotating on its axis once a day and revolving around the Sun once a year).[49] Furthermore, poets such as Callimachus of Cyrene, Theocritus of Syracuse, Apollonius of Rhodes and Posidippus were paid to compose works that glorified the Ptolemaic dynasty, and Ptolemy may also have commissioned the Egyptian priest Manetho to write his *Aegyptiaca* (History of Egypt).[50] The expectation that authors would glorify the Ptolemaic dynasty in exchange for its patronage is demonstrated by the words of Callimachus of Cyrene, who associated Ptolemy II with the Greek gods Zeus and Apollo: *'From Zeus come kings, for than Zeus' princes nothing is more divine... We can judge this from our lord [Ptolemy II] since he has outstripped the rest by a wide margin. What he thinks in the morning he accomplishes by evening – by evening the greatest projects, but the lesser one the moment he thinks of them.'*

One of the most notable scholarly activities to be initiated at around this time was the first known Greek translation of the Hebrew Bible, which was undertaken by a group of Jews who came to Alexandria from Jerusalem during Ptolemy II's reign. According to the pseudepigraphical *Letter of Aristeas to Philocrates*, this was instigated by Ptolemy himself, but the true extent of his involvement is uncertain and it is generally thought that only a translation of the Torah (the first five books of the Hebrew Bible) was completed during his lifetime.

Nevertheless, Ptolemy certainly did oversee the completion of the Pharos Lighthouse (which had been started during his father's reign) and is also believed to have assembled a collection of exotic animals in Alexandria, which became its first zoo.

*

---

[49] Euclid is most famous for his 13 books known collectively as *Elements*, which outlined the basics of geometry.
[50] Callimachus compiled countless lists of the works held in the Library of Alexandria. Known collectively as the *Pinakes*, it was 120 volumes long and is often regarded as the first library catalogue in the West. Unfortunately, it has not survived to the present-day.

On 28 January 246 BC, Ptolemy II died peacefully, bringing his reign of over three and a half decades to a close. He was buried in the royal quarter in Alexandria and was succeeded by his son and heir, Ptolemy III, in what proved to be a smooth transition of power.

Ptolemy II was a skilled general who was unafraid to use military force to expand his power and influence, but had mixed military fortunes and should perhaps be best remembered as a prudent and enlightened ruler with a particular talent for diplomacy. He used his diplomatic skills to mitigate the impact of the various military losses he suffered during his reign, and his success as a ruler can be evidenced by many observations: the wealth and power of his kingdom, the internal stability in Egypt, the expansion of Ptolemaic influence and territories in the Mediterranean, the completion of major projects initiated by Ptolemy I (namely the Musaeum of Alexandria and Lighthouse of Pharos), and the fact that he laid the foundations for the Ptolemaic Kingdom to reach its greatest extent under his successor.

*

Ptolemaic government

The Ptolemaic Kingdom was governed by a complex bureaucracy. It is likely that much of this administrative structure was developed during the reign of Ptolemy I, although most of the surviving evidence comes from the time of Ptolemy II at the earliest.

In the Ptolemaic capital – Alexandria – a small group of officials (selected from amongst the pharaoh's *philoi* or 'friends') occupied the top of the hierarchy. They held the most important posts in government, such as the *hypomnematographos* (who served as chief secretary), the *epi ton prostagmaton* (who was responsible for drafting royal edicts), the *epistolographos* (who was in charge of diplomacy), and the *dioiketes* (the chief finance minister, who controlled taxation and provincial administration), as well as the top military leaders.[51]

For the majority of Ptolemy II's reign (between approximately 262 and 245 BC) a wealthy merchant and landowner named Apollonius served as his *dioiketes*. Thanks to the extensive writings of Apollonius' private secretary Zenon of Kaunos (discovered

---

[51] The *dioiketes* essentially replaced the position of vizier, who had traditionally been the highest official in Egypt after the pharaoh.

during the winter of 1914/1915 AD) a great deal is known about the work Apollonius carried out for Ptolemy II, and it also provides valuable information about the region's population, economy and administration between 261 and 229/228 BC. The collection includes approximately 3,000 papyri, 1,700 of which are legible, and came from the ancient town of Philadelphia (which had been founded by Ptolemy II on the north-eastern edge of the Fayum).

At a local level, Egypt was divided into 39 nomes (districts) – the number having been increased from 36 by Ptolemy II. The dominant figure in each nome was the *strategos*, who commanded the region's military. They were normally Greek, were subordinate to the *dioiketes*, and appointed directly by the pharaoh. Traditionally, the *nomarch* (provincial governor) had been the dominant political figure in Egypt's nomes. However, during the second half of the third century BC the *strategos* exerted growing influence over civil matters in addition to their military duties. Consequently, they eventually became the most senior administrator in their respective nomes, while the importance of the *nomarch* declined.[52]

Beneath the *strategos*, each nome was administered by three key officials of equal rank, all of whom answered to the *dioiketes*. These were the *nomarch* (who was responsible for agricultural production), the *oikonomos* (who oversaw finances), and the *basilikos grammateus* or 'royal scribe' (who was in charge of record-keeping, as well as the surveying, registration and administration of land). This division of power was intended to prevent ambitious officials from establishing regional power bases and undermining the authority of the central government, as well as to extract as much wealth from the nomes as possible.

Most nomes were divided into a number of *topoi* (districts), which were in turn divided into a series of *kōmai* (villages). These subdivisions had their own officials, including the *toparch* (district leader) and *topogrammateus* (district scribe) in the *topoi* and the *komarch* (village leader) and *komogrammateus* (village scribe) in the *kōmai*.

The village scribe was the lowest ranking official in the government hierarchy. They were primarily responsible for maximising the profit generated by state land – calculating farm yields and how much land could be rented out to tenant farmers.

---

[52] Traditionally, the office of *nomarch* had been held by native Egyptians. However, when Egypt was brought under Ptolemaic rule, the position was typically held by Greeks rather than Egyptians.

Every scribe was summoned to the capital of their respective nome twice a year to report to the governor. The first of these meetings took place in February so the annual survey of agricultural production could be prepared, and the second meeting took place about four weeks later in order to report on the survey's findings. In the early summer, the village scribes then travelled to Alexandria to answer to the *dioiketes*.

Even at the very bottom of the chain of command there was a separation of powers to prevent officials from getting too big for their boots, with the *toparchs* and *komarchs* being subordinate to the *nomarch* and the *topogrammateus* and *komogrammateus* reporting to the *basilikos grammateus*. The lower levels of local government, particularly at the village level, remained largely in Egyptian hands, and many Egyptians even served as the *oikonomos* and *basilikos grammateus*.

In addition to the nomes, there were three autonomous Greek cities (*poleis*) in Ptolemaic Egypt that had special privileges under Ptolemaic law, enabling them to blossom as vibrant commercial centres. These were the ancient trading post of Naucratis in Lower Egypt, the newly-established city of Ptolemais Hermiou in Upper Egypt (which Ptolemy I had founded to counter the influence of Thebes), and the capital city Alexandria. The citizens of these cities benefitted from tax privileges and the right to elect their own magistrates, and it was in these places that Egypt's Greek population was centred. All three cities were incredibly multi-ethnic and attracted immigrants from all over the Mediterranean world, who saw Egypt as a place of opportunity where fortunes could be made in finance and commerce.[53]

Outside these key commercial centres, the Egyptian countryside was primarily inhabited by the native Egyptian population and was largely immune to immigration. While the minority Greek population dominated Ptolemaic society and prospered as soldiers, officials, merchants and scholars, the majority native population was expected to do all the hard work – tilling fields and paying crippling taxes – for little in return. Most of the Greek population in Egypt never bothered to learn the Egyptian language and maintained their own cultural traditions. It is alleged that only the last Ptolemaic ruler, Cleopatra VII, knew how to speak the native language, and this reflects the fact that the Ptolemies' primary interest in Egypt was to exploit it for all it was worth.

---

[53] The Greek, Jewish and Egyptian populations were legally segregated in these cities. They lived in different areas and were forbidden from intermarrying.

Unsurprisingly, this cultural and ethnic divide between the Greek cities and the Egyptian countryside caused constant friction, and Ptolemaic rulers had to suppress native rebellions on numerous occasions.

In addition to shaking up the structure of local and central government, Ptolemy II oversaw judicial reforms to promote the centralisation of the legal system, although he was careful to respect local traditions and many of the reforms may have merely amounted to the codification of existing legal practices. The Greek population had imported their legal system from their homeland and this operated alongside the traditional Egyptian one. Consequently, there were three main courts: the *Laokritai*, which was presided over by Egyptian priests and heard cases involving Egyptians; the *Dikasteria*, which handled cases concerning Greeks; and the *Chrematistai*, which was made up of royal judges who dealt with judicial matters by delegation of the king and was open to everyone.

Another way Ptolemy II managed to consolidate royal authority and maximise his revenue was by reforming the currency and tax system. He strengthened his authority over the levying and collection of taxation by stripping the temples of the authority to collect the *hekte* (one-sixth tax) and giving it to tax farmers instead. Even more significantly, he widened the circulation of bronze coinage and introduced new denominations, as well as imposing a new salt tax. This tax applied to both men and women, and only a few groups were exempted from it.

While such policies helped to increase the crown's revenue, it should not be ignored that they failed to prevent the rampant bribery and tax evasion that occurred throughout the Ptolemaic era. Egypt's government under the Ptolemies was like so many others throughout history. It was not run for the benefit of the masses, but for the enrichment and empowerment of a privileged few. And despite the various native uprisings that occurred in Ptolemaic Egypt, that wasn't going to change.

Ptolemy III: The Benefactor

Egypt's third Ptolemaic ruler, Ptolemy III Euergetes, acceded to the throne in 246 BC.[54] During his reign of almost two and a half decades, the Ptolemaic Kingdom reached the height of its power, both militarily and economically.

The future Ptolemy III was born sometime around 280 BC in Egypt or on the Greek island of Kos. Despite him growing up to become one of the most successful Ptolemaic rulers, very little is known about his youth.

As the eldest son of Ptolemy II and his first wife Arsinoe I, Ptolemy III was removed from the line of succession when his mother was accused of treason and forced into exile (sometime after 275 BC).[55] It is probably for this reason that he appears to have been raised on the Greek island of Thera (present-day Santorini) rather than in Alexandria.[56] However, he was later restored as his father's heir in the early 250s BC, after Ptolemy II's nephew and co-regent Ptolemy Epigonos took part in a failed rebellion against him.

When Ptolemy II died on 28 January 246 BC, Ptolemy III was proclaimed pharaoh and took the Egyptian name Iwaennetjerwysenwy Sekhemankhre Setepamun ('Heir of the [two] Benificent Gods, Chosen of Ptah, Powerful is the South of Re, Living Image of Amun'). He benefited from a smooth and peaceful rise to power and married the queen of Cyrenaica, Berenice II, as per the betrothal arranged by his father several years before.[57] Cyrenaica had declared itself independent from the Ptolemaic Kingdom in the early stages of Ptolemy II's reign, but was now brought back under Ptolemaic control as a result of this union. The royal couple are known to have had a number of children: Arsinoe III, Ptolemy IV, an unknown son (possibly named Lysimachus), Alexander, Magas, and Berenice. Many of these children met unfortunate ends. Berenice died as an infant in 238 BC, Magas was put to death in a hot bath as part of a purge of the royal family in 221 BC, and the unknown son and Alexander were probably killed during or prior to this purge too.

---

[54] Euergetes means 'benefactor'.
[55] Ptolemy III had two younger full siblings: Lysimachus and Berenice. They were also removed from the line of succession after their mother's fall from grace.
[56] One of Ptolemy III's tutors was the poet Apollonius of Rhodes, who went on to serve as the head of the Library of Alexandria during his student's reign.
[57] Berenice II was the only child of Ptolemy II's rebellious half-brother, Magas of Cyrene. Therefore, Berenice II was Ptolemy III's half-cousin.

Within a matter of months of becoming pharaoh, Ptolemy found himself at war. Fought against the Seleucid Empire between 246 and 241 BC, it is known as the Third Syrian War (or Laodicean War) and was triggered by a dispute over the Seleucid succession.

In July 246 BC, just a few months after Ptolemy III's accession to the Egyptian throne, the Seleucid king Antiochus II died in suspicious circumstances. Possibly after learning of Ptolemy II's death, Antiochus had left his wife Berenice and their infant son Antiochus in Antioch and moved to Ephesus to live with his ex-wife Laodice. Even after her divorce, Laodice had remained an incredibly powerful figure and never stopped scheming to make herself queen again, which naturally led to accusations that she poisoned Antiochus II while he was living at her residence. In any event, the sudden death of the Seleucid king triggered a succession dispute between supporters of Seleucus II (his teenage son by his first wife, Laodice) and Antiochus (his infant son by his second wife, Berenice). Both Laodice and Berenice were determined to have their sons installed as the new king. Berenice asserted her son was the legitimate heir on the basis that she had been Antiochus II's wife at the time of his death, while Laodice claimed her ex-husband had named her eldest son as his heir on his deathbed. Given that Berenice was Ptolemy's sister, the Egyptian king naturally backed her son's claim to the Seleucid throne and came to her aid by launching an invasion of Syria.[58]

Upon the outbreak of war, Berenice and Antiochus were in Antioch (giving them control of the heart of the Seleucid Empire), while Laodice and Seleucus II were in western Asia Minor (and had possession of a large portion of Anatolia). Meanwhile, Ptolemy faced little resistance as his army marched along the coast of the Levant, bound for Antioch.

One of Berenice's first acts in the war was to send a naval force to Cilicia, which succeeded in capturing the city of Soli (with the assistance of its citizens). The Seleucid governor of Cilicia, Aribazos, attempted to take the contents of the local treasury (which amounted to 1,500 talents) to Laodice in Ephesus, but the treasure was seized by Berenice's forces and Aribazos was captured and beheaded by local inhabitants while trying to escape across the Taurus Mountains.

---

[58] Ptolemy appointed his wife and queen, Berenice II, to serve as head of state in his absence.

By the late autumn of 246 BC Ptolemy III had landed with a small fleet at Seleucia Pieria, where he is reported to have received an enthusiastic welcome from the city's priests, magistrates and citizens, as well as Seleucid military officers and soldiers. Unfortunately, he was too late. When he proceeded to Antioch and entered the royal palace, he found Berenice and Antiochus had been murdered by supporters of Laodice.

The deaths of his sister and nephew did not deter Ptolemy, who continued his campaign. Unwilling to go home empty-handed, he took up official duties in their name and allegedly sacked Antioch as an act of revenge for their murders. He then marched to Mesopotamia via Syria, where he achieved a remarkable victory by seizing control of Babylon in late 246 BC or early 245 BC.

Ptolemy probably hoped to permanently incorporate this region into his kingdom. This was signalled by him appointing a *strategos* (governor) to administer the region he had conquered 'on the other side' of the Euphrates, as well as a second *strategos* to govern the recently acquired territory of Cilicia. As things turned out though, his gains ended up being short-lived, thanks to domestic unrest within his domains.

Not long after the capture of Babylon, Ptolemy was compelled to return to Egypt with an enormous amount of loot to suppress a rebellion, which enabled the Seleucids to recapture Mesopotamia.[59] Despite being a relatively minor and short-lived revolt, it was a sign of worse to come and turned out to be the first of a series of native Egyptian rebellions that plagued the reigns of Ptolemy III and his successors. One of the main causes of this rebellion was the heavy tax burden Ptolemy's Syrian war had placed on the Egyptian people, who were already under immense pressure from the oppressive and unjust Ptolemaic administrative and economic system. The absence of the pharaoh from Egypt during his campaign would have also encouraged them that it was the opportune moment to rise up, and the situation was made worse by famine (caused by the low level of the Nile in 245 BC).

While Ptolemy had his hands full in Egypt, there were important developments in the Aegean. In 246 BC Seleucid-controlled Ephesus was captured by an illegitimate son

---

[59] Ptolemy did not return to Egypt emptyhanded. He is reported to have brought back 40,000 talents of silver and sacred Egyptian statues which had been looted from Egypt by the Persian king Cambyses II in the sixth century BC. This pious deed helped the Ptolemies in their continued efforts to present themselves as legitimate Egyptian pharaohs who had liberated the country from the Persian conquerors.

of Ptolemy II named Ptolemy Andromachou, who installed a substantial garrison there, although things went downhill from here. At an uncertain date in about 246 or 245 BC, a Ptolemaic fleet under the command of Ptolemy Andromachou was defeated by a Macedonian fleet led by Antigonus II at the Battle of Andros. The outcome of the battle seriously undermined Ptolemy's power in the Aegean. However, it did not deter him from continuing to provide financial support to Macedonia's enemies in mainland Greece for the remainder of his reign.[60]

*

Ptolemy's sudden return to Egypt enabled the Seleucids to regain much of the territory they had lost so far in the Third Syrian War. As news of the death of Berenice and her son spread, public opinion throughout the Seleucid Empire shifted in Seleucus II's favour, as most of its inhabitants preferred to have a legitimate Seleucid ruler rather than Ptolemy. Mesopotamia was back in Seleucid hands by July 245 BC and Seleucus II then marched through Syria, where he regained control of Antioch, followed by other important cities in the region. Consequently, the interior of northern Syria was back in Seleucid hands by 242 BC, which gave them the capability to launch raids into the area surrounding Damascus (in Ptolemaic Syria).

Back in Egypt, Ptolemy could at least find satisfaction in the fact that he had successfully suppressed the native rebellion.

As soon as this had been taken care of, he deployed both Greek and Egyptian propaganda to exaggerate the scale of his conquests against the Seleucids. He also had himself and his wife Berenice II deified as the *Theoi Euergetai* ('Benefactor Gods') and inducted into the Ptolemaic cult in 243 BC, which meant they were now worshipped alongside Alexander the Great and the Ptolemies who had preceded them. This title was granted by the Egyptian priesthood, partly in recognition of Ptolemy's campaign against the Seleucids, which had resulted in the return of Egyptian religious statues that had previously been stolen by the Persians. More broadly, it acknowledged the royal couple's generous contributions to Egyptian religious cults, particularly those that concerned sacred animals (such as the Apis bull at Memphis and the Mnevis bull at Heliopolis).

---

[60] After his defeat at Andros, Ptolemy Andromachou is believed to have invaded Thrace, where he conquered Aenus and various other cities. His life came to a bloody end though in 243 BC, when he was assassinated by mutinous Thracian mercenaries under his command in Ephesus.

In 242 BC there was some further fighting near Damascus, but the Third Syrian War was finally brought to an end in 241 BC when Ptolemy negotiated a peace settlement with the Seleucids. During these negotiations Ptolemy's bargaining position was strengthened by Seleucus II's younger brother, Antiochus Hierax, who had defied his sibling's authority by demanding control of Seleucid territories in Asia Minor and declaring their independence soon thereafter. As a consequence of this lack of unity amongst the Seleucids, the peace settlement favoured Ptolemy, who was allowed to retain all the territory he had conquered in Thrace, Asia Minor and northern Syria, including Seleucia Pieria, Lebedus and Ephesus.[61]

Seleucia Pieria was the seaport of Antioch. Allowing this to remain in Ptolemaic hands was a serious loss for the Seleucids – both economically and symbolically – given that it controlled a great deal of the city's trade and was home to the tomb of the first Seleucid ruler, Seleucus I. The city was a terminus for long-distance trade routes and arguably the most important port in the Seleucid Empire: serving as a gateway to the Mediterranean and equipped with a major fortress, naval base and shipyards. Now in Ptolemy's hands, its location offered convenient connections by sea with Ptolemaic Cyprus and Coele-Syria, in addition to the recently conquered territories of Cilicia and Pamphylia.

In exchange for these territorial concessions, Ptolemy recognised Seleucus II as the rightful king of the Seleucid Empire and the Eleutherus River was restored as the recognised border between the Ptolemaic Kingdom and the Seleucid Empire.

By the end of the Third Syrian War, the Ptolemaic Kingdom had almost the entire eastern Mediterranean coastline under its control – from Maroneia (in Thrace) all the way to Libya – making it the most powerful Hellenistic state. With the benefit of hindsight though, this marked the height of Ptolemaic power, and its empire had reached its greatest extent.

*

The Egyptian rebellion served as an important reminder of the collective power of the native population and prompted Ptolemy to seek closer ties with Egypt's priestly elite. These efforts were recorded in the Decree of Canopus, which was inscribed in three languages (Egyptian hieroglyphs, Demotic and Greek) and refers to a major assembly of Egyptian priests at Canopus on 7 March 238 BC.

---

[61] Lebedus was renamed Ptolemais in Ptolemy III's honour.

This decree was one of a series of decrees issued by the Egyptian priesthood, known collectively as the Ptolemaic Decrees. The other decrees were the Decree of Alexandria (under Ptolemy III), the Raphia Decree (under Ptolemy IV), and the Decree of Memphis and the two Philae decrees of 186 and 185 BC (under Ptolemy V).

In the Decree of Canopus, the priests presented Ptolemy as the ideal pharaoh, on a number of grounds. They praised him for his support for the priesthood, such as through his donations to temples and his endorsement of the Apis and Mnevis cults. They commended his good governance, particularly regarding him importing grain from Syria, Phoenicia, Cyprus and many other places at his own expense to alleviate a famine caused by an inadequate inundation of the Nile in 245 BC. And last but not least, they applauded his military achievements, which had kept Egypt safe and led to the recovery of Egyptian religious statues from the Seleucids.[62] The decree also deified Ptolemy's deceased infant daughter Berenice and instituted a series of reforms, including the introduction of a leap day every four years to the 365-day Egyptian calendar.

The Egyptian calendar was composed of 12 months (each lasting 30 days) and five epagomenal days. In accordance with the reform, there were six epagomenal days instead of five once every four years, which would have made it the most accurate calendar in the ancient world. However, this reform failed to achieve popular acceptance and was ultimately rejected by the Egyptian priesthood, who were reluctant to abandon thousands of years' worth of tradition in favour of Greek rationalism. It was not until 29 August 22 BC that the calendar change was officially implemented in Egypt by the Roman Emperor Augustus.

Like the Ptolemies who preceded and succeeded him, Ptolemy III made an effort to present himself in the guise of a traditional Egyptian pharaoh to his native subjects. While his father (Ptolemy II) and grandfather (Ptolemy I) had followed Alexander the Great's example by favouring the worship of Amun (at Karnak, in Thebes), Ptolemy III prioritised the worship of the god Ptah (at Memphis). As a consequence of this, the sacred Apis bull (which was worshipped as a living manifestation of Ptah) began to play a key role in both New Year and coronation festivals. And Ptolemy III's preference for Ptah was also reflected in two elements of his royal title: in his golden Horus name *Neb khab-used mi ptah-tatenen* ('Lord of the Jubilee-festivals as well as

---

[62] The statues had been stolen in the sixth century BC during the reign of the Persian king Cambyses II, who conquered Egypt and became its pharaoh. The return of these statues earned Ptolemy III his nickname Euergetes ('Benefactor').

Ptah Tatjenen') and his nomen, which included the phrase *Mery-Ptah* ('beloved of Ptah').

In general, however, Ptolemy continued his father's and grandfather's policy of sponsoring temple construction and restoration projects across Egypt. The best-known of these projects was the Temple of Edfu, which was dedicated to Horus and built on the site of a smaller existing temple dedicated to the same god. Construction began on 23 August 237 BC and its grand scale is reflected in the fact that work continued at the site until its completion in 57 BC (during the reign of Ptolemy XII).[63]

Another major project Ptolemy initiated was the construction of a temple devoted to the worship of the Greco-Egyptian deity Serapis, known as the Serapeum of Alexandria. The Serapeum became the largest and most magnificent temple in Alexandria's Greek quarter and went on to house an offshoot collection of the Library of Alexandria.

Suffice it to say Edfu and the Serapeum were merely the tip of the iceberg. True to his epithet – Benefactor – a great deal of religious building work was sponsored by Ptolemy III during his reign, including: the construction of a temple of Osiris at Canopus, the erection of a great gateway and enclosure wall at the temple of Khonsu (at Karnak) and a birth house at the temple of Isis at Philae, restoration work on the temple of Khnum at Esna, decorative work on the temple of Isis at Behbeit El Hagar, and the creation of a sacred lake and the construction of a chapel by the temple of Montu at Medamud.

In addition to his religious patronage, Ptolemy picked up from where his father had left off in the Fayum Oasis by continuing his efforts to boost the amount of arable land there. And most notably of all, he maintained and expanded his dynasty's reputation as a generous sponsor of literature and scholarship throughout his reign.

Ptolemy was unafraid of using dishonest means to expand the Library of Alexandria's burgeoning collection, including outright theft. Any manuscripts contained on board ships that docked in Alexandria were seized and copied. The original manuscript would then be retained by the Library and the copied version given to the owner. In

---

[63] Today the Temple of Edfu is one of the best preserved Ancient Egyptian temples and the finest surviving building of the Ptolemaic period. The main temple was finished in 231 BC (during the reign of Ptolemy IV), the full complex was opened in 142 BC (during the reign of Ptolemy VIII), and much of the decorative work was not completed until the reign of Ptolemy XII.

one famous incident, he obtained the official copies of classic works by the three Greek tragedians (Aeschylus, Sophocles and Euripides) from Athens on loan, but opted to forfeit the hefty deposit of 15 silver talents instead of returning them.

Some of the most prominent scholars who were active in Alexandria during Ptolemy's reign were the polymath Eratosthenes, the astronomer Conon of Samos, and the geometer Apollonius of Perga.

Eratosthenes of Cyrene was best known for calculating the circumference of the Earth with remarkable accuracy. He became the chief librarian at the Library of Alexandria and served as a tutor to Ptolemy III's children, including his successor Ptolemy IV.

Conon of Samos is primarily remembered for naming the constellation Coma Berenices ('Berenice's Hair') in honour of Ptolemy III's wife, Berenice II, who famously vowed to sacrifice her long hair as a votive offering if her husband returned safely from his campaign against the Seleucids in the Third Syrian War.[64]

Last but not least, Apollonius of Perga was most famous for his work on conic sections. He coined mathematical terms which are still in use today, such as 'ellipse', 'parabola' and 'hyperbola', and he also dabbled in astronomy (for which the Apollonius crater on the Moon was named in his honour).

*

After the conclusion of the Third Syrian War, Ptolemy did not take any more direct military action against Seleucus II. However, he did make life hard for his rival by continuing to offer financial aid to the Seleucid king's opponents. This included support for Seleucus' rebellious younger brother Antiochus Hierax (who had

---

[64] The Alexandria-based scholar Callimachus of Cyrene wrote a poem entitled *The Lock of Berenice*, which tells the story of how Berenice II fulfilled her promise to give a lock of her hair as a votive offering to Aphrodite, in thanks for her husband's safe return from the Third Syrian War. The offering was made at the temple at Cape Zephyrium to the east of Alexandria (where Arsinoe II was worshipped as Aphrodite) and was said to have disappeared the following morning. It was eventually rediscovered among the stars by the astronomer Conon of Samos, who claimed Aphrodite had placed it in the sky in recognition of Berenice's sacrifice.
A second poem by Callimachus, called the *Victory of Berenice*, celebrates Berenice II's victory in the four-horse chariot race at the Nemean Games (one of the four Panhellenic Games held in Ancient Greece). This was such an impressive feat that Berenice commissioned the poet Posidippus to write an epigram, claiming she had 'stolen' the fame of Cynisca (the first woman to win an Olympic event, in the 396 BC four-horse chariot race).

established his own kingdom in Asia Minor) and Attalus I (the king of Pergamon, who took advantage of the conflict between the two brothers to seize control of Seleucid territories in Asia Minor).[65]

The shift from direct military intervention to more indirect forms of hostility can also be seen in Ptolemy's policy towards Macedonia. Following the Ptolemaic navy's defeat against the Macedonians at the Battle of Andros, Ptolemy returned to his previous strategy of financing Macedonia's enemies in mainland Greece – most significantly the Achaean League, which Ptolemy ended up being elected the leader (*hegemon*) of in 243 BC.

Although Ptolemy's relationship with the Achaean League endured for many years, it fell apart when the League went to war against Sparta for control of the Peloponnese, in a conflict known as the Cleomenean War (229-222 BC).[66]

Spartan successes in the early stages of the war convinced Ptolemy that Sparta would prove to be a more useful ally against Macedonia than the faltering Achaean League, so he abandoned the Achaeans and shifted his financial support to the Spartans instead.

By 226 BC, continued Spartan gains had compelled the *strategos* of the Achaean League, Aratus of Sicyon, to strengthen his poor hand by seeking an alliance with his former enemy, the Macedonian king Antigonus III. This was a serious development for the Spartans and marked a key turning point in the war, as it caused the tide to start turning against Ptolemy's ally.

In 224 BC, the Macedonians invaded the Peloponnese to bring the Spartans to heel. By then most of the Greek states had become part of Antigonus III's 'Hellenic League', with the notable exceptions of Athens and the Aetolian League, who allied themselves with Ptolemy. To show their gratitude for Ptolemy's support, the Athenians established a religious cult in which the Egyptian king and his wife were worshipped as gods and a festival (called the Ptolemais) was celebrated in their honour every four years from 224/223 BC. Just in case this wasn't enough, they also named a new *phyle* (tribe) in Ptolemy's honour (called Ptolemais) and a new *deme* (subdivision of Athens) after his wife Berenice II (called Berenicidae), as well as

---

[65] Following the assassination of Seleucus II in 223 BC, the Seleucid general Achaeus reconquered the Seleucid territories in Asia Minor that had been seized by Attalus I.
[66] The Cleomenean War was named after the Spartan king Cleomenes III.

erecting two statues of the Egyptian king – one at the Agora of Athens and another at Delphi – and naming a gymnasium that Ptolemy III had established near the Agora of Athens 'Ptolemaion' after its founder.

Meanwhile, fortune started to turn against the Spartan king Cleomenes III. With the Macedonians closing in, he was compelled to request financial assistance off Ptolemy near the end of 224 BC so he could afford to recruit additional troops. Although the request was granted, Cleomenes was required to send his mother and children to Alexandria as hostages in return, and between 223 BC and the summer of 222 BC the Macedonians dealt a series of defeats to the Spartans on the Peloponnese that ultimately forced them to retreat all the way home to Laconia.

These setbacks convinced Ptolemy that Sparta was no longer worth supporting. He was reluctant to commit troops to the war in Greece, which would have been required in large numbers to maintain the Spartan war effort. Sending in an army would have contradicted the established Ptolemaic policy towards Greece (which favoured financial assistance over direct military intervention) and left his empire (particularly Coele-Syria) vulnerable to a potential attack from the Seleucids. For these reasons, the Egyptian king was persuaded by Antigonus to withdraw his financial support for Sparta (perhaps in exchange for some territory in Asia Minor) in the early summer of 222 BC. Given that this money had been used by Cleomenes to pay for mercenaries, Ptolemy's decision dealt a serious blow to the Spartan cause. Just ten days after Cleomenes received this disappointing news from the Ptolemaic court in Alexandria – informing him that the financial support had been suspended and encouraging him to open peace negotiations with the Macedonians – the Cleomenean War came to an end when the Macedonian alliance routed the Spartans at the Battle of Sellasia.

In the aftermath of the battle, Cleomenes fled into exile. He sought asylum at Ptolemy's court in Alexandria, which was granted, and the Egyptian king also promised to help him regain his throne.[67] However, as things turned out Ptolemy did not live long enough to keep this promise. In November or December 222 BC, soon after Cleomenes' arrival in the Egyptian capital, Ptolemy III died. He was presumably

---

[67] Cleomenes III did not prosper during the reign of Ptolemy III's successor. Ptolemy IV's chief minister, Sosibius, had Cleomenes placed under house arrest on trumped-up charges of conspiring against the king. Cleomenes eventually managed to escape (in 219 BC), but committed suicide along with his friends after trying and failing to instigate an uprising against Ptolemy IV.

buried in the royal quarter in Alexandria and was succeeded by his eldest son Ptolemy IV.

Although no one could have known it at the time, the Ptolemaic Kingdom had reached the height of its power and influence under Ptolemy III's rule. By reunifying Egypt and Cyrenaica and conducting a successful campaign against the Seleucids in the Third Syrian War, he increased his territorial possessions. Just as importantly, he proved to be a prudent ruler who maintained peace at home through competent governance and deterred threats from external enemies by maintaining a strong national defence system. Admittedly, he did face the first native revolt against Ptolemaic rule, but this was quickly suppressed and he handed a kingdom to his successor that was both prosperous and internally stable.

Alas, even though his dynasty clung onto power for a further two centuries, it would be all downhill from here for the Ptolemies.

Ptolemy IV: The Fratricidal King

The fourth ruler of the Ptolemaic dynasty, Ptolemy IV Philopator, was the eldest son of Ptolemy III and Berenice II.[68] He acceded to the throne after the death of his father in late 222 BC and was deified at the same time as the *Theos Philopator* ('Father-loving God'). Although he couldn't have known it at the time, his reign marked the beginning of a long-term decline in Ptolemaic Egypt's power and influence that would ultimately result in its absorption into the Roman Empire. Unlike the Ptolemies who had preceded him, many ancient sources criticise Ptolemy IV for neglecting his duties in government in favour of luxury and royal pageantry. He led a dissolute life, became grossly obese, and was heavily influenced by his favourites at the royal court.

Ptolemy IV was probably a little over 20 years old when he became king. Unlike the relatively peaceful successions of his father and grandfather, Ptolemy IV's rise to power coincided with an extensive and bloody purge of the royal family. This was orchestrated by two prominent courtiers named Sosibius and Agathocles, who exerted considerable influence over the young pharaoh and sought to eliminate anyone who might attempt to oppose their newly acquired authority.[69]

The reason for Agathocles' influence is fairly obvious, as he was the brother of Ptolemy IV's favourite mistress – a noblewoman named Agathoclea.

Agathocles and his sister had been introduced to Ptolemy IV by their greedy and ambitious mother Oenanthe, who used her son and daughter to gain considerable influence over Ptolemy IV's government throughout his reign.[70] By contrast, very little is known about Sosibius' origin or how he came to exercise so much influence over the young Ptolemy IV, although his father may have been Sosibius of Tarentum (one of Ptolemy II's bodyguards). Sosibius was clearly a highly intelligent individual and was apparently an accomplished athlete from his early youth, which is evidenced by him being the victor at various games, including in the *diaulos* (boys' foot race) at

---

[68] Philopator is translated as 'lover of his father'.
Ptolemy IV also adopted the Egyptian name Iwaennetjerwy-menkhwy Setepptah Userkare Sekhemankhamun, which means 'Heir of the [two] Beneficent Gods, Chosen of Ptah, Powerful is the Soul of Re, Living Image of Amun'.
[69] Sosibius managed to maintain his preeminent position in government throughout Ptolemy IV's reign, although some power was shared with Agathocles.
[70] Agathocles served in the prestigious position of priest of Alexander the Great for the year 216/215 BC.

the Ptolemaia, in the *agéneioi* ('beardless') wrestling at the Panathenaic games and in chariot racing at the Isthmian and Nemean games.

The purge that Sosibius and Agathocles presided over occurred in 221 BC, with the pharaoh's approval, and had a number of high profile victims. Ptolemy's uncle Lysimachus was put to death, followed by his younger brother Magas, who was scalded to death in a bath. Soon after this, his mother Berenice II was murdered, probably by poisoning. Other potential victims of the purge were Ptolemy IV's two other younger brothers – Alexander and a brother whose name is unknown (possibly Lysimachus) – both of whom appear to have died either before or during the purge.

It is possible that Berenice II felt her eldest son was not fit to inherit the throne and wanted Magas (who held important military positions and was popular with the army) to succeed her husband instead. If that was indeed the case, then it would explain the ruthless and decisive action Ptolemy took against so many of his immediate family members.

Only one of Ptolemy's siblings was lucky enough to survive the purge. This was his elder sister, Arsinoe III, who he married at some point between his accession to the throne and the autumn of 220 BC. Their marriage produced just one child – a son named Ptolemy V, who was born in 210 BC – and Ptolemy's mistress Agathoclea continued to be his favourite lover.

After the purge, Sosibius and Agathocles emerged as the dominant figures in Egypt's government. Like many corrupt royal favourites throughout history, they used their power to further their own interests, to the displeasure of the people.

According to numerous ancient sources, Sosibius took over the day-to-day running of the kingdom while the young king indulged in debauchery and luxurious living, encouraged by his mistress Agathoclea. Under Sosibius' supervision, the state of Egypt's military and finances declined significantly. As a result of this, when war broke out with the Seleucids once again, it took Ptolemy's government a considerable amount of time to muster and train an army that was capable of countering the Seleucid threat.

Between 219 and 217 BC the Ptolemaic Kingdom became embroiled in yet another conflict with the Seleucid Empire, called the Fourth Syrian War.

The stage was set for this conflict in 223 BC, when Antiochus III acceded to the Seleucid throne. The new Seleucid king was determined to reverse the losses his kingdom had suffered at the hands of Ptolemy III in the Third Syrian War and sought to take advantage of the domestic instability caused by Ptolemy IV's bloody purge at the Ptolemaic court by launching an invasion of Ptolemaic Coele-Syria in the summer of 221 BC. This initial attack was repelled by the Aetolian general Theodotus (who was in command of Ptolemaic forces in the region), although soon after this Ptolemy made the mistake of alienating Theodotus against him.

Rather than rewarding Theodotus for his successful defence of Coele-Syria, Ptolemy recalled the victorious general to Alexandria, where he was ill-treated by a number of the king's favourites at the royal court and quickly became disgusted by Ptolemy's vices and extravagant living. As a result of this, when Theodotus resumed his duties in Coele-Syria in 219 BC, he opened secret negotiations with Antiochus to surrender the province to him.

The real war began in the spring of 219 BC, when Antiochus launched a second invasion that resulted in the capture of the important seaport of Seleucia Pieria, which had been in Ptolemaic hands since 246 BC. This bad situation became even worse for Ptolemy when Theodotus officially defected to Antiochus, causing parts of Coele-Syria and a substantial portion of the Ptolemaic navy to fall into the hands of the Seleucids. This included the surrender of the important coastal cities of Tyre and Ptolemais in Phoenicia (present-day Acre, Israel), and left Egypt vulnerable to a Seleucid invasion via Palestine. However, the efforts of another Aetolian general in Ptolemy's service called Nicolaus undermined Theodotus' plans. Antiochus was forced to engage in prolonged (and ultimately futile) sieges at Sidon and Dora, and these obstacles prevented the Seleucids from taking control of the entirety of Coele-Syria.

Meanwhile, another threat to Ptolemy's rule emerged much closer to home when the exiled Spartan king Cleomenes III attempted to stir up a rebellion against him in Alexandria.

From the very start of his reign, Ptolemy had no intention of honouring his father's promise to provide Cleomenes with troops to regain his throne. He did initially try to keep Cleomenes happy so he could be used as a counterweight to his younger brother Magas, but once Magas had been killed Cleomenes' usefulness waned and Ptolemy had him placed under house arrest, probably at the instigation of Sosibius (who succeeded in making the pharaoh suspicious of the former Spartan king). This situation came to a head in 219 BC, when Cleomenes escaped from imprisonment by deceiving his guards and attempted to incite a revolt against Sosibius' government. He went through the streets of the Egyptian capital with his men, urging its citizens to rise up, and planned to break into the fortress and release the prisoners being held there. However, he failed to gain the support of the people of Alexandria and the revolt came to nothing. Realising the hopelessness of their cause, Cleomenes and his supporters committed suicide, most likely in the spring of 219 BC.

Back in Coele-Syria, Antiochus had been kept busy consolidating the gains he had made. By the end of 219 BC, Ptolemy and Antiochus had agreed to a ceasefire and entered formal peace negotiations at Seleucia Pieria. The negotiations took place in the winter of 219/218 BC, during which both sides argued over who was entitled to Coele-Syria, while Antiochus rejected Ptolemy's demands to return Seleucia Pieria to Ptolemaic control and to recognise the authority of the separatist king Achaeus in Asia Minor.[71] It is clear that neither side negotiated in good faith or had any desire to secure peace, and were essentially playing for time. Antiochus was busy preparing a new offensive, while Ptolemy needed to buy himself some time to get the Ptolemaic army into shape.

To finance the war effort taxes were increased to even more extortionate levels, placing a heavy burden on an already suffering and cash-strapped population. Meanwhile, the task of recruiting and training the Ptolemaic army was delegated to Sosibius. Soldiers were recruited from all of the Ptolemaic Kingdom's foreign territories, in addition to various other places, including Greece, Crete, Thrace and Galatia. In a break with tradition, the army was not just composed of Greeks, but also included approximately 20,000 native Egyptian troops. The fact that Ptolemy was willing to enrol a large force of Egyptians into his army and train them in phalanx tactics for the first time in Ptolemaic history shows just how serious the situation had become. In the short term, this innovation would help the Ptolemaic Kingdom to prevail in its war against the Seleucids, but had serious consequences for the kingdom's long-term stability.

---

[71] Achaeus was a Seleucid general who had been appointed commander of the Seleucid Empire's territories in Asia Minor to the west of the Taurus Mountains by Antiochus III. However, when he was falsely accused of planning a revolt, he declared himself a king in self-defence and became the region's de facto ruler.

The peace negotiations at Seleucia Pieria soon broke down and the anticipated Seleucid offensive began in early 218 BC when the Seleucids defeated Ptolemaic forces on both land and sea at Berytus. The attack led to the capture of Philadelphia (present-day Amman, Jordan) and paved the way for a full-scale invasion of Coele-Syria, although the Seleucids failed to gain control of the southern part of the Beqaa Valley, Damascus or Sidon.

The war came to a head in 217 BC when Ptolemy, accompanied by his wife Arsinoe III and chief minister Sosibius, led the Ptolemaic army north from Pelusium into the Levant to meet Antiochus and the Seleucids in battle. The Battle of Raphia, as it is known, was fought on 22 June 217 BC near Rafah (in present-day Palestine) and turned out to be one of the largest battles fought in the Hellenistic period.[72]

The battle was preceded by a series of minor skirmishes and a failed attempt to assassinate Ptolemy. The attempted assassination was carried out by Theodotus, who snuck into the Ptolemaic camp with two companions, but the Egyptian king was absent and he ended up killing Ptolemy's physician instead.

On the eve of the battle, Ptolemy tried to motivate his forces by addressing them in the manner of a traditional Egyptian pharaoh, although the 20,000 Egyptians who had been recruited wouldn't have been fooled by the performance. Like the Ptolemies who had preceded him, he had made no effort to learn the Egyptian language, so he delivered his speech in Greek and had to rely on an interpreter to translate it into Egyptian.

If Polybius' account of the Battle of Raphia is to be believed, the Ptolemaic army was composed of 70,000 infantry, 5,000 cavalry and 73 African war elephants, while the Seleucid army numbered 62,000 infantry, 6,000 cavalry and 102 Indian war elephants. In terms of formation, both Ptolemy and Antiochus placed their phalanx in the centre when they prepared their armies for battle. Mercenaries and more lightly armed troops were positioned on the right and left wings (led by their war elephants), as well as the cavalry (who were positioned at the far side of either wing).

Despite it being a relatively even match in terms of numbers, the battle got off to a disastrous start for Ptolemy's army. At the beginning of the battle, the wings of each

---

[72] The Hellenistic period refers to a period of history in the Greek Mediterranean world, lasting from the death of Alexander the Great in 323 BC until the defeat of Cleopatra and Ptolemaic Egypt at the hands of the Romans in 30 BC.

army charged, led by their war elephants. Crucially, the African elephants in the Ptolemaic army were smaller and weaker than the Asian ones used by the Seleucids, which scared them and prompted them to turn and flee.[73] As they did so, they ploughed through the friendly infantry lined up behind them, sowing panic and disorder in their own ranks. Antiochus took advantage of this by leading his cavalry against the left wing of the Ptolemaic army. He succeeded in breaking their ranks and forcing them to retreat, but this promising start caused him to reach the premature conclusion that the battle was as good as over and he neglected what was happening on the other fronts.

With both the right and left wings of the Ptolemaic army consumed by chaos, the situation only improved when Ptolemy rode to his phalanx in the centre and encouraged them to attack the phalanx of the Seleucid army. As Polybius reports: 'Suddenly Ptolemy, who earlier had retreated under the protection of his phalanx, came on the scene in the middle of his ranks and showed himself to both armies, spreading fear among his opponents and powerfully reviving the courage and lust for battle on his own side.'

Ptolemy's inspiring actions are commonly presented as being the decisive turning point in the battle. While Antiochus was busy pursuing the fleeing Ptolemaic left wing, the centre of the Seleucid army was routed and started to retreat. As soon as this was brought to Antiochus' attention, he tried to come to their aid, but by the time he arrived they had already been defeated. It was clear that he would not be able to keep up the fight without his phalanx, so the Seleucid king opted to live to fight another day and retreated to Antioch.

One of the main contributing factors to Ptolemy's victory was the incorporation of a large number of well trained and equipped native Egyptians in his army for the first time in the dynasty's century-long existence. Doing this had the obvious benefit of ending the issue of manpower shortages. However, it also had serious long-term consequences. Now the Egyptians had been armed, trained and experienced success in battle, they were emboldened, and it was not long before they started to cause trouble for the Ptolemaic authorities: seeking to reassert their independence and determined not to be treated like second-class citizens in their own country any longer.

---

[73] Given that the African bush elephant is larger than the Asian elephant, the elephants used by the Ptolemaic army were probably either African forest elephants, North African elephants (now extinct), or a more diminutive variety of African bush elephant that can still be found in Eritrea in the present day.

*

The decisive Ptolemaic victory at the Battle of Raphia ended the threat of a Seleucid invasion of Egypt and brought the Fourth Syrian War to a close. In the aftermath of the battle, Ptolemy dispatched Sosibius to negotiate with the Seleucid king, and pressured Antiochus into accepting a peace treaty by invading and plundering Seleucid-controlled territories in Syria in the summer of 217 BC. Under the terms of the treaty that was agreed, Ptolemy received a large amount of gold and maintained possession of all the territories he had held at the start of the war (with the exception of Seleucia Pieria).

In October 217 BC Ptolemy made his triumphant return to Egypt. His victory in battle against the Seleucids was immortalised in the Raphia Decree, which was issued by a synod of Egyptian priests at Memphis.[74][75] Nevertheless, he has been criticised by some scholars in the present day for not forcing Antiochus to accept harsher peace terms and for failing to make the most of his victory by launching an offensive military campaign to conquer parts of the Seleucid Empire or – at the very least – to reclaim Seleucia Pieria. Some attribute the swiftness of Ptolemy's return to his desire to resume his cushy, luxurious life in Alexandria. However, Ptolemy's decision not to press his advantage and continue the war might also have been prompted by practical considerations: namely a decline in the population and overseas trade, which had led to a shortage of silver. In light of such economic problems, it is understandable why Ptolemy would have been reluctant to spend money on the additional mercenaries that would be required to sustain an aggressive foreign policy.

In the aftermath of the Fourth Syrian War, Ptolemy tried to rebuild the influence his father had lost in mainland Greece as a consequence of the Cleomenean War, as well as focusing on maintaining friendly relations with various states in preparation for potential future clashes with the Seleucid Empire. Ptolemaic diplomats – along with delegates from Byzantium, Chios and Rhodes – helped to arbitrate the Peace of Naupactus between the Hellenistic League (led by Macedonia) and the Aetolian League, which brought the Social War (220-217 BC) to an end, and Ptolemy gained

---

[74] By doing this Ptolemy IV followed his father's example, who had called a synod of Egypt's priests at Canopus.
[75] The Raphia Decree was inscribed on a stone stela and written in three different scripts: Egyptian hieroglyphs, Demotic and Greek. Issued on 15 November 217 BC, it was one of a series of decrees issued by synods of Egyptian priests in the Ptolemaic Kingdom, known collectively as the Ptolemaic Decrees.

the support of a number of Greek cities by providing them with generous financial assistance. Places such as the island of Rhodes and the town of Oropus (in Boeotia) showed their gratitude for his patronage by erecting statues in the Egyptian king's honour, and Ptolemy had particularly good relations with the Cretan city of Gortyn, where he initiated the construction of the city walls. However, the efforts of Ptolemy's emissaries (and representatives from other neutral states) to mediate a peace agreement between Macedonia and the Roman Republic on three separate occasions in the First Macedonian War (215-205 BC) proved to be far less successful.[76]

To the west of his domains, Ptolemy maintained cordial relations with both Carthage and the Roman Republic by remaining neutral during the Second Punic War (218-201 BC). He also continued his predecessors' friendly policy towards the tyrant of Syracuse, Hiero II (r. 275-215 BC). Given that Syracuse was caught between two great powers – Rome and Carthage – Hiero understood he would need to secure all the foreign support he could get if he wanted to maintain his city's independence. As part of his efforts to butter up the Ptolemaic Kingdom, he had a luxurious ship loaded with grain and sent it to the Ptolemaic ruler as a gift (probably during the reign of Ptolemy III). However, relations with Syracuse did admittedly cool during the brief reign of Hiero II's successor, Hieronymus (r. 215-214 BC).[77] Hieronymus' plans to abandon Syracuse's alliance with Rome in favour of one with Carthage and his repeated attempts to persuade Ptolemy to enter the Second Punic War (218-201 BC) on the Carthaginian side risked undermining the careful balancing act the Ptolemaic king was engaged in to stay on the good side of both Rome and Carthage. This awkward situation resolved itself when Hieronymus was assassinated just over a year into his reign, in 214 BC. A republican government was restored by the Syracusans (known as the Fifth Democracy), but it did not save Syracuse from the wrath of the Romans, who captured the city two years later.

*

In 216-215 BC, soon after the festivities that were held to celebrate the Ptolemaic victory in the Fourth Syrian War, Ptolemy IV and Arsinoe III were officially integrated into the Ptolemaic cult as the *Theoi Philopatores* ('Father-loving gods'). Ptolemy also tried to promote the unity of the cults of Alexander the Great and the Ptolemies by moving the remains of Alexander the Great and his Ptolemaic

---

[76] These attempts were made between 210 and 207 BC.
[77] Hieronymus was the grandson of Hiero II. He was only a teenager when he became king and was essentially a puppet of his guardians.

predecessors from their existing individual tombs to a new pyramidal structure within Alexandria's royal quarter. This new tomb – where Alexander the Great and his Ptolemaic successors would rest side by side for eternity – was probably consecrated during the Ptolemaia festival of 215/214 BC, and it is likely that he also established a new cult in Ptolemais Hermiou (Upper Egypt) dedicated to the founder of the dynasty (Ptolemy I) and the current reigning monarch at about the same time. A few years later, in 211 BC, Ptolemy appears to have started promoting a cult devoted to his late mother, Berenice II. As part of this, a new temple was established in honour of *Berenice Sozousa* ('Berenice who saves') near the shore in Alexandria, which fit in well with her association with the protection of sailors. It is likely that Berenice II's cult was modelled off the one that already existed for Ptolemy IV's grandmother Arsinoe II, which can be seen in their many similarities. For example, both of the deified queens were supposedly able to offer safety to sailors and came to be equated with the Egyptian goddess Isis and the Greek goddess Aphrodite.

Ptolemy showed particularly strong support for the Greek god of wine, Dionysus, which is hardly surprising considering the opulence and luxury of the Ptolemaic court and the fact that Dionysus was the god that best represented the ideal of *tryphé*. Various areas of Alexandria were renamed after Dionysus during Ptolemy's reign. He had himself depicted with attributes of Dionysus in works of art, referred to himself as the *Neos Dionysos* ('New Dionysus'), and also established several festivals in the god's honour, many of which he took part in – leading the procession with a *tympanon* (hand drum) at hand.

Dionysus was not the only god that Ptolemy was equated to in royal imagery. For example, on a famous collection of gold *octodrachms* (eight-drachma coins) Ptolemy is shown wearing the rayed crown of Apollo or Helios and holding the trident of Poseidon and the aegis of Athena, Zeus and Alexander the Great.

As a member of the Ptolemaic cult, he was also worshipped in his own right. During his reign various Greek cities that were either allied with him or under his direct control inaugurated cults in his honour. Such cults were commonly granted to monarchs and other powerful individuals by Greek cities in the Hellenistic period to give thanks for a specific benefaction, and Ptolemy received similar honours in Jaffa and other Levantine cities following his victory at Raphia.

Like the Ptolemies who preceded him, Ptolemy IV had himself depicted as a traditional Egyptian pharaoh and maintained the support of Egypt's powerful priestly elite by taking part in religious rituals, making generous donations, and funding the construction and restoration of temples. Much of the work he sponsored was a continuation of projects that had been initiated by his predecessors, such as the Temple of Edfu (where construction had started during the reign of Ptolemy III).[78] Other notable religious construction work carried out under Ptolemy IV included: a shrine dedicated to Harpocrates within the Serapeum of Alexandria; a chapel of Khonsu-Neferhotep at Karnak; a shrine for Hathor and Maat at Deir el-Medina (west of Thebes); the east gate of the temple of Ptah at Memphis; a new temple for Hathor at Cusae, Nemty at Tjebu, Thoth at Dakka, and Arensnuphis at Philae; additions to the temple of Min and Isis at Coptos (present-day Qift); decorative work on the temple of Hibis in the Kharga Oasis, the great gateway at Karnak, and the temple of Isis at Philae (all continued from Ptolemy III); work on the temple of Montu at Medamud (also started by Ptolemy III); and the reconstruction of the naos of the temple of Mut, Khonsu and Astarte at Tanis.[79][80][81]

Throughout the Ptolemaic dynasty its rulers became closely associated with the Greek term *tryphé*. There is no definitive translation for this word, but it essentially refers to extravagance, excess, luxury and femininity. Although *tryphé* came to be regarded as a negative thing by the Romans, it was presented as a virtue in the Ptolemaic Kingdom. There, the king's wealth was considered an indicator of their success as a ruler, so the Ptolemies put it on public display at every opportunity, such as through their opulent palaces, the luxury of their court, and the extravagant festivals, processions and banquets they were able to hold. Furthermore, *tryphé* demonstrated a monarch's willingness and ability to make benefactions, and bestow wealth and good fortune on their kingdom. These things were particularly visible during the reign of Ptolemy IV, who took the Ptolemaic dynasty's love of luxury to a whole new level. One of the most stunning examples of this was a giant galley known as the *tessarakonteres*, which he is believed to have ordered the construction of.[82] The *tessarakonteres* was allegedly 128m long and required 4,000 rowers to power it, but

---

[78] Work on the Temple of Edfu was brought to a halt in 206 BC as a result of Horwennefer's rebellion.
[79] Harpocrates was developed by the Ptolemies in Alexandria. He was the god of silence, secrets and confidentiality, and was inspired by the Egyptian god Horus.
[80] Naos: The sanctuary or central room of a temple, where statues of gods were kept.
[81] The temple of Hibis was consecrated to the Theban triad: a group of three gods who were particularly popular in the region surrounding Thebes. The triad was composed of Amun, his consort Mut and their son Khonsu.
[82] *Tessarakonteres* means 'forty' and refers to the number of rowers required on each column of oars to propel the vessel.

these figures may be an exaggeration. Nevertheless, it is possible that this was both the largest ship to be built in the ancient world and the largest human-powered vessel ever constructed.

Although it is not entirely certain what the vessel looked like, there is a general consensus amongst scholars that it was used as a pleasure barge rather than for military purposes. Its vast size would have prevented it from being used as an effective warship and demonstrates that it was built as a status symbol. It was fitted with a range of facilities that made it look more like a villa than a ship, including shrines, dining and state rooms, and promenades along both decks.

The *tessarakonteres* is referred to in a number of ancient sources, including a work by Ptolemy's contemporary, Callixenus of Rhodes. This text is now lost, but part of it has been preserved in an early third century AD work by the Greek grammarian Athenaeus, called the *Deipnosophistae*: 'Philopator built a ship with forty ranks of rowers, being two hundred and eighty cubits long and thirty-eight cubits from one side to the other; and in height up to the gunwale it was forty-eight cubits; and from the highest part of the stern to the water-line was fifty-three cubits; and it had four rudders, each thirty cubits long . . . And the ship had two heads and two sterns, and seven beaks . . . And when it put to sea it held more than four thousand rowers, and four hundred supernumeraries; and on the deck were three thousand marines, or at least two thousand eight hundred and fifty. And besides all these there was another large body of men under the decks, and a vast quantity of provisions and supplies.'

Ptolemy's elaborate ship is also referenced in the *Life of Demetrius*, which was written by the Greek historian Plutarch in the late first century AD as part of his *Parallel Lives* series: 'Ptolemy Philopator built [a ship] of forty banks of oars, which had a length of two hundred and eighty cubits, and a height, to the top of her stern, of forty-eight; she was manned by four hundred sailors, who did no rowing, and by four thousand rowers, and besides these she had room, on her gangways and decks, for nearly three thousand men-at-arms. But this ship was merely for show; and since she differed little from a stationary edifice on land, being meant for exhibition and not for use, she was moved only with difficulty and danger.'

*

Despite Ptolemy's victory in the Fourth Syrian War, his kingdom continued to weaken in the years that followed. In addition to economic problems, nationalist sentiments were on the rise amongst the native Egyptian population. This particularly applied to the Egyptian soldiers who had taken part in the Battle of Raphia, given that they had been armed and trained, and emboldened by the experience of winning a stunning military victory.

Ever since the Ptolemies had become the masters of Egypt, the native population had only grudgingly accepted the authority of what was clearly a foreign dynasty. This is hardly surprising considering the Egyptian populace were essentially second class citizens in their own land and the Ptolemies ruled Egypt as a private estate for their own enrichment. While the resentful Egyptians had been largely kept in line during the firm and competent rule of Ptolemy I, Ptolemy II and Ptolemy III, they lunged at the opportunity to revolt when the central government weakened under the rule of Ptolemy IV and his clique of favourites.

Sometime after Raphia the Egyptian soldiers who had fought in the Ptolemaic army mutinied. Disaffected peasants also began leaving their villages in droves, in favour of living a life of banditry. Consequently, a string of violent revolts broke out in both the Nile Delta and Upper Egypt intended at re-establishing traditional pharaonic rule and shifting the centre of power from Alexandria back to Memphis or Thebes. While the precise cause of these rebellions continues to be a matter of debate, two of the main contributing factors were probably social injustice (in particular, the heavy taxation that had been imposed on lower class Egyptians to fund the Fourth Syrian War) and Ptolemy's decision to arm and train Egyptian soldiers to fight in his army at the Battle of Raphia.

What is certain is that the revolt in Upper Egypt was the most severe. The rebellion there prevented Ptolemy's forces from effectively defending southern Egypt against incursions by the Nubians, which enabled the Kushite king of Meroë, Arqamani, to seize control of the Dodekaschoinos in about 207-206 BC. Various temple construction projects Ptolemy had sponsored in the region were hijacked by Arqameni (or his successor Adikhalamani), who completed the work or simply stole all the credit by removing Ptolemy's name from inscriptions and replacing it with Arqameni's.[83]

---

[83] Ptolemaic temple building in the Dodekaschoinos was aimed at consolidating Ptolemaic rule in the area, by demonstrating royal power and assimilating local Nubian gods into the Egyptian pantheon.
During Ptolemy IV's reign he confirmed Ptolemy II's gift to the temple of Isis at Philae, which granted the income generated by the Dodekaschoinos to that temple. He was also involved in

The situation in Upper Egypt became even more serious in late 206 BC, when Thebes (Upper Egypt's principal city) fell to the rebels, who proclaimed their leader – Horwennefer – pharaoh. An Egyptian text, known as the *Demotic Chronicle* and likely composed during the reign of Ptolemy III, had prophesised that a native king would lead an uprising to overthrow the Ptolemaic dynasty, and this now seemed to be coming true.

The secessionist regime Horwennefer created in Upper Egypt stretched from Abydos in the north to Pathyris (present-day Gebelein) in the south and retained its independence for two decades, giving Egypt its first native pharaoh since the rebel pharaoh Khabash over a century earlier (in the 330s BC). Under Horwennefer the oppressive Ptolemaic tax system was abolished, land records were destroyed, and Greek inhabitants were forced to abandon their homes and property. The most important god of this new Theban state was the patron god of Thebes, Amun, which stressed its ideological opposition to the High Priests of Ptah in Memphis, who were close allies of the Ptolemaic monarchy. The priesthood of Amun at Thebes officially recognised Horwennefer as the rightful pharaoh and may even have presided over the rebel dynasty's coronation ceremonies.

The native rebellions deprived Ptolemy of tax revenue and farm yields and took a heavy toll on the already faltering Egyptian economy. And his financial woes were made even worse by the need to spend large amounts of money on mercenaries to fight the rebels.

It was during this period of domestic unrest – in July or August 204 BC – that Ptolemy IV died in mysterious circumstances, perhaps as a result of a fire in the royal palace. He was almost certainly laid to rest alongside Alexander the Great and his Ptolemaic ancestors in a grand tomb in Alexandria's royal quarter.

Ptolemy's wife, Arsinoe III, also died around this time, probably as a result of foul play. The Latin historian Justin claims Ptolemy's mistress Agathoclea persuaded him to divorce and murder Arsinoe shortly before his own death, while the Greek historian Polybius recorded she was murdered by Ptolemy's chief minister Sosibius. The most likely explanation is that Ptolemy's favourites were determined to hold onto their positions of power and were anxious that Arsinoe would be named regent. To prevent

---

the construction of temples dedicated to Thoth at Dakka and the Nubian god Mandulis at Talmis (present-day New Kalabsha), in addition to the enlargement of a temple devoted to the Nubian god Arensnuphis at Philae.

her from attempting to rule Egypt through her son, Agathocles and Sosibius had her murdered in a palace coup before she learned of her husband's death and claimed the regency for themselves.

No matter which of these theories is correct, it is clear that Arsinoe had a far less peaceful death than the Ptolemies who had preceded her – and this reflected the dynasty's declining stability and fortunes.

Ptolemy's death was kept secret by Agathocles, Agathoclea and their allies for a few days before his five-year-old son Ptolemy V was proclaimed the new pharaoh in accordance with tradition.[84] They used this delay to plunder the royal treasury and secure their hold on power by arranging a regency government led by Sosibius and Agathocles.

The Greek historian Polybius, writing in the second century BC, portrayed Ptolemy IV as the archetypal bad king who was responsible for the decline of his empire.[85] He allegedly dedicated his time to royal pageantry and luxurious living, and neglected his administrative duties by delegating most political, diplomatic and military business to his chief minister Sosibius. Polybius attributes the disasters that occurred during Ptolemy's reign (including the loss of southern Egypt and even his own death) to these failings, especially his disregard for government business.

Ptolemy is cast in a similarly negative light in the deuterocanonical book *3 Maccabees*. Composed at some point between the first century BC and the first century AD (likely by an Alexandria Jew writing in Greek), it presents the Egyptian king as an oppressive tyrant and tells the story of Ptolemy's persecution of the Jews. In the story, Ptolemy visits Jerusalem after his victory at the Battle of Raphia. Here, he defies divine law by attempting to enter the Second Temple in Jerusalem, but is prevented from doing so. This incident causes Ptolemy to develop a hatred for the Jews. Upon his arrival back in Alexandria he attempts to wipe out the Jewish population in his kingdom by gathering them in the city's hippodrome, where he plans to have them trampled to death by intoxicated elephants. However, Ptolemy's plans are ultimately thwarted when God intervenes to make the elephants trample the

---

[84] Ptolemy V had been named his father's co-regent shortly after his birth in 210 BC. He was the only child of Ptolemy IV and Arsinoe II.
[85] Given that Polybius was not alive during Ptolemy IV's reign, he would have consulted earlier works (which have long since been lost) when writing his history. This included the *Histories* of the Greek historian Phylarchus (of which Polybius was critical).

pharaoh's men instead. After witnessing this divine intervention, Ptolemy has a dramatic change of heart. He releases the Jews and grants them extensive privileges. The contents of this story are generally regarded as having a symbolic purpose – demonstrating the superiority of divine authority over secular authority – rather than relating real events, and it has also been argued that Ptolemy's character in the story was actually inspired by the Roman Emperor Caligula (who disregarded Jewish sensibilities). If this is true, then the writer probably used the long-dead Ptolemy IV as a cover for criticising contemporary Roman policies.

One thing that continued to prosper under Ptolemy IV's rule was scholarship. He shared his predecessors' passion for the arts – evidenced by him establishing a temple and cult in Alexandria dedicated to the Greek poet Homer and allegedly composing a tragedy about Adonis – and continued their generous sponsorship of scholarship and literature.[86] However, the overall picture of Egypt under Ptolemy IV is not a positive one. He proved to be a weak ruler and a poor administrator, and allowed a handful of favourites to dominate the government. This undermined not just Egypt's empire and international reputation but its internal stability too, and marked the beginning of a long-term decline in Ptolemaic power and influence. In the decades that lay ahead declining military fortunes, economic crises, domestic unrest, the rising influence of Rome, and power struggles within the Ptolemaic dynasty itself would mar the Ptolemaic Kingdom and sow the seeds of its demise.

*

Ptolemy's victory at Raphia marked the end of the Ptolemaic Kingdom's glory days. After the Fourth Syrian War, Ptolemy's kingdom went into a sharp decline. The Egyptian economy was severely weakened by the cost of the Fourth Syrian War, as well as the loss of tax revenues in the south of the country due to the establishment of a breakaway pharaonic state in Upper Egypt. The internal instability created by these native revolts, as well as by infighting and power struggles at the royal court in Alexandria, significantly weakened the Ptolemaic state and made it vulnerable to hostile foreign powers, causing it to lose its preeminent status in the Mediterranean.

---

[86] Adonis was a mortal lover of the goddess Aphrodite in Greek mythology.

Ptolemy V: The Boy King

The only child of Ptolemy IV and Arsinoe III, Ptolemy V Epiphanes Eucharistos, succeeded his father at just five years of age in the summer of 204 BC.[87]

The Ptolemaic dynasty's first boy king had the misfortune of acceding to the throne at a time of considerable unrest. Part of southern Egypt had seceded from the Ptolemaic Kingdom under a rival native Egyptian pharaoh. Both of his parents had died in suspicious circumstances. As a minor, he would not be ready to rule in his own right for many years. And his government was in the hands of the same self-serving courtiers who had presided over the misfortunes of Ptolemy IV's reign.

All of these things were a recipe for disaster and set the stage for a continuation of the Ptolemaic dynasty's declining fortunes. During his time on the throne almost all of the Ptolemaic Kingdom's overseas possessions were lost, including the long contested region of Coele-Syria.

When Ptolemy IV died, his passing was kept secret for a few days by his advisors. Ptolemy IV's mistress Agathoclea and her brother Agathocles were concerned the boy king's mother Arsinoe III would attempt to have herself named regent and rule through her son, which would spell the end of their own influence at the royal court. To prevent this from happening, they worked with Ptolemy IV's corrupt chief minister Sosibius to have Arsinoe murdered.

Once this bloody deed had been carried out the royal bodyguard and senior army officers were summoned to the royal palace, where Sosibius announced the deaths of Ptolemy IV and Arsinoe III. He then officially proclaimed their son, Ptolemy V, pharaoh by wrapping a diadem around the boy's head.

The removal of the new king's mother had enabled Sosibius and Agathocles to forge Ptolemy IV's will, which Sosibius now read out to those gathered before him. In accordance with the contents of this will, Sosibius and Agathocles were named regents of Ptolemy's government and the young pharaoh was placed in the care of Agathoclea and her mother Oenanthe. However, there are no further references to Sosibius after this event, which suggests he died soon thereafter. It is possible that he was murdered by Agathocles (who may have desired to be sole regent), and if this was indeed the

---

[87] Epiphanes Eucharistos can be translated as 'the Manifest, the Beneficent'.

case then it proved to be a fatal mistake. With the benefit of hindsight, the regency had a pitifully short lifespan, and some historians have argued that the loss of Sosibius (along with his ruthlessness, shrewdness, and exceptional diplomatic and organisational abilities) was one of the main reasons for this.

*

Agathocles was well aware of his unpopularity and took a number of measures to secure his regency. He granted two months' pay to all the soldiers in Alexandria to keep the army on side and sent leading members of the aristocracy overseas on diplomatic missions, hoping to gain international recognition for Ptolemy V's succession and to keep powerful aristocrats away from the Ptolemaic court (where they might have attempted to challenge the new regime).

As part of these efforts the Ptolemaic governor of Cyprus, Pelops, was dispatched to Asia Minor, where he was tasked with persuading the Seleucid king Antiochus III to honour the terms of the peace treaty that had been agreed at the end of the Fourth Syrian War.[88] Antiochus was busy regaining territory in the region and had exploited the turmoil in Alexandria by seizing several Ptolemaic possessions in Caria (including Amyzon in the spring of 203 BC), which Pelops protested was a breach of the agreement reached after the Battle of Raphia. Meanwhile, a son of the late Sosibius named Ptolemy was sent to the court of the Macedonian king Philip V with instructions to negotiate an anti-Seleucid alliance and arrange a marriage between Ptolemy V and one of Philip V's daughters. Ptolemy of Megalopolis (who later served as the governor of Cyprus, between 197 and 180 BC) was dispatched to Rome, most likely with orders to make the Senate aware of the change in government in Alexandria and to warn them of the Seleucid king's military activities in Asia Minor. And Philammon (the man allegedly hired to murder Arsinoe III) was sent to assert Ptolemaic authority in Cyrene and serve as its governor.

These missions achieved little and failed to neutralise the mounting Seleucid threat. Antiochus III continued his attacks on Ptolemaic lands in Caria and by the end of 203 BC had reached a secret agreement with Philip V of Macedon to conquer and share the Ptolemaic Kingdom's overseas territories, leaving Egypt on the brink of all-out war with two of the biggest powers in the Mediterranean.

---

[88] Pelops served as *strategos* (governor) of Cyprus under Ptolemy IV. He was appointed to the position in 217 BC and probably remained in the post until Ptolemy IV's death in 203 BC.

Agathocles is reported to have begun preparations for a potential conflict by sending an embassy to Greece to hire mercenaries. However, according to Polybius his real motivation was to replace the existing Ptolemaic troops (whose loyalty to his regency was questionable) with mercenaries who would be loyal to him.

Despite these efforts to cling onto power, Agathocles' tenure as regent did not last long. He and his family had earned the resentment of the people of Alexandria during the previous reign for their greed and corruption. Instead of changing his ways after becoming regent, he repeated the same mistakes by appointing friends and family members to high offices. To make matters worse, the Alexandrians' hatred for Agathocles was heightened by the widespread belief that he had been directly involved in the death of Arsinoe III and the murder of various other high profile courtiers.

One of Agathocles' main opponents was the general Tlepolemus, who was the *strategos* of the key border fortress at Pelusium. He had been subjected to a series of indignities by the new regent, including his mother-in-law being arrested and publicly shamed, and soon became a figurehead of the mounting opposition to Agathocles' rule.

In October 203 BC Agathocles assembled the army and royal bodyguard to hear a proclamation, but was insulted by the troops and lucky to escape with his life. Instead of trying to ease the growing tensions, Agathocles escalated the situation by having a member of the royal bodyguard named Moeragenes (who was suspected of having links with Tlepolemus) arrested and tortured. This backfired dramatically when Moeragenes managed to escape custody and persuaded the army to rebel against the regent. Many angry Alexandrians also joined the revolt and the city rapidly descended into anarchy, prompting Oenanthe and her daughters (including Agathoclea) to seek asylum in the temple of Demeter, where they hoped to protect themselves by gaining the support of the gods.

That night, an Alexandrian mob besieged the royal palace and demanded that the young pharaoh be brought before them. By dawn the army had arrived and forced their way inside the palace, leaving Agathocles with no choice but to surrender.

That same morning, Oenanthe and her daughters were dragged out of the temple where they had been seeking refuge by the furious Alexandrian mob. To maximise the humiliation of their downfall, they were completely naked. Oenanthe and her daughters were then taken to the city's stadium on horseback, along with their family and partisans, to meet their fate.

Meanwhile, Ptolemy had been removed from his regent's custody and taken to the stadium, where he was seated on a throne before the people of Alexandria. Suffice it to say the seven-year-old king received a far warmer reception than Agathocles did and was treated with all the reverence his rank demanded. While Agathocles had gained power by usurpation, Ptolemy was their rightful ruler, and as a mere child he was innocent of the crimes committed by his regency government. After a short trial, Ptolemy was urged by the crowd and one of his courtiers (Sosibius' son Sosibius) to order the execution of his mother's killers, and the confused king is said to have nodded or allowed an officer standing behind him to raise one of his arms. The vengeful mob took this as a sign that royal approval had been given for the executions and did not hesitate to have Agathocles dragged into the stadium and killed. He perished alongside his family (including his mother Oenanthe and his sister Agathoclea) and anyone else implicated in the murder of Arsinoe III.

The executions were such a grisly sight that one of Ptolemy's officers is said to have covered the young king's eyes. In an appropriately graphic account, the Greek historian Polybius recorded the manner in which the bloodthirsty mob sought out and killed the relatives and associates of the deposed regent when he wrote: 'All of them were then handed over together to the mod, and some began to bite them, others to stab them, others to gouge out their eyes. As soon as any of them fell, the body was torn limb from limb until they had mutilated them all.'

*

Even after Ptolemy IV's greedy favourites had been removed from power, the situation did not improve. In the years that followed Ptolemy V's government was led by a series of incompetent regents, leaving the kingdom in disarray. The first of these was Agathocles' opponent, Tlepolemus, who arrived in Alexandria shortly after the bloody purge. In addition to being selected as Ptolemy's new regent, he also served jointly with Sosibius' son Sosibius as the boy's guardian, although he did not retain the support of the masses for long. The people soon became disaffected with Tlepolemus for wasting many hours of the day drinking and sparring with his troops, and were unhappy with his decision to give large amounts of money to embassies he received from the city-states of mainland Greece.

Sosibius' son Ptolemy sought to exploit the regent's declining popularity by attempting to set his brother Sosibius against Tlepolemus, but this backfired when the plot was discovered and Sosibius was removed from his position as Ptolemy's co-guardian.

As usual, the Ptolemaic Kingdom's Seleucid and Macedonian rivals (Antiochus III and Philip V) did not hesitate to take advantage of Egypt's weakened state by declaring war in 202 BC. Known as the Fifth Syrian War (202-196 BC), unlike most of the previous Syrian Wars this conflict did not go in the Ptolemies' favour.

Ever since his defeat at the Battle of Raphia in 217 BC, the Seleucid king Antiochus III had been waiting for the opportune moment to get his revenge on the Ptolemaic Kingdom. As mentioned earlier on in this chapter, he took advantage of the ongoing internal unrest in Egypt and the feeble state of Ptolemy's regency government by seizing control of Ptolemaic possessions in western Asia Minor in 203 BC and making a secret pact with Philip V of Macedon to jointly conquer the Ptolemaic Kingdom's territories in Asia and the Aegean. However, the real war did not start until 202 BC, when the Seleucids launched an invasion of Coele-Syria and took control of Damascus.

When Tlepolemus received word of this significant escalation in hostilities he dispatched an embassy to Rome to plead for assistance, although his incompetent regency collapsed soon after this.

At some point during the winter of 202/201 BC Tlepolemus was replaced as regent with a member of the royal bodyguard named Aristomenes of Alyzia, who had previously been a supporter of Agathocles but also played a key role in removing Ptolemy from Agathocles' custody.

Meanwhile, things were continuing to go badly in the war against the Seleucids. In 201 BC they invaded Palestine and took control of Gaza, while the Ptolemaic governor of Coele-Syria (Ptolemy son of Thraseas) saw which way the wind was blowing and opted to defect to Antiochus. In the Aegean and Asia Minor the situation was just as bleak for the Ptolemaic cause, thanks to the efforts of Philip V, who had started attacking Ptolemaic territories in accordance with his pact with Antiochus. The Macedonian king seized control of the island of Samos and launched an invasion of Caria (in south-western Asia Minor), which also led to conflict with Rhodes and Pergamon, who sent their own embassies to Rome to ask for support. Philip then went on to conquer Ptolemaic possessions in the Hellespont and Thrace, in addition to independent cities there.

It was at this point that Rome finally decided to intervene by declaring war on Macedonia, marking the beginning of the Second Macedonian War (200-197 BC).[89] This would have been welcome news to Ptolemy and his ministers, although they still had their hands full with their primary enemy – the Seleucids.

Back in Coele-Syria, an Aetolian general under Ptolemaic service named Scopas spent the winter of 201/200 BC leading a successful reconquest of Palestine, although Damascus remained under Seleucid control and his success was short-lived.[90] In the summer of 200 BC, all of Scopas' work was undone when he was defeated by Antiochus at the Battle of Panium. Although the Romans did respond to the Ptolemaic government's pleas for assistance by sending an ambassador to negotiate peace between Ptolemy and Antiochus, these negotiations came to nothing and Rome essentially left the Ptolemaic Kingdom to its fate. The Romans were primarily interested in deterring the Macedonians and Seleucids from invading Egypt itself in order to prevent any disruption to the supply of Egyptian grain, which the people of Italy were heavily reliant on to feed their large population. As neither Antiochus nor Philip had planned to take on the arduous task of conquering Egypt, they happily complied with Rome's demand and proceeded with their work of carving up Ptolemy's overseas empire.

After his defeat at the Battle of Panium, Scopas retreated behind the walls of Sidon (in present-day Lebanon) with 10,000 troops. He was besieged here from the winter of 200/199 BC until he was starved into surrender, early in the summer of 199 BC.

Despite this failure, Scopas appears to have remained in good favour at the Ptolemaic court and was sent to his native Aetolia with a large sum of money and orders to recruit a mercenary force to help defend Egypt in the event that the Seleucids invaded.

---

[89] Rome entered the Second Macedonian War at the request of Pergamon and Rhodes, who were concerned about Macedonia's aggressive expansionism. It resulted in a Roman victory that forced Philip V of Macedonia to surrender all his possessions in southern Greece, Thrace and Asia Minor. The war significantly boosted the Roman Republic's power and influence in the eastern Mediterranean, setting the stage for its eventual conquest of the Greek world.
[90] Prior to serving as a general in the Ptolemaic army (during the Fifth Syrian War), Scopas had served his native Aetolian League during the Social War (220-217 BC) against a Macedonian-led coalition.

According to the Roman historian Livy, Scopas was incredibly successful when carrying out this task. He is reported to have returned to Alexandria with an army of 6,000 Aetolian youths, but the power soon got to his head and ultimately brought about his downfall. Emboldened by the large military force he had at his disposal and the vast wealth he had accumulated as a result of his service to Ptolemy, his ambition reached a dangerous level and he allegedly plotted to seize control of the Ptolemaic government. However, his plans were discovered before he was in a position to execute them and Scopas was taken by surprise when Ptolemy's regent Aristomenes dispatched an armed force to arrest him. As soon as he was in Aristomenes' custody, Scopas was brought before Ptolemy's council and sentenced to death.[91]

Fortunately for Ptolemy, the anticipated Seleucid invasion of Egypt never materialised. Rather than extending the war into Egypt, Antiochus focused on consolidating his territorial gains in Coele-Syria and Judea during 198 BC. As time would tell, these two territories had been lost permanently and were never reabsorbed into the Ptolemaic Kingdom. Nevertheless, Antiochus still wasn't satisfied by the gains he had made, and in the spring of 197 BC his attention turned to what territories the Ptolemaic Kingdom still possessed in Asia Minor. Here the Seleucids managed to conquer Ptolemaic-controlled cities in Cilicia (Mallus, Zephyrium, Soli, Aphrodisias, Anemurium, Selinus and Korasion) and several others in Lycia (Telmessus, Corycus, Andriake, Limyra, Arycanda, Patara and Xanthus) and Ionia (Ephesus).

By 195 BC ongoing domestic issues – including economic hardship and the native Egyptian rebellion – compelled Ptolemy to seek a quick (and therefore disadvantageous) peace with the Seleucid Empire. That year Ptolemy and Antiochus signed a treaty which formally ended the Fifth Syrian War. Under the terms of this agreement, Antiochus' possession of Coele-Syria was confirmed and Ptolemy agreed to marry one of the Seleucid king's daughters, Cleopatra I.[92] As a result of the war, all of Ptolemy's territories in the Levant and Asia Minor had been lost, along with the majority of his kingdom's influence in the Aegean Sea. The loss of these territories (and in particular the port cities of Tyre and Sidon) had serious economic consequences for the Ptolemaic Kingdom. Egypt had been humbled in a big way. And Antiochus' revenge for Raphia was complete.

*

---

[91] Scopas was executed the night after he was sentenced to death (in 196 BC).
[92] Ptolemy V and Cleopatra I had three children together: Ptolemy VI (c. 186 BC), Cleopatra II (c. 185 BC) and Ptolemy VIII (c. 184 BC).

In 196 BC Ptolemy V came of age, marked by him being crowned pharaoh at Memphis and adopting the Egyptian name Iwaennetjerwy-merwyitu Setepptah Userkare Sekhem-ankhamun.

The timing of this declaration was influenced by his kingdom's failings in the Fifth Syrian War, which had crippled the authority of his regent, Aristomenes. At some point during the autumn of 197 BC the Ptolemaic *strategos* (governor) of Cyprus, Polycrates of Argos, travelled to Alexandria, where he was warmly received and made arrangements for Ptolemy to be declared an adult. Although the king was only 13 or 14 years old at the time, he believed this measure was needed to alleviate the kingdom's internal instability.[93] Ptolemy's entry into adulthood was made official by holding an *anacleteria*: a feast that was celebrated in Ancient Greece when a ruler assumed full control over the running of their state. As Polybius explained in *The Histories*, the boy king's courtiers hoped 'that the kingdom would gain a certain degree of firmness and a fresh impulse towards prosperity, if it were known that the king had assumed the independent direction of the government.'

Ptolemy's initiation into adulthood was followed by his coronation as pharaoh on 26 March 196 BC. In accordance with tradition, the coronation ceremony took place in Memphis and Ptolemy was crowned by the High Priest of Ptah.

Given that Ptah was the principal deity of Egypt's traditional capital (Memphis), the High Priest of Ptah had been one of the most important religious figures in the country since the old kingdom and their prominence continued under Ptolemaic rule. Technically the High Priest of Ptah was appointed by the pharaoh, although it became customary for the office to be passed from father to son. Indeed, the position was held by the same family throughout the Ptolemaic dynasty. They achieved this by demonstrating unwavering loyalty to the Ptolemies, unlike the High Priests of Amun in Thebes (the traditional religious capital of Egypt) whose enthusiasm for their foreign Greek rulers was lukewarm at best. In other words, the High Priests of Ptah had a mutually beneficial arrangement with the Ptolemies: bestowing legitimacy and divine authority on the pharaoh in exchange for royal favour that made them the most powerful and influential native family in Egypt.

---

[93] Polycrates was born into a distinguished family from Argos. He served as a general in the Ptolemaic army at the Battle of Raphia and became an incredibly influential figure at the Ptolemaic court. Sometime after Raphia, he was appointed governor of Cyprus by Ptolemy IV.

On the day after Ptolemy was crowned pharaoh, a synod of Egyptian priests who had gathered in Memphis for the coronation issued a decree. Known to posterity as the 'Decree of Memphis' or the 'Rosetta Stone decree', it was inscribed on stelae, two of which have survived to the present-day: the Nubayrah Stele and – more famously – the Rosetta Stone.

The decree was written in three languages (Egyptian hieroglyphs, Demotic and Greek), which led to the Rosetta Stone playing a pivotal role in the deciphering of Egyptian hieroglyphs approximately 2,000 years later.[94][95][96] This is common knowledge to people all over the world, although the actual contents of the stone are less well known.

The trilingual decree established the new pharaoh's divine cult and was aimed at reasserting Ptolemaic authority over the entirety of Egypt. It recorded gifts of grain and silver that Ptolemy gave to temples, as well as him having excess water dammed for the benefit of farmers when the Nile flooded at an unusually high level during the eighth year of his reign. In addition to praising the pharaoh's benefactions for the people of Egypt, it celebrated Ptolemy's victory over the native Egyptian rebels at Lycopolis and granted tax exemptions to Egyptian temples. In return for his generous patronage, the Egyptian priesthood pledged to celebrate the days of his birth and coronation annually, awarded him religious honours, and agreed to erect a statue of him in the shrine of every Egyptian temple. At the end of the decree an instruction is

---

[94] In 1798 AD Napoleon invaded Egypt with the intention of annexing it as a French colony. Doing so would enable him to dominate global trade and weaken Britain's hold on India, but the expedition was thwarted by an Anglo-Ottoman coalition and became famous not for its military significance but for the birth of a new academic discipline – Egyptology.
In 1799, during the Egyptian campaign, the Rosetta Stone was discovered by an officer in the French army (Pierre-François Bouchard). Named after the Egyptian port city where it was found, the stone was seized by the British in 1801 when they defeated Napoleon's Egyptian expedition. The following year it was put on public display in the British Museum in London and has remained there ever since.

[95] In ancient times, the Rosetta Stone was probably kept in a temple somewhere inland (possibly at Sais), before being used in the construction of a fortress at Rosetta. Materials from many other Egyptian temples met a similar fate after the end of pharaonic rule in Egypt.

[96] One of the most important figures in the deciphering of Egyptian hieroglyphs was the nineteenth-century AD French philologist Jean-François Champollion. This was made possible by the Rosetta Stone containing a decree in Ancient Greek (a known language) along with two almost identical passages in Egyptian hieroglyphs and Demotic. However, the stone is damaged and doesn't contain the full stela, meaning none of the three texts are complete. Nor is it unique in the present day due to the discovery of additional trilingual artefacts, including copies of the same Memphis decree on the Philae obelisk and Nubayrah Stele.

given for a copy of it to be kept in every temple and inscribed in the 'language of the gods' (Egyptian hieroglyphs), the 'language of documents' (Demotic), and the 'language of the Greeks'.

The fact that the decree was issued at Memphis (Egypt's ancient capital) rather than at Alexandria (the centre of the Ptolemaic government) demonstrates that Ptolemy V was as eager as his predecessors to gain the support of Egypt's powerful priestly elite. However, the decree is not just a sign of the continuing importance of the Egyptian priesthood, but also of their growing power during Ptolemy V's reign. With part of Egypt occupied by rebels and an inexperienced teenager on the throne, the priests were well aware that Ptolemy was far more dependent on their support than his predecessors had been, and the remission of their taxes was the price he had to pay to maintain their support against the rebels.

At some point after the coronation Aristomenes was supplanted by Polycrates of Argos as the leading figure at the royal court. Aristomenes apparently fell into disfavour with the young king (for unknown reasons) and was eventually compelled to commit suicide by taking poison in 192 BC.

During this period, Ptolemy sealed the peace agreement he had reached with the Seleucids to end the Fifth Syrian War by marrying Cleopatra I (a daughter of Antiochus III) in the winter of 194/193 BC. Antiochus arranged for the wedding to take place at Raphia for symbolic purposes – as the location of his ignominious defeat at the hands of Ptolemy IV would now become the place where he made his conquest of Coele-Syria official. Ptolemy (now 16 years of age) had previously been initiated into the Ptolemaic cult when he received the title *Theos Epiphanes Eucharistos* or 'Manifest, Beneficent God' (probably during the Ptolemaia festival in 199/198 BC), but now the pharaoh and his new wife were deified as the *Theoi Epiphaneis* ('Manifest Gods').[97] Egypt's new queen (aged about ten years old at the time) was nicknamed 'the Syrian' in Alexandria, in recognition of her Syrian roots, and Ptolemy apparently received the revenues of Coele-Syria (but not ownership of that territory) as her dowry.

Ptolemy's decision to make peace with Antiochus unintentionally angered the Romans. Probably near the end of 197 BC, the Ptolemaic government had complained to Rome about the Seleucid king's conquests and appealed to the Senate to intercede

---

[97] Ptolemy V continued the tradition of honouring former Ptolemaic queens with cults devoted to their worship by establishing one for his mother Arsinoe III in the Ptolemaia of 199/198 BC).

with Antiochus on its behalf. The Romans were initially preoccupied fighting the Second Macedonian War, but were able to turn their attention to the Seleucid Empire after they decisively defeated the Macedonians at the Battle of Cynoscephalae (in 197 BC). As Philip V's ally and the other major expansionist power in the eastern Mediterranean, the Seleucid king now posed the biggest threat to Rome's interests, so the Senate sent an embassy to meet with Antiochus at the Thracian town of Lysimachia at some point between the autumn of 196 BC and early 195 BC. The embassy was led by Lucius Cornelius Lentulus and was tasked with negotiating an end to the conflict between the Seleucid Empire and the Ptolemaic Kingdom. During these peace negotiations, Lentulus demanded (among other things) that Antiochus return the Ptolemaic territories he had seized to Ptolemy's control. However, Lentulus had a rude awakening when the Seleucid king informed him that he was in the process of concluding a peace treaty with Ptolemy, which they planned to seal through a marriage alliance. This revelation, as well as a false rumour that the young Egyptian king had died, appears to have halted the conference between Lentulus and Antiochus, and the Roman envoy ended up leaving with little to show for their efforts.

The Romans eventually had a golden opportunity to get their own back on Ptolemy when they fought a war against the Seleucids between 192 and 188 BC, in response to Antiochus' continued policy of aggressive expansion in the eastern Mediterranean. Hopeful of renewing its ties with Rome and regaining some of the territories it had lost to Antiochus, the Ptolemaic administration offered to provide Rome with both financial and military support soon after the outbreak of war (in 191 BC). Unfortunately, the Romans were still angry about Ptolemy's decision to make a separate peace with the Seleucids at the end of the Fifth Syrian War, so the Senate rejected the assistance offered by his embassy. A second embassy sent by Ptolemy to Rome later the same year (191 BC) to congratulate the Romans on their victory at the Battle of Thermopylae and to reiterate their willingness to assist them in the ongoing war received an even frostier reception when the Senate completely ignored it. However, it was not until the end of the Roman-Seleucid War in 188 BC that the full consequences of the poor state of Roman-Ptolemaic relations were felt, when the victorious Romans decided to grant the former Ptolemaic territories they had seized off Antiochus in Asia Minor to Rhodes and Pergamon instead of returning them to Ptolemy.[98]

---

[98] After emerging victorious in the Roman-Seleucid War, the Romans imposed the Treaty of Apamea on Antiochus III. Under the terms of this peace agreement, the Seleucid king surrendered all his European possessions and all the territories he held west and north of the

The loss of the majority of Ptolemy's overseas empire in the Fifth Syrian War resulted in Cyprus playing an increasingly important role in the Ptolemaic Kingdom. This was reflected by the centralised religious structure that was established on Cyprus and its governor (*strategos*) being made the island's high priest (*archiereus*). This meant the *strategos* was now not only the most important secular official on Cyprus, but the most important religious official too.

*

Ptolemy continued the religious policy of his predecessors by presenting himself as a traditional Egyptian pharaoh and seeking to maintain the support of Egypt's priestly elite. However, the number and scale of temple construction and restoration projects declined significantly during his reign, as a consequence of financial difficulties and large portions of Egypt being under rebel control. The construction work that did take place was focused on northern Egypt (where Ptolemy's authority was at its strongest), including at the sanctuary of the Apis Bull at Memphis and the temple of Anubis at nearby Saqqara, although he did sponsor some work as far south as Philae, where the temple of Imhotep was established and the existing temple of Arensnuphis was extended. In addition to practical considerations, this northern focus has been interpreted as an attempt by Ptolemy to help Memphis supersede Thebes (the epicentre of the revolt against his authority) as Egypt's most important religious centre.

One possible example of the Ptolemies' attempts to associate themselves with the traditional Egyptian pharaohs is an inscription called the Famine Stela, which was probably carved during Ptolemy V's reign. Located on Sehel Island in the River Nile (near Aswan), the inscription is written in Egyptian hieroglyphs and describes the action taken by the Third Dynasty pharaoh Djoser to tackle a seven-year period of drought and famine: 'My heart was in sore distress, for the Nile had not risen for seven years. The grain was not abundant, the seeds were dried up, everything that one had to eat was in pathetic quantities, each person was denied his harvest. Nobody could walk any more: children were in tears; the young people were struck down; the old people's hearts were sad and their legs were bent when they sat on the ground, and their hands were hidden away. Even the courtiers were going without, the temples

---

Taurus Mountains (in Asia Minor). Antiochus was also required to pay war reparations, give up all his war elephants, agree to restrictions on the size of his navy, and place a number of high profile hostages in Roman custody as a guarantee of future good behaviour. These terms enabled Rome to gain hegemony over the Greek city-states and Asia Minor.

were closed and the sanctuaries were covered in dust. In short, everything in existence was afflicted.' Desperate to alleviate the suffering of his subjects and to restore order to his kingdom, Djoser turned to his high priest Imhotep for assistance – asking him to find out where Hapi (the god of the annual flooding of the Nile) was born and which god lived there. During his investigations, Imhotep searched through the archives of the temple of Thoth at Hermopolis, where he discovered the annual flooding of the Nile was controlled by the ram-headed god Khnum from a sacred spring on the island of Elephantine. As soon as he had found this out, Imhotep travelled to the temple of Khnum at Elephantine. Here he prayed and made offerings to the god. After falling asleep, Imhotep was visited in a dream by Khnum, who was kind to him and promised to make the Nile flood: 'I will cause the Nile to rise up for you. There will be no more years when the inundation fails to cover any area of land. The flowers will sprout up, their stems bending with the weight of the pollen.' When Imhotep woke up from the dream, he wrote everything down and went straight to Djoser with the good news.

There remains considerable debate amongst historians over who created the Famine Stela and for what purpose. It is possible that Ptolemy was involved in its creation. If this was the case, then he was probably referring to himself in the story (albeit in the guise of Djoser), and his role in tackling the combined challenges of famine and rebellion in southern Egypt. However, the most likely explanation is that it was produced by the priests of Khnum, who struggled with rival priesthoods for power and influence in the Elephantine region and used the story as a means of boosting their legitimacy.

*

The failings of Ptolemy V's government on the world stage had severely diminished his kingdom's influence and territorial possessions, but he faced an equally serious situation at home due to the continued Egyptian rebellion that had started during Ptolemy IV's reign.

As explained in the previous chapter, the rebellion had resulted in the loss of most of Upper Egypt and parts of Lower Egypt. This deprived Ptolemy of a substantial portion of his Egyptian revenues for the majority of his reign and compelled him to pay for large numbers of mercenaries to help quell the disorder, which in turn led to economic stagnation and instability.

The Upper Egyptian revolt was led by the self-proclaimed native Egyptian pharaoh Horwennefer. He appears to have died in c. 200 BC, but was succeeded by another native Egyptian named Ankhwennefer, who continued the fight.[99] At around this time, Ptolemy's regency government initiated a large-scale military campaign in Upper Egypt, during which their forces recaptured Ptolemais Hermiou (in early 199 BC), besieged Abydos (in August 199 BC) and brought Thebes back under Ptolemaic control (at some point between late 199 and early 198 BC). Unfortunately for Ptolemy this key victory was followed by a series of setbacks. After losing Thebes, Ankhwennefer made the daring decision to head north with his troops. As he did so he engaged in an orgy of plundering and destruction, aimed at damaging the rural economy, as well as isolating the Ptolemaic forces in Thebes by depriving them of supplies and disrupting their lines of communication with Alexandria. Meanwhile, a separate group of rebels in the Nile Delta (presumably with links to Ankhwennefer) seized control of the city of Lycopolis (present-day Asyut).

Lycopolis was restored to Ptolemaic control after being besieged by Ptolemy's army in 197 BC. To their credit, the Delta rebels believed passionately in their cause and had a well-stocked and fortified headquarters, but ultimately proved no match for the Ptolemaic army's superior numbers and weaponry. The leaders of this rebellion were publicly executed in Memphis on 26 March 196 BC, during the celebrations that followed Ptolemy's coronation.

At some point in the mid-190s BC Ankhwennefer struck a deal with the Kushite king of Meroë, Adikhalamani. In exchange for ceding control of the city of Syene (present-day Aswan) to the Kushites (which they occupied from 196/195-187 BC), Ankhwennefer received assistance off Adikhalamani in his struggle against Ptolemy. This helped Ankhwennefer to recapture Thebes, which was back in his possession by the autumn of 195 BC. Despite the rebel pharaoh's success in regaining control of the Thebaid, Ankhwennefer remained under immense pressure from Ptolemaic forces to the north (who were determined to restore their kingdom's territorial integrity) and the Kushites to the south (who sought to exploit Egypt's civil war to enlarge their own kingdom, particularly in the Dodekaschoinos). Without control of the richer and more fertile lands of northern Egypt, Ankhwennefer's ability to resist gradually weakened, enabling the Ptolemaic army to push southward and gradually retake territory. Violent

---

[99] Although Ankhwennefer's relationship to Horwennefer is unknown, he may have been his son or another relative.
An alternative theory claims Horwennefer and Ankhwennefer were the same person and he had simply changed his name.

clashes occurred between Ptolemaic and rebel forces in the vicinity of Asyut, and by early 190 BC Thebes appears to have been brought back under Ptolemaic control once again following a successful campaign by the Ptolemaic general Comanus. After achieving this key objective, the Ptolemaic authorities prioritised returning neglected and war-torn land to cultivation as quickly as possible. Doing so enabled them to boost their war effort by increasing tax revenues and keeping their army well supplied with grain from all over Egypt.

The loss of Thebes forced Ankhwennefer to retreat south, all the way to the border with the Kingdom of Kush, where he managed to keep his cause on life support by securing the service of some Nubian troops. However, his cause was further weakened in 187 BC when Adikhalamani withdrew from Syene and stopped giving support to the rebel pharaoh.

The rebellion in Upper Egypt finally came to an end in late August 186 BC when Ankhwennefer launched an attack on Thebes with his Egyptian-Nubian army but failed to retake the city. As a result of the battle (fought against Ptolemaic forces under the command of Comanus) Ankhwennefer's son was killed and the rebel leader himself was defeated and captured. Ankhwennefer was then taken north to Alexandria, where he was imprisoned but may have avoided the death penalty, after a synod of Egyptian priests intervened on his behalf. The priests probably persuaded Ptolemy that executing Ankhwennefer would merely turn him into a martyr. Even though it was a tough pill to swallow after so many years of hard fighting, Ptolemy understood that the best way of placating Egyptian opposition in the south of the country was to discredit Ankhwennefer by branding him an enemy of the gods, while also offering him a pardon to avoid adding fuel to the fire.

At the same time as Ankhwennefer's fate was being decided, the synod of Egyptian priests issued the Philae Decree II (on 6 or 12 September 186 BC), in which they denounced Ankhwennefer for rebelling against Ptolemy and for committing numerous crimes against both humanity and the gods. By rebelling against the government in Alexandria, he had gone against the official ideology which asserted the Ptolemaic ruler was the sole legitimate pharaoh in Egypt, and he had also been compelled to milk the temples and his subjects for all they were worth in his regime's desperate fight for survival. Once this had been said, the priests gave orders two new feast days to be observed – one on the day of Ankhwennefer's defeat and another on the day the victory was announced – and for a statue of Ptolemy V as 'Lord of Victory' to be installed in every temple sanctuary in Egypt.[100]

A month later (on 9 October 186 BC) Ptolemy issued an additional decree which pardoned all fugitives for any crimes or rebellious activity committed prior to September 186 BC (with the exception of premeditated murder and temple theft) and ordered them to return to their homes. This amnesty was prompted by the need to placate native Egyptian sentiments and restore large swathes of land to cultivation, which had been neglected during the many years of civil war. He also resumed work at the Temple of Edfu (which had been suspended as a result of the war) and spent lavishly on other temples in the region. However, he was well aware that acts of mercy and patronage alone would not be enough to prevent further native rebellions breaking out, so he also sought to impose absolute military control over the south. To do this, Ptolemy established a new military governorship in Upper Egypt (headed by an *epistrategos*) and settled Greek soldiers across the southern part of the country by giving them land grants in local communities. As a reward for his services during the war, the first person to be appointed to the position of *epistrategos* was Comanus.

Ankhwennefer's demise enabled Ptolemy to re-establish his authority over the entirety of Upper Egypt and the Triakontaschoinos. To symbolise this, inscriptions on temple walls bearing the names of the Kushite rulers who had occupied the region since 206 BC were erased.

Meanwhile, the rebels in Lower Egypt maintained their fierce resistance into 185 BC, but were eventually suppressed as a result of an act of deception by Polycrates of Argos.

When Polycrates reassured the rebel leaders that they would be treated leniently if they surrendered, they agreed to travel to Sais to engage in negotiations. However, as soon as they arrived in the city (in October 185 BC) they were placed under arrest. Seeking to make an example of them, the Ptolemaic authorities had the rebels stripped naked and forced them to drag carts through the city like oxen, before torturing them to death.

*

---

[100] A further decree was issued by a synod of priests at Memphis in the autumn of 185 BC, following the enthronement of a new Apis bull. Known as the Philae Decree I, it regranted the various honours Arsinoe II, Ptolemy IV and Arsinoe III had received in Upper Egyptian temples, which had been revoked during Ankhwennefer's occupation of the region. In addition to this, Ptolemy V's wife, Cleopatra I, received the same honours that had been granted to her husband in the Memphis Decree of 196 BC.

Outside Egypt, Ptolemy spent the remainder of his reign attempting to restore his kingdom's prestige on the world stage after the humiliating conclusion of the Fifth Syrian War.

An opportunity to do this arose in 187 BC, when Antiochus III died shortly after coming to terms with the Romans in the Roman-Seleucid War. He was killed by enraged local inhabitants while pillaging a temple of Bel near Susa and was succeeded by his son, Seleucus IV (r. 187-175 BC), who proved to be a weak king.

Now his rival was dead, Ptolemy started planning a campaign to recapture Coele-Syria off the Seleucids. As part of these preparations, he dispatched a childhood friend (the eunuch Aristonicus) to Greece in 185 BC with instructions to recruit an army of mercenaries.[101] He also revived his kingdom's alliance with the Achaean League (which had fallen apart during the Cleomenean War of 229-222 BC) by giving its members generous gifts and pledging to provide them with ships in 185 BC. And as someone who took an interest in athletic games and was accomplished at physical activities such as hunting, riding and fencing, he attempted to raise his profile in Greece by entering a chariot team in the 182 BC Panathenaic Games (which won a four-horse chariot race).

Ptolemy's plans for a new campaign against the Seleucids never materialised due to his sudden death in 180 BC. He was apparently poisoned by his own courtiers, who were concerned he was planning to seize their property to fund the war (although an alternative theory suggests they preferred to have a juvenile king who would be easier to manipulate).

Ptolemy's body was presumably buried in a tomb in the royal quarter of Alexandria, alongside the remains of Alexander the Great and the previous Ptolemies. In accordance with tradition, he was succeeded by his eldest son, Ptolemy VI, who was only about six years old at the time.

Ptolemy V's reign marked the end of the Ptolemaic Kingdom's influence in the wider Mediterranean, leaving its empire fatally weakened. During his time on the throne, ambitious courtiers and members of the priestly elite exploited the domestic unrest to secure an increasingly prominent role in political life at the expense of the monarch,

---

[101] Aristonicus had been raised alongside Ptolemy V from a young age. The Greek historian Polybius praised him as a generous man, who was skilled in both warfare and politics, and had served as the priest of Alexander the Great for the year 187/186 BC.

and this trend continued under most of the Ptolemies who followed. However, it would be unfair to say Ptolemy was completely to blame for the declining strength of the Ptolemaic monarchy. He came to the throne as a minor and spent most of his reign trying to stamp out fires that had been started by the poor administration of his father's greedy courtiers: including threats from dissident subjects internally and hostile foreign powers externally. Consequently, the kingdom he left to his successor was significantly smaller than the one he had inherited. Its overseas territories had been reduced to Cyrenaica, Cyprus, and its garrisons at Itanos, Thera and Methana in the Aegean, although Ptolemy at least managed to stabilise Egypt by suppressing the native rebellions and bringing some semblance of order to the administration of state. He proved himself to be a cruel and ruthless ruler when suppressing the Egyptian rebellions and some accounts portray him as a tyrant. Nevertheless, that was not an unusual characteristic for an Egyptian pharaoh to have, and to bring some balance to his character he is also known to have been an accomplished athlete.

Rather than improving in the years and decades that followed Ptolemy V's death, the internal crises affecting the Ptolemaic dynasty only got worse. Native rebellions became increasingly common. Infighting at the royal court and amongst the royal family itself became increasingly frequent and severe. Alexandrian aristocrats and the Egyptian priesthood continued to whittle away the monarch's authority. And the growing power of Rome started to threaten Egypt's autonomy.

All these things reveal the painful truth that the kingdom's best days were behind it. Even though the Ptolemies would cling onto their throne for a further century and a half, the power of the Ptolemaic monarchy would never be restored to its former glory.

Ptolemy VI and Ptolemy VIII: The Warring Siblings

When Ptolemy V died just shy of his thirtieth birthday in 180 BC, he was succeeded by his eldest son, Ptolemy VI Philometor.[102] Like his father, Ptolemy VI was a young boy when he came to the throne and had a series of regents to govern the kingdom on his behalf during his minority. Conflict within the royal family, which would continue to undermine the Ptolemaic Kingdom from within for the remainder of the dynasty, was rife during his time on the throne. This is reflected by him being the first Ptolemaic monarch to be deposed and restored to the throne, ruling from 180 BC to 164 BC and from 163 BC to 145 BC. Far from being a time of peace and prosperity, his reign was marred by continued conflict with the Seleucid Empire over control of Coele-Syria and a power struggle with his younger brother, Ptolemy VIII, over the Ptolemaic throne.

As he acceded to the throne at just six years of age, Ptolemy's mother, Cleopatra I, was appointed to serve as his regent.

During Cleopatra I's regency all coinage was minted under the joint authority of the regent and pharaoh and Cleopatra's name preceded Ptolemy's on official documents, which clearly indicates that it was the mother rather than the son who was in charge of the kingdom at this time. Despite her late husband's intention to fight a new war against the Seleucid Empire, Cleopatra abandoned these plans and instead sought to maintain the uneasy peace that had been established between Egypt and its longtime rival. This policy made sense considering Cleopatra's Seleucid ancestry (which would have undermined her regency if war broke out with the Seleucids), in addition to the fact that the current Seleucid king, Seleucus IV, was her brother.

Cleopatra remained in control of the regency until her death at some point between 178 and 177 BC (although some scholars have dated her death as late as 176 BC). Under her leadership some degree of stability had been maintained in the kingdom, but instability and infighting returned to the Ptolemaic government soon after her passing.

Given that Cleopatra's son was still a child and too young to rule in his own right at the time of her death, she appointed two close associates named Eulaeus and Lenaeus to succeed her as Ptolemy's regent.[103] Their appointment as joint regents was accepted

---

[102] Philometor means 'mother-loving'.

by rival factions at the royal court, who were eager to avoid a member of the opposing faction gaining control over the regency (or even someone with the lineage and sufficient backing to attempt to usurp young Ptolemy's throne). The more senior out of the two regents was the eunuch Eulaeus. He had served as one of Ptolemy VI's tutors and even went on to have coinage minted in his own name. Ptolemy's more junior regent, Lenaeus, appears to have been primarily responsible for the kingdom's finances and had a far more humble background. Originally a Syrian slave, it is thought that he came to Egypt as part of Cleopatra I's retinue after she married Ptolemy V.

When they came to power they tried to secure their regency (which they had tenuous constitutional grounds to lead) by strengthening the young pharaoh's authority. One of the main ways they did this was by arranging for Ptolemy to marry his younger sister Cleopatra II (who also became his co-regent) in early 175 BC. This adhered to the practices of the traditional native Egyptian pharaohs and the legitimacy of the newlyweds was further emphasised by them being incorporated into the Ptolemaic dynastic cult as the *Theoi Philometores* ('Mother-loving Gods'). This epithet was selected in honour of their late mother, Cleopatra I, and was also a subtle reference to the relationship between Horus (the first divine king of Egypt, who the pharaohs claimed descent from) and his mother Isis in Egyptian mythology.

It is clear that Ptolemy VI and Cleopatra II did not consummate their marriage until a number of years after their wedding as they were only young children at the time. However, they went on to have at least four children together later on in life: Ptolemy Eupator, Cleopatra Thea, Cleopatra III, and another son named Ptolemy.[104][105]

---

[103] Eulaeus and Lenaeus held the regency cooperatively until 169 BC.
[104] Ptolemy VI and Cleopatra II may have also had a daughter named Berenice, who died young.
[105] The identity and reign of Ptolemy VII Neos Philopator is shrouded in uncertainty and continues to be debated by scholars. The traditional theory is that he was the youngest son of Ptolemy VI and Cleopatra II and reigned briefly after his father's death, but was supplanted by his uncle Ptolemy VIII and murdered sometime after.
An alternative (and more likely) theory argues Ptolemy VII Neos Philopator was the son of Ptolemy VIII and Cleopatra II, Ptolemy Memphites. Although he never became pharaoh, he is believed to have been the person who was posthumously incorporated into the Ptolemaic cult as Theos Neos Philopator in 118 BC. If this is indeed the case, then the VII assigned to him by historians merely reflects his place in the list of deified Ptolemies – between Ptolemy VI and Ptolemy VIII – rather than being a regnal number.

Between 170 and 168 BC, the Ptolemaic Kingdom engaged in the Sixth (and final) Syrian War against the Seleucid Empire. While Cleopatra I's regency government and the Seleucid king Seleucus IV had both pursued relatively peaceful policies towards each other, this had all changed after Cleopatra's death (c. 178-176 BC) and Seleucus IV's murder in 175 BC.

The assassination of Seleucus IV triggered a power struggle in his kingdom. Within two months the dead king's younger brother, Antiochus IV, had managed to have himself installed on the Seleucid throne, but the situation remained unsettled and the pro-war faction at the Ptolemaic court sought to take advantage of this, hoping to regain control of Coele-Syria and perhaps even conquer the Seleucid Empire.

Without the commanding presence of Cleopatra I to oppose these forceful voices, her peace policy went out the window. Eulaeus and Lenaeus were greedy individuals and proved either unable or unwilling to reject the growing calls for action to be taken against the Seleucids. With the benefit of hindsight, this was a great folly on their part. They clearly underestimated the difficulty of winning such a war, and its disastrous outcome would ultimately bring about their downfall.

Initially, Ptolemy's ministers bided their time, but by 172 BC they had started preparing for a potential war, judging the opportune moment for a military campaign against the Seleucids was near. The timing of this decision was partly influenced by Rome's preparations for war against Macedonia, which was attempting to form a large Hellenistic coalition against the Romans. These tensions ultimately resulted in the outbreak of the Third Macedonian War between the Roman Republic and Macedonia in 171 BC, which kept both of these major Mediterranean powers distracted and reduced their ability to interfere with Ptolemaic affairs.[106]

As part of the preparations for war, Ptolemy's younger brother Ptolemy VIII was elevated to the position of co-regent in October 170 BC. He was also incorporated into the Ptolemaic cult as one of the *Theoi Philometores* ('Mother-loving Gods'), alongside Ptolemy VI and Cleopatra II (who were already worshipped under this title). Not long after this, the seniority of Ptolemy VI was emphasised when he was declared an adult in a coming-of-age ceremony and took the Egyptian name Iwa-en-netjerwy-per Setep-en-Ptah-khepri Ir-maat-en-amun-re ('Heir of the [two] Houses of the Gods,

---

[106] The Third Macedonian War lasted from 171 BC until 168 BC. It ended with the decisive Roman victory at the Battle of Pydna and resulted in Macedonia being divided into four client republics that were subservient to Rome.

Chosen of Ptah, Truth is the Form of Amun-Re'). Officially, this meant that Ptolemy would rule in his own right from this point forward, but in reality Eulaeus and Lenaeus were still in charge of everyday government business.

Some scholars believe Ptolemy VI and Ptolemy VIII had become the figureheads of rival factions at the royal court and that the younger brother's promotion was motivated by a desire to promote unity within the Ptolemaic government before it went to war against the Seleucids. By the time of Ptolemy V's death, two prominent factions had formed at the royal court: one calling for a new war against the Seleucids (to restore the kingdom's prestige on the world stage) and the other preferring to maintain peace (to avoid the costs of war and allow the government to focus on domestic issues). Given that Cleopatra I had been closely associated with the peace faction when serving as Ptolemy VI's regent, it is unsurprising that members of the pro-war faction sought to make the pharaoh's younger brother, Ptolemy VIII, the figurehead of their movement.

In any event, the year of Ptolemy VIII's elevation to co-regent and Ptolemy VI's assumption of full royal powers was declared the first year of a new era.

In the winter of 170/169 BC the long-anticipated war with the Seleucid Empire finally broke out. Known as the Sixth Syrian War, this turned out to be the last of the so-called 'Syrian Wars' and began when Ptolemy's army departed the border fortress of Pelusium with the intention of launching an invasion of Palestine.

Unfortunately for Ptolemy, Antiochus was aware of the Ptolemaic preparations for war and had been busy assembling an army of his own. Before the Ptolemaic invasion force had even reached Palestine, it was intercepted by the Seleucid army on the Sinai Peninsula. This took the Ptolemaic army completely by surprise. They hadn't expected Antiochus to be so well prepared for war and were consequently defeated in the battle that followed.

The Seleucids added to their victory by marching on Pelusium. The city quickly capitulated and they then set off in pursuit of the remnants of the Ptolemaic army, which had retreated to the Nile Delta.

The botched invasion and the fall of Pelusium left Egypt wide open to attack and had grave consequences for the government in Alexandria. In a futile attempt at clinging on to power, Eulaeus tried to send Ptolemy to the Greek island of Samothrace (in the Aegean Sea) along with the royal treasury. However, before the plan could be set in motion, Eulaeus and Lenaeus were deposed in a military coup. The coup was led by two prominent Ptolemaic generals named Comanus and Cineas, who took control of the government.

Meanwhile, Antiochus IV's forces continued to advance deeper into Egyptian territory. They took control of Naucratis, where Antiochus attempted to win over the Greek inhabitants with gifts, and set up a camp near Alexandria, potentially threatening a siege of the capital.

The situation was now so serious that Ptolemy departed Alexandria in order to conduct negotiations with the Seleucid king (who also happened to be his uncle).

When Ptolemy arrived in the Seleucid camp, he became a virtual prisoner of Antiochus, who took his young nephew under his guardianship and planned to use him as a puppet through which he could rule Egypt. The agreement of friendship that was reached as a result of the one-sided negotiations essentially reduced Ptolemy to a vassal of the Seleucids, but such humiliating terms were unacceptable to the people of Alexandria, who rioted as soon as they received word of what had been agreed.

Comanus and Cineas shared the people's anger and rejected the agreement in the most explicit way possible: by renouncing their allegiance to Ptolemy VI and declaring his brother and co-regent, Ptolemy VIII, to be sole king.[107]

These developments gave Antiochus an excuse to besiege Alexandria, which he was able to claim he was doing in the name of the rightful king of Egypt (Ptolemy VI). However, he failed to seize the city and opted to withdraw from Egypt in September 169 BC (with the exception of Pelusium, where he maintained a garrison, and Memphis, where he installed Ptolemy VI as a puppet ruler). This decision was prompted by the approach of winter and the need to suppress yet another Jewish rebellion in Palestine, but his absence from Egypt gave time for the rift within the Egyptian royal family to be patched up.

*

When Judea had been part of the Ptolemaic Kingdom, the Ptolemies had been careful to respect Jewish culture and institutions. This policy had continued under Seleucid rule, until the reign of Antiochus IV, who banned many traditional Jewish practices

---

[107] Cleopatra II's status was not affected by the coup and retained her position as co-regent.

and persecuted devout Jews. As a result, the Jews rebelled against the Seleucid king's authority throughout his reign. During Antiochus' invasion of Egypt, the deposed High Priest of Israel, Jason, launched a surprise attack on Jerusalem and removed his successor, Menelaus, from power (who had been appointed to the position by Antiochus).

The deuterocanonical book *2 Maccabees* records the ruthlessness with which Antiochus suppressed the rebellion and restored Menelaus as High Priest upon his return from Egypt in 168 BC: 'When these happenings were reported to the king, he thought that Judea was in revolt. Raging like a wild animal, he set out from Egypt and took Jerusalem by storm. He ordered his soldiers to cut down without mercy those whom they met and to slay those who took refuge in their houses. There was a massacre of young and old, a killing of women and children, a slaughter of virgins and infants. In the space of three days, eighty thousand were lost, forty thousand meeting a violent death, and the same number being sold into slavery.'

*

Less than two months after being forced into exile, Ptolemy VI was reconciled with his co-regents (Ptolemy VIII and Cleopatra II) and returned to Alexandria. The reunited government started recruiting mercenaries from Greece to fill the Ptolemaic army's depleted ranks in the expectation of another Seleucid invasion and overturned the peace agreement Ptolemy VI had made with his Seleucid counterpart.

The unexpected reconciliation between the royal siblings prompted Antiochus to invade Egypt once again in the spring of 168 BC – hoping to take his enemy by surprise and inflict a crushing defeat on them while Rome was still distracted by its war against Macedonia. Officially, he presented his campaign as a righteous struggle to restore Egypt's rightful pharaoh (Ptolemy VI), whose authority had been usurped by his younger brother. However, his real motivation was anything but selfless. He had not given up on his plan to subjugate the Ptolemaic Kingdom to Seleucid domination by using Ptolemy VI as a client ruler, and therefore desired to regain control of Ptolemy VI and remove his younger brother's supporters from power.

At first everything went according to plan in Antiochus' campaign. His fleet quickly seized Ptolemaic Cyprus and his army reoccupied Memphis, where he allegedly had himself crowned pharaoh of Egypt, although it is more likely that he attempted to establish a Seleucid protectorate over Egypt in the name of Ptolemy VI, which would have given his actions more legitimacy.[108] Antiochus then marched north with his army, bound for the Egyptian capital, but was stalled on the outskirts of Alexandria by the timely arrival of a Roman embassy.

The embassy had come to Egypt at the request of the Ptolemaic government, which had appealed to Rome for help during the winter of 169/168 BC.[109] Its leader – the politician and general Gaius Popillius Laenas – confronted the Seleucid king at Eleusis (a suburb of Alexandria) in July 168 BC and brought the Sixth Syrian War to an end by forcing Antiochus to agree to a peace settlement, which included the withdrawal of his troops from Egypt and Cyprus. By doing so he prevented the Ptolemaic and Seleucid kingdoms from being unified and preserved the Roman Republic's status at the greatest power in the Mediterranean.

According to the Roman historian Livy: 'After receiving the submission of the inhabitants of Memphis and of the rest of the Egyptian people, some submitting voluntarily, others under threats, [Antiochus] marched by easy stages towards Alexandria. After crossing the river at Eleusis, about four miles from Alexandria, he was met by the Roman commissioners, to whom he gave a friendly greeting and held out his hand to Popilius. Popilius, however, placed in his hand the tablets on which was written the decree of the senate and told him first of all to read it. After reading it through, he said he would call his friends into council and consider what he ought to do. Popilius, stern and imperious as ever, drew a circle round the king with the stick he was carrying and said, "Before you step out of that circle give me a reply to lay before the senate." For a few moments he hesitated, astounded at such a peremptory order, and at last replied, "I will do what the senate thinks right." Not till then did Popilius extend his hand to the king as to a friend and ally. Antiochus evacuated Egypt at the appointed date, and the commissioners exerted their authority to establish a lasting concord between the brothers, as they had as yet hardly made peace with each other.'

---

[108] The Ptolemaic *strategos* (governor) of Cyprus, Ptolemy Macron, entered Antiochus' service after surrendering the island to him.

[109] The Romans were too busy fighting Perseus of Macedonia in the Third Macedonian War (171-168 BC) to send an immediate response to the Ptolemaic plea for assistance against the Seleucids. It was not until they had brought the war with Macedonia to a close by decisively defeating Perseus' forces at the Battle of Pydna (in June 168 BC) that they were in a position to send an embassy to Alexandria.

Polybius gave a slightly more detailed account in *The Histories*: 'At the time when Antiochus approached Ptolemy and meant to occupy Pelusium, Caius Popilius Laenas, the Roman commander, on Antiochus greeting him from a distance and then holding out his hand, handed to the king, as he had it by him, the copy of the senatus-consultum, and told him to read it first, not thinking it proper, as it seems to me, to make the conventional sign of friendship before he knew if the intentions of him who was greeting him were friendly or hostile. But when the king, after reading it, said he would like to communicate with his friends about this intelligence, Popilius acted in a manner which was thought to be offensive and exceedingly arrogant. He was carrying a stick cut from a vine, and with this he drew a circle round Antiochus and told him he must remain inside this circle until he gave his decision about the contents of the letter. The king was astonished at this authoritative proceeding, but, after a few moments' hesitation, said he would do all that the Romans demanded. Upon this Popilius and his suite all grasped him by the hand and greeted him warmly. The letter ordered him to put an end at once to the war with Ptolemy. So, as a fixed number of days were allowed to him, he led his army back to Syria, deeply hurt and complaining indeed, but yielding to circumstances for the present. Popilius after arranging matters in Alexandria and exhorting the two kings there to act in common, ordering them also to send Polyaratus to Rome, sailed for Cyprus, wishing to lose no time in expelling the Syrian troops that were in the island. When they arrived, finding that Ptolemy's generals had been defeated and that the affairs of Cyprus were generally in a topsy-turvy state, they soon made the Syrian army retire from the country, and waited until the troops took ship for Syria. In this way the Romans saved the kingdom of Ptolemy, which had almost been crushed out of existence: Fortune having so directed the matter of Perseus and Macedonia that when the position of Alexandria and the whole of Egypt was almost desperate, all was again set right simply owing to the fact that the fate of Perseus had been decided. For had this not been so, and had not Antiochus been certain of it, he would never, I think, have obeyed the Roman behests.'

Antiochus' decision to comply with the Roman demands was probably driven by the knowledge that a large number of Roman troops had been freed up following their recent victory against Macedonia in the Third Macedonian War, which meant they were well-prepared to back up their demands with military force. He could not ignore the fact that Rome was now a major power in the Mediterranean and was surely eager to avoid a repeat of the humiliation his kingdom had suffered at the hands of the Romans during the Roman-Seleucid War.

Even though the imposed peace and Seleucid withdrawal humiliated Antiochus and marked the end of his plans to absorb Egypt into his empire, the Ptolemaic Kingdom was severely weakened by the war and the factional conflict that continued to play out between Ptolemy VI and Ptolemy VIII. This has led to some historians presenting the alternative argument that the actions of the Roman embassy were actually a blessing in disguise for Antiochus, as it gave him an excuse to abandon what could have turned out to be a long, costly and risky siege of the Egyptian capital. Instead, he was able to return to his own domain, weighed down with loot from his campaign and reassured by the knowledge that he had weakened his Ptolemaic rival.

The disastrous events of the Sixth Syrian War left the Ptolemaic monarchy's prestige in tatters. Ptolemy VI, Ptolemy VIII and Cleopatra II continued to rule the kingdom jointly, but a permanent rift had developed between the two brothers that soon led to further infighting at the very top of the Ptolemaic government. The situation started to come to a head in 165 BC, when Dionysius Petosarapis (a prominent courtier, presumably of native Egyptian origin) appeared before the people of Alexandria in the city's stadium and warned them that Ptolemy VI was plotting to murder his younger brother. Dionysius Petosarapis was clearly trying to exploit the mutual distrust between the royal siblings to improve his own position, but Ptolemy VI successfully convinced Ptolemy VIII that the allegations were false. As a show of unity, the two kings made a joint appearance at the stadium, while Dionysius Petosarapis was forced to flee Alexandria. Nevertheless, this initial setback did not deter the ambitious courtier, and he wasn't finished causing trouble yet.

Soon after his departure from the Egyptian capital, Dionysius Petosarapis managed to persuade some units in the Ptolemaic army to mutiny but was defeated.[110] This was followed by fierce fighting in the Fayum – triggered by social conditions – that ended at some point in 164 BC. Meanwhile, a separate rebellion had broken out in the Thebaid. This was a native Egyptian revolt that appears to have had no links to Dionysius Petosarapis' rebellious activity further north. It may have been sparked by a decree that Ptolemy VI, Ptolemy VIII and Cleopatra II had issued in the autumn of 165 BC, aimed at bringing land back into cultivation that had been abandoned during the many years of civil war and conflict with the Seleucids. It was hoped that these measures would protect their agricultural revenue, but they faced widespread resistance from their subjects. Nevertheless, the revolt was eventually suppressed after

---

[110] The final fate of the rebel Dionysius Petosarapis is unknown.

Ptolemy VI marched south with an army and successfully besieged the city of Panopolis (present-day Akhmim).

At some point in the autumn of 164 BC, soon after Ptolemy VI had arrived back in Alexandria from his campaign against the native Egyptian rebels in southern Egypt, Ptolemy VI and Cleopatra II were deposed by Ptolemy VIII, who marked the beginning of his sole rule by adopting the epithet *Euergetes* ('Benefactor') to distance himself from his older brother and highlight his ties with his illustrious ancestor, Ptolemy III. How this happened is uncertain, although one of the main instigators appears to have been a man named Timotheus, who went on to become the chief minister in Ptolemy VIII's government.

After being ousted from power, Ptolemy VI travelled to Rome – accompanied by a meagre party, composed of a eunuch and three servants – in the hope of securing assistance to regain his throne. In the end he had no luck, so he proceeded to the Ptolemaic island of Cyprus, which was still loyal to him (and where his wife, Cleopatra II, may have travelled after his deposition).

Fortunately, Ptolemy VI did not have to languish in exile for long. In his absence, Ptolemy VIII and Timotheus governed the kingdom ruthlessly and tyrannically. They attempted to consolidate their hold on power by torturing and executing opponents of the new regime, but such arbitrary measures alienated the people against them. By the summer of 163 BC the Alexandrians had had enough. They rioted against Ptolemy VIII and invited Ptolemy VI to return to power.

When Ptolemy VI was restored to his rightful position as pharaoh, the Romans persuaded him to grant his younger brother control of Cyrenaica as a concession prize.[111] Meanwhile, the rest of the Ptolemaic Kingdom (Egypt and Cyprus) was brought back under the joint rule of Ptolemy VI and Cleopatra II. This arrangement pleased the Romans, who saw the partitioning of the Ptolemaic Kingdom as a means of preventing it from getting too powerful. However, it was unacceptable to Ptolemy VIII, who was not content with Cyrenaica by itself and desired to gain control of Cyprus too. For this reason, he visited Rome (in late 163 or early 162 BC), where he brought his case before the Senate and sought its support.[112]

---

[111] When Ptolemy VIII became king of Cyrene, he was also appointed to serve as the priest of Apollo (the most important religious position in Cyrene). During his reign here, he sponsored extensive construction projects in the city and sought to demonstrate the Hellenistic royal virtue of *tryphé* (luxury). These were all efforts at improving his poor image.

As the Romans preferred to keep the Ptolemaic Kingdom divided and weakened rather than unified, the Senate agreed that the division was unfair and dispatched an embassy to the Ptolemaic court. Headed by Titus Manlius Torquatus and Gnaeus Cornelius Merula, it was tasked with persuading Ptolemy VI to sweeten the deal by giving his brother control of Cyprus. However, the Egyptian king had no intention of surrendering to his brother's demands. He procrastinated over the issue, dragging out the negotiations, and the ambassadors ended up returning to Rome empty-handed near the end of 162 BC.

Upon their return, Torquatus and Merula were determined to retaliate against Ptolemy VI for his defiance. They persuaded the Senate to repudiate Rome's alliance with Ptolemy VI, to expel his ambassadors from the city, and to give Ptolemy VIII permission to seize control of Cyprus by force. However, their blessing did not include any practical support to help Ptolemy VIII achieve this, so Cyprus remained under Ptolemy VI's control.

While Torquatus and Merula had been conducting their futile negotiations in Egypt, Ptolemy VIII had kept himself busy. After leaving Rome, he travelled to Greece to begin recruiting mercenaries for an invasion of Cyprus. However, he only made it as far as Rhodes, where he crossed paths with Torquatus and Merula on their way to Egypt. The ambassadors persuaded him to discharge his troops and return to Cyrenaica, but when he arrived there he lingered by the Egyptian border with a force of 1,000 Cretan mercenaries, awaiting news of the outcome of the Roman negotiations with his brother. He remained there for well over a month and only withdrew when he was distracted by a revolt in Cyrene. The perpetrator of the uprising was none other than Ptolemy Sempetesis (the man who Ptolemy VIII had appointed to serve as governor of the city in his absence), although it had been suppressed by the end of 162 BC.

---

[112] Ptolemy VIII benefitted from close relations with the Roman Republic throughout his time as ruler of Cyrenaica. He was declared a 'friend and ally' of Rome in 162 BC and is said to have met Cornelia (a daughter of the renowned Roman general Scipio Africanus) during his stay in the city. After the death of Cornelia's husband Tiberius Sempronius Gracchus (in about 152 BC) Ptolemy VIII is said to have sought her hand in marriage, but she rejected his advances (perhaps because she desired to maintain her newly acquired independence and freedom). However, there is no hard evidence to support this, and it is likely that the story of his marriage proposal is little more than a legend.

It is unclear whether Ptolemy VIII achieved this by military or diplomatic means. What can be said for certain though is that his attention returned to Cyprus as soon as the situation in Cyrenaica had been stabilised.

At some point in 161 BC, Ptolemy VIII sent a military expedition to the island. This might have lasted as long as a year, but he was ultimately forced to abandon the invasion after facing fierce Cypriot resistance. Without active military resistance from Rome, he simply did not have sufficient manpower to achieve his objectives.

Despite having his hands full with his younger brother's schemes, Ptolemy VI managed to find the time to immerse himself in a plot to destabilise the Seleucid Empire. When Antiochus IV died in 164 BC, he was succeeded by his son Antiochus V, who was only about nine years old at the time. Like many child rulers throughout history, his young age left him vulnerable to rival claimants to the throne. The biggest threat was posed by his cousin, Demetrius I, who had been held as a hostage by the Romans since the reign of his father (Seleucus IV), but eventually managed to escape captivity.[113] Once he was at liberty, Demetrius sought to seize control of the Seleucid Empire. He received assistance off Ptolemy VI and by approximately November 162 BC had succeeded in usurping Antiochus' throne.[114]

Almost as soon as Demetrius was in power, the interests of the Seleucid and Ptolemaic kings diverged, making it increasingly likely that war would break out between their kingdoms yet again. Tensions became particularly high when it came to Ptolemy VI's attention that his governor of Cyprus, Archias, had opened secret negotiations with Demetrius to sell Cyprus to the Seleucid ruler for 500 talents. The plot's discovery in 155 BC caused the negotiations to fall through and Archias hanged himself after being caught.

In 154 BC, Ptolemy VIII made a second appeal to the Roman Senate, following a failed assassination attempt that he claimed had been masterminded by his older brother but may in fact have been carried out by his own Cyrenean subjects seeking to depose him.[115] To give substance to his claims, he showed the gathered senators the

---

[113] Under the terms of the Treaty of Apamea (which had ended the Roman-Seleucid War), various prominent members of the Seleucid royal family had been sent to Rome as hostages.
[114] Antiochus V (who was aged just 10 or 11 years old at the time of his deposition) was put to death along with his regent Lysias shortly after being deposed.
[115] According to an inscription carved after the assassination attempt on Ptolemy VIII (in 155 BC), he bequeathed his kingdom (without specifying what that included) to the Roman Republic in his will, in the event that he died without a legitimate heir. Although there is no

scars he had sustained as a result of the attempt on his life, and the Romans responded to his request for assistance by sending another embassy to the Ptolemaic court (despite the opposition of Cato the Elder, who favoured Ptolemy VI).

The embassy was led by Gnaeus Cornelius Merula and Lucius Minucius Thermus, who received the same instructions as Torquatus and Merula had before them: to order Ptolemy VI to surrender Cyprus into Ptolemy VIII's custody. Unlike the first embassy, this time the Senate was prepared to back up its decision with force and provided some token military support to Ptolemy VIII so he could make a second bid at taking Cyprus. Nevertheless, the assistance (five ships, some advisors, and permission for their allies in Greece and Asia to support the campaign) was only a token show of support and nowhere near enough to tip the balance in Ptolemy VIII's favour. Preoccupied with conflict in Spain and aware that a war with Carthage was on the horizon, the Romans had no desire to entangle themselves in a full-scale war with Egypt, and Ptolemy VI was well aware of this, which strengthened his hand in the negotiations.

On Cyprus, Ptolemy VIII occupied the town of Lapethus, but failed to extend his control over the entire island. Before long, he was being besieged by Ptolemy VI, which resulted in the fall of the town and Ptolemy VIII's capture.

Once he had Ptolemy VIII in his custody, Ptolemy VI was able to coerce him into withdrawing his forces from Cyprus. In return, he allowed Ptolemy VIII to remain in control of Cyrenaica, as well as promising to grant him an annual grain subsidy and to arrange for him to marry one of his young daughters (most likely Cleopatra Thea) once they came of age.[116]

Ptolemy VI's decision to treat his brother leniently was almost certainly prompted by the fear of provoking Roman aggression if he had him killed or tried to overturn the status quo. At the same time, his prolonged conflict with Ptolemy VIII made him particularly eager to promote his eldest son, Ptolemy Eupator, as the rightful heir to the throne. The prince was appointed to serve as the priest of Alexander the Great for 158/157 BC, even though he was only about seven years old at the time, and by the spring of 152 BC he had been promoted to the rank of co-regent alongside his parents. However, any hope of Ptolemy Eupator one day ruling the Ptolemaic Kingdom in his

---

reference to this in any literary source, the practice was adopted by many Hellenistic monarchs during this period to deter their subjects from attempting to assassinate or overthrow them.
[116] This marriage never took place.

own right was shattered when he died just a few months into his co-rule, aged about 12 or 13.[117] Given that Ptolemy VI's other son (also named Ptolemy) was very young at the time, Ptolemy Eupator's premature death left a big question mark hanging over the succession. This prompted him to start grooming his daughter Cleopatra III as a potential successor (or to serve as her younger brother's regent in the event their parents died before he came of age). As part of these efforts, he made the unprecedented decision to deify her and appoint a priest for her worship in Ptolemais Hermiou in c. 146 BC. This was the first time a female member of the Ptolemaic dynasty who was not a queen had an eponymous cult established in their honour and reveals Ptolemy's determination to prevent his younger brother from regaining control of Egypt after his death.

*

In 153 BC yet another rival claimant to the Seleucid throne – Alexander Balas – arrived on the scene and attempted to assert his claim against Demetrius I. Balas claimed to be a son of Antiochus IV Epiphanes and Laodice IV and may have received assistance off Ptolemy VI, although there is no hard evidence for this. If help was given it probably included financial aid, the provision of naval transport, and support in gaining control of Ptolemais in Phoenicia, where Balas landed his army of mercenaries.

Alexander Balas' other allies included the Roman Republic and the Kingdom of Pergamon. Neither cared whether he was an imposter or not, and were eager to use him to destabilise the Seleucid Empire.

After gaining recognition from the Roman Senate as king of the Seleucids in 153 BC, Balas recruited a mercenary army and began his invasion by attacking the coastal city of Ptolemais in Phoenicia. Once he had successfully occupied Ptolemais (in 152 BC), he had himself officially proclaimed king of the Seleucids. This meant the Seleucid Empire now had two rival kings, and the kingdom was plunged into civil war.

During this conflict Balas relied heavily on foreign allies to bankroll his mercenary army (namely the Roman Republic and the Kingdom of Pergamon) as well as on the support of the many of Demetrius' domestic enemies (including a group of rebellious Jewish warriors called the Maccabees).[118] The fighting dragged on for three years, but

---

[117] Ptolemy Eupator is believed to have died on Cyprus, where his father had sent him to govern.

the support given by his allies paid off when Balas defeated and killed Demetrius in battle in the summer of 150 BC.

Even if Ptolemy VI didn't assist Balas during the civil war, he certainly did form an alliance with him soon after Demetrius' defeat by marrying his daughter Cleopatra Thea to the new Seleucid king. The wedding ceremony took place at Ptolemais in Phoenicia and was attended by Ptolemy VI himself, which highlights the importance of the occasion. There is no doubt that this was a significant diplomatic victory for the Ptolemaic king, who had the satisfaction of seeing a competent, ambitious and hostile Seleucid king in Demetrius replaced by the opportunistic Balas (who was now his own son-in-law). However, as time would tell, this arrangement was pitifully short-lived.

*

The Seleucid Empire did not remain at peace for long, thanks to the efforts of Demetrius I's son, Demetrius II, who was determined to claim his birthright. In about 147 BC civil war broke out once again when the disinherited prince sought to overthrow the Seleucid king by invading Syria with an army of Cretan mercenaries while Balas had his hands full with a revolt in Cilicia.

Soon after the resumption of hostilities, the alliance between Ptolemy VI and Alexander Balas started to fall apart. The Egyptian king began amassing an army, with the intention of intervening in the Seleucid civil war, and invaded Syria in 147 BC. Balas was still busy suppressing the rebellion in Cilicia at the time and his Jewish ally Jonathan Maccabee made no effort to prevent Ptolemy's forces from passing through Judea, so Ptolemy's forces were able to occupy most of the coast of Coele-Syria with relative ease.

The Egyptian king justified his actions by claiming he was intervening to support Balas against Demetrius II. However, his decision to seize Seleucid cities along the cost of Coele-Syria and stamp his authority on these settlements (possibly by minting his own coinage there) revealed he wasn't doing anything of the sort. Rather, he was taking advantage of the turmoil in the Seleucid Empire to regain former Ptolemaic possessions that had been lost during the reign of his father.

---

[118] The Maccabees were led by Jonathan Apphus at this time. They supported traditional Judaism and opposed the growing influence of Hellenistic Judaism. In order to do this, they fought for control of Judea (which was part of the Seleucid Empire at the time) and established the Hasmonean dynasty.

The alliance between Ptolemy VI and Alexander Balas officially came to an end when Ptolemy allegedly learned that Balas' chancellor Ammonius was plotting to assassinate him. He is said to have discovered the plot while he was staying at Ptolemais in Phoenicia, although it is highly likely that the charges were false and had been fabricated by Ptolemy to give him an excuse to switch sides in the civil war. If this is true, then Demetrius II had presumably offered to formally recognise Ptolemaic rule in Coele-Syria if Ptolemy defected to his cause, and Ptolemy may have also been encouraged to do so by the assumption that he'd be able to exert more influence over Demetrius (who was only a teenager at the time) than Balas. Alternatively, Balas may have seen Ptolemy's 'assistance' for what it was (an attempted land grab) and plotted to have the Ptolemaic king assassinated to prevent him from making these territorial gains permanent.

No matter what really occurred, Balas rejected Ptolemy's demands for Ammonius to be brought to justice and the Egyptian king retaliated by switching his support to Demetrius II.

While the Ptolemaic army continued to advance north, Balas was still preoccupied suppressing the revolt in Cilicia (in Asia Minor), which left the Seleucid capital – Antioch – vulnerable to attack. The two commanders who were left in charge of the city, Diodotus and Hierax, surrendered Antioch to Ptolemy when he arrived and tried to ingratiate themselves with the Egyptian king by having him crowned 'king of Asia'. However, after a short period Ptolemy decided to abandon this title in favour of Demetrius II (who he remarried his daughter Cleopatra Thea to) and restrained his ambition to the annexation of Coele-Syria and ruling the Seleucid Empire informally through his new son-in-law. This was prompted by his fear that the Romans would intervene if he attempted to unify the Ptolemaic Kingdom and the Seleucid Empire.

In Antioch, Ptolemy was reunited with his daughter Cleopatra Thea. Shortly after their reunion, he had her marriage to Alexander Balas annulled so she could be remarried to Demetrius II. Under the terms of this marriage alliance, Ptolemy agreed to help Demetrius II take the Seleucid throne from Balas in exchange for Coele-Syria being returned to the Ptolemaic Kingdom.

Meanwhile, Balas and his supporters returned to Syria after quelling the Cilician revolt and put pressure on Ptolemy's occupying force by pillaging the countryside around Antioch. Eventually, Ptolemy and Demetrius sought to put an end to the raids by departing the Seleucid capital with a joint army and meeting Balas in battle just outside the city. This engagement took place in the summer of 145 BC and is known as the Battle of the Oenoparus, after the river where it was fought.

Ptolemy and Demetrius' coalition force won a decisive victory in the fighting. Balas managed to escape to Arabia, where he planned to seek asylum with his Nabataean allies, but was killed soon thereafter. Depending on the account, he was either killed by two of his own men (who were eager to get in Demetrius' good books) or a Nabataean prince named Zabdiel (who wanted to gain the favour of Ptolemy), and the deposed king's severed head was sent to Ptolemy VI as a trophy of his victory.

The Battle of the Oenoparus was a major victory for the Ptolemaic army and effectively united Egypt and Syria. However, it came at a high price for their king who died from wounds he had sustained in the battle just three days later.[119] Apparently Ptolemy's horse had fallen on him after being startled by a war elephant, fracturing his skull. Nevertheless, the precise circumstances of his death are far less significant than its consequences.

The sudden deaths of Alexander Balas and Ptolemy VI left Demetrius II as the unexpected victor of the battle. Now his powerful father-in-law was no longer around to restrain his ambitions, Demetrius turned against his Ptolemaic ally and rapidly restored Syria to Seleucid control. By the end of 145 BC, he had successfully pushed all the occupying Ptolemaic forces out of Syria, and asserted his authority in the region by marching with his army all the way to the Egyptian border. This was a shocking reversal in fortune for the Ptolemaic Kingdom, which had regained possession of Coele-Syria and reduced its bitter Seleucid rival to a client state, only to lose it all in the blink of an eye.

*

When looking back on Ptolemy VI's time as pharaoh there is no doubt that his second reign (163-145 BC) was far more successful than the first (180-164 BC), both in terms of his conflict with the Seleucids and his power struggle with Ptolemy VIII. For the majority of his first reign he was reliant on regents to govern on his behalf, and when he came of age things could not have gone much worse: with Egypt being humiliated by the Seleucids in an ill-advised war and Ptolemy suffering the indignity of being sidelined by supporters of his younger brother. It was only after he was restored to

---

[119] Ptolemy VI was almost certainly buried in the royal quarter in Alexandria, along with the other Ptolemies.

power that Ptolemy turned things around and started building a legacy to be proud of. Within the Ptolemaic Kingdom, he had Ptolemy VIII exiled to Cyrenaica and thwarted multiple attempts by him to take control of Cyprus, despite intervention by the Roman Senate in his younger brother's favour. Outside his domains, he offered his support to a series of rival claimants for the Seleucid throne, which resulted in a civil war that lasted for multiple generations and ultimately brought about the downfall of the Seleucid dynasty.[120]

The fact that he was just as capable of forging alliances as he was at making enemies was emphasised by the erection of a bronze statue of Ptolemy VI on horseback in the Acropolis at Athens. The Athenians did this to show their gratitude for gifts they had received off the Egyptian king, which included a library and perhaps a gymnasium. Such donations were common at this time and were a key element of Ptolemy VI's foreign policy. Doing so helped him to foster amicable relations with various states, as well as making them feel obliged to support him during times of war.

At home Ptolemy VI followed the example of his Ptolemaic predecessors by presenting himself to his Egyptian subjects as a traditional pharaoh and maintaining good relations with the Egyptian priestly elite. He took part in religious rituals and was closely associated with the worship of Ptah and the Apis bull at Memphis in particular. Every New Year, Ptolemy VI and his wife (Cleopatra II) appear to have travelled to Memphis to take part in the New Year festival that was held there, during which they stayed in the city's Serapeum. The royal couple also called a meeting of Egypt's priests in the summer of 161 BC. During this synod Ptolemy continued a tradition that had been established during the reign of Ptolemy III by passing a decree which granted tax exemptions and other benefits to the Egyptian priesthood, which reflected his eagerness to gain the support of the clergy. In return, the royal couple's cult received honours in Egyptian temples.

It is known from various inscriptions that Ptolemy VI made many other religious benefactions throughout his reign. In September 157 BC he reconfirmed a grant that had originally been made during the reign of Ptolemy II, which gifted all of the tax revenue generated by the Dodecaschoenus region to the Temple of Isis at Philae. Over a decade later, in about 145 BC, he donated all the tribute payments made by a Nubian vassal to the priests of the Nubian god Mandulis at Philae. Such gestures were part of

---

[120] The Seleucid Empire was defeated and dissolved by the Roman general Pompey in 63 BC.

a broader effort to legitimise Ptolemaic rule in Lower Nubia and to reassert the dynasty's authority there.

However, the most obvious way Ptolemy VI promoted good relations with the Egyptian priesthood was by funding religious construction projects. Building work that took place during his time on the throne included: the construction of a new temple of Satet on the island of Elephantine and the Temple of Kom Ombo; the foundation of the temple of Hathor at Philae; continued work on the temple of Arensnuphis at Philae and the temple of Khnum at Esna; the enlargement of the temple of Nemty at Qaw el-Kebir; and the resumption of work at the Temple of Edfu (in 152/151 BC).[121][122]

After taking all these things into consideration, the image we get of Ptolemy VI is generally positive. This is certainly the case when comparing him to his ruthless younger brother, Ptolemy VIII – as you will see in the second half of this chapter. According to Polybius, Ptolemy VI never sentenced anyone to death. If this is true, this was remarkably humane conduct by the standards of the time, considering the casualness and regularity with which most of his Ptolemaic kin resorted to murder.

Unfortunately, those days were now over – never to return.

*

There was already a Jewish presence in Egypt when the Ptolemies came to power, but their population had grown significantly since 311 BC, when Ptolemy I reportedly seized Jerusalem by a ruse and brought a large number of its Jewish inhabitants back to his kingdom – using some to serve in his army and enslaving the rest. Those who became slaves were later freed, and by the time Ptolemy VI came to the throne Jews enjoyed similar privileges to Egypt's Greek and Macedonian population, as well as having a well-established presence in the Ptolemaic army. Alexandria had a sizeable Jewish community and even had its own dedicated quarter in the city (which may have been established during Ptolemy VI's time on the throne). The Jewish quarter had some degree of self-governance and was led by an *ethnarch*, who was selected by its Jewish inhabitants.

---

[121] Work on the Temple of Edfu was suspended between 206 and 186 BC as a result of the rebellion in Upper Egypt. With the exception of some minor details on the gates from the time of Cleopatra I, no significant work was undertaken at the site until 152/151 BC.
[122] The Temple of Kom Ombo was a double temple dedicated to Haroeris ('the elder Horus') and Sobek.

According to the first century AD Roman-Jewish historian Josephus, Ptolemy VI took a personal interest in the wellbeing of his Jewish subjects. In approximately 160 BC a particularly large group of Jewish immigrants arrived in Egypt and were given permission by Ptolemy VI to settle in and around the city of Leontopolis (in the Nile Delta) in return for military service.[123] They were fleeing an ongoing conflict between the Seleucid Empire and the Maccabees and were led by Onias IV (the son of a former Jewish High Priest, Onias III, who had been deposed and murdered during the reign of the Seleucid king Antiochus IV, perhaps on suspicion of having Ptolemaic sympathies). Onias IV had hoped that the Maccabees would prevail in their revolt and appoint him to his rightful position as High Priest, or that the Seleucids would make him High Priest in order to quell the rebellion and legitimise their rule in the eyes of the populace. Unfortunately, neither of these things happened. The Seleucids chose an opponent of the Maccabean Revolt named Alcimus to serve as High Priest in about 162 BC, and in 152 BC the Maccabean leader Jonathan Apphus made a deal with Alexander Balas to secure the title of High Priest for himself. Now it was clear that Onias IV was not going to be recalled to Judea to inherit his father's position, his attitude towards the Maccabees hardened. At an unknown date he was granted permission by Ptolemy VI to build a Jewish temple in Leontopolis, which he presided over as a rival High Priest to the one in Jerusalem.[124] Ptolemy VI's support can be explained by his continued desire to regain control of Coele-Syria and Judea, and Onias IV prospered as a result. He was appointed to a distinguished position in the Ptolemaic army and his family became honoured members of the Ptolemaic court.

*

Ptolemy VI had probably intended for his son, also named Ptolemy, to succeed him. However, the young prince was only about seven years old at the time of his father's death and the Alexandrians invited Ptolemy VIII to return from Cyrenaica and become their king once more.

Given that the majority of the Ptolemaic army was still in Syria at this time (and a large portion of it were mercenaries, who joined Demetrius II after Ptolemy VI's sudden death), Cleopatra II and her young son were left with little protection in

---

[123] The area where they settled became known as the 'Land of Onias'. It was named after their leader, Onias IV.
[124] The temple was closed on the orders of the Roman emperor Vespasian in 73 AD, in the aftermath of the First Jewish-Roman War.

Alexandria. Fearing for their safety, they sought refuge in Memphis when Ptolemy VIII returned to Egypt, although they did not remain there for long.

In order to secure his hold on power, Ptolemy VIII arranged a reconciliation with his newly widowed sister, who agreed to marry him (in 145 BC).[125][126] To mark the change in leadership, the newlyweds were incorporated into the Ptolemaic cult as the *Theoi Euergetai* ('Benefactor Gods'), even though they had both already been incorporated into the cult with Ptolemy VI as the *Theoi Philometores* ('Mother-loving Gods').

It is widely believed that Ptolemy VIII had his young nephew, Prince Ptolemy, put to death, although the exact timing and circumstances are uncertain. The Roman historian Justin claims the young boy died in Cleopatra II's arms after being murdered by her new husband on the night of their wedding. However, surviving documentary evidence reveals that Prince Ptolemy did not die immediately. He initially served as his uncle's heir and was probably only murdered sometime after the birth of Ptolemy VIII and Cleopatra II's son, Ptolemy Memphites, who had replaced him as the heir apparent to the throne by the end of 140 BC.[127]

Ptolemy VIII is also known to have had an illegitimate son named Ptolemy Apion (probably born at some point between 150 and 145 BC). The mother of this child was a concubine from Cyrenaica, perhaps named Eirene. Eirene was Ptolemy VIII's mistress between 150 and 127 BC and travelled with her lover from Cyrenaica to Egypt when he succeeded Ptolemy VI as pharaoh in 145 BC. Therefore, it is safe to assume that Ptolemy Apion was born in Cyrene (the capital of Cyrenaica), but was raised and educated at the Ptolemaic court in Alexandria after his father's accession to the Egyptian throne.

Ptolemy VIII was officially crowned pharaoh at a ceremony in Memphis in either 144 or 143 BC.

---

[125] Ptolemy VIII and Cleopatra II are thought to have had at least one child together – a son named Ptolemy Memphites.
[126] Ptolemy VIII was probably born around 184 BC.
[127] Ptolemy Memphites was born at some point between 144 and 142 BC. Some scholars believe he is the same person as Ptolemy VII Neos Philopator, who was posthumously deified in 118 BC.

Ancient sources present Ptolemy VIII in a very unflattering light. He is characterised as a cruel tyrant and derided as a fat, morally corrupt individual. This was in sharp contrast to his elder brother, Ptolemy VI, who enjoyed a much better reputation.

After returning to Alexandria from his coronation in Memphis, Ptolemy VIII is reported to have presided over a bloody purge of his late brother's supporters. Various anecdotes appear in the ancient sources about this incident, including him letting his soldiers loose on the streets of Alexandria, where they murdered citizens indiscriminately, and him giving orders for the city's gymnasium to be set on fire while people were taking refuge inside.[128] He dished out severe punishments to the Jewish military commanders who had helped to overthrow his previous regime and banished large numbers of Greek intellectuals from Alexandria (including the director of the Library of Alexandria, Aristarchus of Samothrace), leaving the Ptolemaic capital a changed city. As a result of the brutality and injustice that became synonymous with Ptolemy VIII's rule, the people of Alexandria started to refer to him by the derisive nicknames *Kakergetēs* ('Malefactor') and – later – Physcon ('Fatty' or 'Potbellied'). The first of these was a pun on his official epithet Euergetes ('Benefactor'), while the second was a reference to his obesity, which allegedly became so severe later on in his reign that he had to be carried everywhere in a litter. As the Greek author Athenaeus wrote in the *Deipnosophistae* (in the early third century AD): 'Through indulgence in luxury his [Ptolemy VIII's] body had become corrupted with fat and with a belly to measure it with one's arm…'

To compensate for the many enemies he made amongst the Ptolemaic Kingdom's influential immigrant population, Ptolemy tried to ingratiate himself with the native Egyptian masses by issuing amnesty decrees and bestowing generous patronage on their temples.

Within a few months of acceding to the throne, Ptolemy pulled his troops out of the few Ptolemaic bases that remained in the Aegean – in Methana (on the Peloponnese), Itanos (on Crete), and on the island of Thera (present-day Santorini). This decision meant the once extensive Ptolemaic Kingdom had now been reduced to Egypt, Cyrenaica, Cyprus, and some strongholds along the coast of the Red Sea.

A few years into his marriage to his sister, Ptolemy VIII caused a scandal when he decided to marry his niece and stepdaughter, Cleopatra III, and promote her to the

---

[128] There is some uncertainty about whether these stories refer to this purge or the purge that occurred when Ptolemy VIII reconquered Alexandria in 126 BC.

rank of co-regent at some point between 142 and 140 BC.[129][130] They may have been in an intimate relationship for a number of years before their wedding (perhaps even as early as his accession to the throne), and it is likely that Cleopatra III agreed to the liaison in return for being made queen. Ptolemy's motivation is less clear, but two credible theories are that he was seeking to prevent her from marrying someone else who might use the union to usurp his throne, or that he was simply captivated by her.

Nevertheless, Ptolemy did not divorce his first wife, and an uneasy arrangement followed where both mother and daughter served as the pharaoh's wife and co-regent.

Ptolemy's actions were a tough pill to swallow for Cleopatra II. It seriously damaged her relationship with her husband (which had already been put under strain by his decision to murder her son Ptolemy) and turned her own daughter into her fiercest rival.

Cleopatra II responded to her brother-husband's marriage to her daughter by supporting a revolt orchestrated by an Athamanian mercenary named Galaestes. Galaestes was the son of a king of the Athamanians and had been a valued commander in the Ptolemaic army during the reign of Ptolemy VI, but had fallen into disfavour with his successor, who had confiscated his property and exiled him to Greece in 145 BC. Since then, He was determined to regain his proper place in society and realised the time was ripe to topple Ptolemy VIII from his throne, so raised an army of fellow Ptolemaic exiles in Greece. To strengthen his cause, he claimed he had Ptolemy VI's young son, Ptolemy, in his care. He declared him to be the rightful king of Egypt and planned to put him on the throne.

When Galaestes launched his attack, Ptolemy VIII's mercenaries were so disaffected about their pay being in arrears that they nearly defected to his side. Disaster was only averted by the efforts of their commander, Hierax, who managed to buy their continued loyalty to Ptolemy VIII by using his own money to pay them the wages they were owed.

Now the support of his mercenaries had been secured, Ptolemy VIII was able to confront Galaestes' army, which was defeated by February 139 BC. He then tried to

---

[129] Cleopatra III was a daughter of Ptolemy VI and Cleopatra II. Shortly before she married Ptolemy VIII, she was added to the Ptolemaic dynastic cult as one of the *Theoi Euergetai* ('Benefactor Gods') alongside Ptolemy VIII and Cleopatra II (who already held the epithet).
[130] Ptolemy VIII and Cleopatra III went on to have five children together: Ptolemy IX, Ptolemy X, Tryphaena, Cleopatra IV and Cleopatra Selene.

secure his position by issuing a decree that confirmed the Egyptian priesthood's rights and privileges and created the illusion that he was ruling harmoniously with his two wives (Cleopatra II and Cleopatra III).

In the same year as Galaestes' rebellion was suppressed, Ptolemy VIII gave an extravagant welcome to a Roman embassy that arrived at his court, headed by the general and statesman Scipio Aemilianus. The embassy had been tasked with undertaking a tour of inspection of states allied to Rome in the eastern Mediterranean (140-139 BC) to ensure everything was in order and behaved in stark contrast to their hosts when they visited Alexandria – being austere in their manner, and snubbing the luxury and immorality that was rife at the Ptolemaic court. Nevertheless, when they conducted a survey of the Nile Delta as far south as Memphis, they were highly impressed by the fertility of the land and the many bustling towns in the region.[131] Upon their return to Rome, they presented their findings to the Senate, which highlighted the immense value of Egypt if it were governed prudently. Rome's ever-growing empire thirsted for that ancient country's fabled wealth. Initially it would try to exploit it indirectly. But one day, just over a century later, that ambition would turn to conquest.

*

In the years that followed Ptolemy VIII's decision to marry his niece, tensions grew between the Egyptian king and his first wife. The situation reached breaking point in late 132 BC when Cleopatra II initiated a rebellion against Ptolemy VIII and Cleopatra III that plunged the kingdom into civil war.

Ptolemy initially remained in control of the capital, but was forced to flee to Cyprus along with Cleopatra III in the autumn of 131 BC when the people of Alexandria rioted against him and set the royal palace on fire. However, he had no intention of remaining in exile for long. Fearing that his son – Ptolemy Memphites – would be acclaimed king in his place, he had him brought to Cyprus from Cyrene as an insurance policy, and planned to reconquer Egypt using newly-recruited soldiers and the troops stationed on Cyprus (who were still loyal to him).

With the support of the Alexandrians, Cleopatra II had herself proclaimed sole queen and adopted the epithet *Thea Philomētōr Sōteira* ('Mother-loving, Saviour Goddess').

---

[131] After departing Egypt, the Roman embassy visited Rhodes, Cyprus, Syria and Pergamon in turn.

As the first woman to take sole possession of the Ptolemaic Kingdom, this title helped to legitimise her position by linking her to both her late husband, Ptolemy VI Philometor ('Mother-loving'), and the dynasty's founder, Ptolemy I Soter ('Saviour'). At the same time, she scorned her second husband and daughter by destroying Ptolemy VIII's statues and having the *Theoi Euergetai* removed from the Ptolemaic cult in Alexandria, although Ptolemy VIII and Cleopatra III had their own rival priest of Alexander during their exile from the Egyptian capital (between 130 BC and 127 BC).[132]

In the conflict that followed, Cleopatra II had the backing of both Alexandria and the majority of the kingdom's Greek and Jewish inhabitants, while Ptolemy and Cleopatra III enjoyed greater popularity with the native Egyptian population. Consequently, the majority of the kingdom outside of Alexandria continued to regard Ptolemy as their ruler, and in the southern part of Upper Egypt a native Egyptian rebel named Harsiesi exploited the conflict between the royal siblings to have himself proclaimed pharaoh.

Following in the footsteps of Horwennefer and Ankhwennefer, Harsiesi briefly seized control of Thebes in August or September 131 BC but only held onto the city for a couple of months.[133] In November of the same year, Thebes was recaptured by the native Egyptian *strategos* of the Thebaid, Paos, and his forces set off in pursuit of Harsiesi. The favour Ptolemy had always shown the native Egyptian population bought their support, and that included Paos, who remained loyal to Ptolemy and played a key role in the civil war.

At the start of 130 BC, Ptolemy and Cleopatra III returned to Egypt from their brief exile in Cyprus, and by spring they had set up a rival government in Memphis. The support of his native Egyptian subjects gave him the perfect springboard to recapture the kingdom and he consolidated this support by promoting Egyptians to senior offices.[134] As a reward for Paos' military successes against Harsiesi, Ptolemy put him

---

[132] Since the death of Arsinoe II, it had become customary for deceased Ptolemaic queens to be honoured with their own cult, including a dedicated priestess (who marched behind the priest of Alexander the Great during religious processions in Alexandria). In 131 or 130 BC Ptolemy VIII took this tradition to the next level by establishing a cult in honour of Cleopatra III even though she was still alive. Another difference between Cleopatra III's cult and those of previous Ptolemaic queens was that it was presided over by a priest rather than a priestess. This priest marched immediately behind the priest of Alexander the Great and therefore ahead of all the priestesses of previous queens (who she took precedence over).
[133] Harsiesi was the last Egyptian to hold the title of pharaoh.
[134] Ptolemy VIII's dependence on the native populace in his power struggle with Cleopatra II

in charge of the entirety of Upper Egypt. This was a significant promotion, as no native Egyptian had held such a prominent position in the Ptolemaic government before.

Ptolemy's confidence in Paos soon paid off when Harsiesi was captured and executed in September 130 BC. However, even though the majority of the country was under Ptolemy's control, Cleopatra II still possessed strongholds throughout Egypt and Ptolemy's attempt to capture Alexandria by laying siege to the city failed.

At around this time, Ptolemy is said to have eliminated two of Cleopatra II's sons to prevent her supporters in Alexandria from proclaiming either of them king. The first of these may have been her last surviving son by Ptolemy VI, also named Ptolemy, who is reported to have been murdered after being summoned from Cyrene.[135] The second victim was Ptolemy's own son with Cleopatra II, Ptolemy Memphites. Then aged somewhere between 12 and 14 years old, his father had him chopped to pieces and sent to Cleopatra II as a birthday present.

Cleopatra II was not the sort of person who would allow personal feelings or grief get in the way of her political objectives, so did not hesitate to put her son's mutilated remains on public display. By doing so, she hoped to turn the populace against Ptolemy, but the Egyptian people were accustomed to the rule of ruthless tyrants and remained steadfastly loyal to their king.

Meanwhile, both sides in the civil war attempted to secure support from Rome, but neither had any luck and the Roman Senate decided to remain neutral. With the majority of the kingdom out of her control and her sons dead, by 129 BC Cleopatra II had become so desperate that she invited her son-in-law (the Seleucid king Demetrius II) to invade Egypt and claim the throne for himself.[136] The Seleucid kings had long

---

resulted in native Egyptians securing positions at the very top of the Ptolemaic government for the first time.

[135] It is uncertain whether the person Ptolemy VIII summoned from Cyrene was Ptolemy VI's son Ptolemy or Ptolemy VIII's son Ptolemy Memphites.
Other sources claim that Ptolemy VI's son Ptolemy was murdered on Ptolemy VIII's orders at an earlier date – perhaps even as early as the day of Ptolemy VIII's and Cleopatra II's wedding.
[136] Between 139 and 129 BC, Demetrius II was held prisoner by the Parthians. During this time, his wife, Cleopatra Thea, married his younger brother, Antiochus VII, who took over as king of the Seleucids. When Antiochus VII died and Demetrius II was restored to the throne in 129 BC, Cleopatra Thea resumed her marriage with her first husband. However, Cleopatra Thea was angered that Demetrius had married a Parthian princess and had children with her during his time in captivity. For the remainder of their marriage, Cleopatra Thea retaliated with acts of

dreamed of absorbing the Ptolemaic Kingdom into their empire, so it is unsurprising that Demetrius gladly accepted the offer. He assembled an army and marched on Egypt in early 128 BC, but his invasion force only made it as far as the border fortress of Pelusium. While the Seleucid king was busy besieging the city, he was forced to abruptly abandon the invasion and return to Syria (in the spring of 128 BC) when his troops mutinied and he received word that his wife (Cleopatra II's daughter, Cleopatra Thea) had rebelled against him.

To prevent Demetrius from returning to Egypt, Ptolemy undermined the Seleucid king's attempts to reassert his authority in his own kingdom. He did this by sending a pretender named Alexander II (who claimed to be a son of Alexander Balas or an adopted son of Antiochus VII) to lead a group of rebels in Syria, which rapidly took control of Antioch and forced Cleopatra Thea to flee to Ptolemais in Phoenicia.[137] This led to further civil war in the Seleucid Empire that kept the Seleucids too busy to intervene in Egyptian affairs and ultimately resulted in Demetrius' defeat and death in 125 BC.

Without the Seleucid military support she desperately needed, Cleopatra II's position continued to deteriorate. At some point in 127 BC she decided to abandon Alexandria and fled with the contents of her treasury to the court of her daughter Cleopatra Thea at Ptolemais in Phoenicia.[138] Although the Egyptian capital continued to hold out for nearly a year, her withdrawal from Egypt paved the way for Ptolemy to recapture Alexandria, which was back in his hands by August 126 BC. This effectively brought the civil war to an end and was marked by a bloody purge of Cleopatra II's supporters in Alexandria.

Now he was back in control of the entire kingdom, Ptolemy opened negotiations with the Seleucid court at Ptolemais in Phoenicia to bring about a reconciliation with Cleopatra II and restore peaceful relations with the Seleucid Empire. As a result of these negotiations, the Egyptian king agreed to withdraw his support for the usurper Alexander II, who had defeated Demetrius II and was now in control of the majority

---

disloyalty.

[137] It is generally believed that Alexander II's claim to be a son of the Seleucid king Alexander Balas or an adopted son of Antiochus VII was false.

[138] Demetrius II was eventually defeated by Alexander II, in a battle fought near Damascus in 125 BC. After his defeat, he fled to Ptolemais in Phoenicia, where his wife and son had established a rival Seleucid regime. However, Cleopatra Thea refused to let him into the city, forcing the beleaguered king to go to Tyre instead. He was reportedly murdered on Cleopatra Thea's orders soon after his arrival.

of the Seleucid Empire (except for the area surrounding Ptolemais in Phoenicia, where Cleopatra Thea ruled). Instead, Ptolemy now recognised Antiochus VIII – a son of Demetrius II and Cleopatra Thea – as the rightful Seleucid king and sealed the agreement by arranging for Antiochus to marry one of his daughters by Cleopatra III, Princess Tryphaena.[139]

The completion of this agreement meant Cleopatra II was now able to return to Egypt from her self-imposed exile at Cleopatra Thea's court. Surviving papyrus documents show she had been restored to the position of co-regent by July 124 BC, and both Cleopatra II and Cleopatra III remained wives and co-regents of Ptolemy VIII for the remainder of his reign. Nevertheless, it took a considerable amount of time and effort to patch up Cleopatra II's relationship with her co-regents, and to restore peace and prosperity across the war-torn kingdom. To help facilitate this, the three rulers issued an amnesty decree in April 118 BC that included a range of measures, such as: encouraging refugees to return to their homes, pardoning fugitives of any crimes committed before 28 April 118 BC (excluding murder and the looting of temples), writing off unpaid taxes, confirming the tax privileges and land holdings of temples, granting the land their soldiers had been promised during the civil war, reducing the duty on goods arriving through the port of Alexandria, and ordering tax officials to use standardised weights and measures when carrying out their duties (on pain of death). In recognition of the growing power of the native Egyptian population, whose support had been vital to Ptolemy during the civil war, the decree also set out how legal disputes between Greeks and Egyptians should be handled. From this point forward, cases that were centred on documents written in Greek would be decided by the *chrematistai* ('money-judges'), while cases centred on documents written in Egyptian would be decided by the *laokritai* ('folk-judges'). Consequently, native Egyptians now stood a better chance of getting a fair trial, as the *chrematistai* were no longer permitted bring Egyptians before their courts on matters that concerned Egyptian documents. These measures were part of a broader effort to bring about peace and

---

[139] After the death of Demetrius II in 125 BC, Cleopatra Thea shared the Seleucid throne with her son Antiochus VIII. With Egyptian military assistance, they decisively defeated Alexander II in 123 BC, ending the civil war, but Cleopatra's co-regent gradually became harder to control and she decided to kill him by offering him a cup of poisoned wine (in 221 BC). This backfired when her son guessed she was trying to kill him and forced her to drink it instead.
While most people would never dream of suspecting their own parents of wishing to murder them, Antiochus VIII had a good reason to do so given that Cleopatra had already murdered her eldest child by Demetrius II, Seleucus V.
Seleucus V had attempted to claim the Seleucid throne after his father's death, but had been killed by his mother, who feared he would seek to avenge his father's murder once in power.

stability, and were aimed at improving conditions for the working population (and in particular farmers of crown land), which was the backbone of the Egyptian economy and therefore had an essential role to play if Ptolemy wanted his kingdom to stand a chance of bouncing back from the economic turmoil inflicted by many years of civil war and unrest.

Due to their power and influence, the priesthood received even greater advantages in the decree than the general population. This included the right of temples to grant asylum being confirmed, the immunity and freedom of temple land being upheld, the burials of the Apis and Mnevis bulls being funded by the crown, the renovation of temples being encouraged, and priests who had bought their position being allowed to retain it (although they did not have the authority to transfer it to another individual).

In addition to the amnesty decree, another move intended at promoting reconciliation in the spring of 118 BC was the decision to incorporate one of the princes Ptolemy VIII had murdered into the Ptolemaic cult under the epithet *Theos Neos Philopator* ('New Father-loving God'). The inductee was either Ptolemy (the son of Ptolemy VI and Cleopatra II) or Ptolemy Memphites (the son of Ptolemy VIII and Cleopatra II). The most likely of the two candidates is Ptolemy Memphites, but this is not certain and continues to be debated by historians.

*

The turbulent events of Ptolemy VIII's reign meant no major temple-building projects were initiated during his reign. Nevertheless, he did sponsor a number of modest religious building programs. This included: finishing the decoration of the inner temple at Kom Ombo and on the interior of the temple in Deir el-Medina (west of Thebes); expanding and decorating the birth house (*mammisi*) in the temple of Isis at Philae; enlarging the sanctuary of Amun (by the mortuary temple of Hatshepsut at Deir el-Bahari) and the temple of Montu at El-Tod (south of Thebes); completing the temple of Satet (started by Ptolemy VI) on the island of Elephantine; decorating the Second Pylon in the Precinct of Amun-Re at Karnak; carrying out construction work on the temple of Opet at Karnak; and constructing a small temple dedicated to Thoth known as Qasr el-Aguz (situated to the south of Medinet Habu), which was never fully completed but is well-preserved in the present day.[140]

---

[140] The extension to the sanctuary of Amun served as a cult for two famous Egyptian holy men who were elevated to healing gods after their deaths: Amenhotep, son of Hapu (an architect who held a number of important offices under Amenhotep III) and Imhotep (the possible architect of

Like his predecessors, Ptolemy VIII presented himself as a traditional Egyptian pharaoh to his native subjects and went to great lengths to stress his devotion to Egyptian religion, such as by promoting animal cults and agreeing to use royal funds to pay for the burials of the Apis and Mnevis bulls.

In addition to his sponsorship of Egyptian religion, Ptolemy also followed in the footsteps of the Ptolemies who preceded him by being actively involved in Greek scholarship. Most notably, he is said to have composed a study of the Greek poet Homer and written 24 books of *Hypomnemata* or 'Notes' (a collection of paradoxography that covered a range of topics, including exotic wildlife and tales of both historical and contemporary monarchs).

In terms of the promotion of academia as a whole, however, Alexandria's reputation as a leading intellectual centre was severely damaged during Ptolemy VIII's reign. This is hardly surprising considering the civil strife that plagued much of his reign and the bloody purges he ordered in Alexandria in 145 and 126 BC. Leading intellectuals such as Aristarchus of Samothrace and Apollodorus of Athens may have been persecuted during first purge and this encouraged large numbers of Alexandrian scholars to go into exile soon thereafter.[141][142][143]

Nevertheless, even though Ptolemy VIII's time on the Egyptian throne was a turbulent one, there are some positives that can be salvaged from it, particularly with regard to trade.

For many generations the Ptolemaic Kingdom had possessed trading posts along the coast of the Red Sea, which enabled it to acquire key commodities from the Horn of Africa such as gold, ivory and war elephants. However, trade with the East (and India in particular) was made considerably easier near the end of Ptolemy VIII's reign, when Greek sailors learned how to exploit the annual reversal of the Indian Monsoon Current, which made it possible to cross the Indian Ocean in the summer and return in

---

Djoser's step pyramid at Saqqara).

[141] Most of the Alexandria-based intellectuals who fled persecution from Ptolemy VIII's regime settled in Athens or Rhodes.

[142] Aristarchus was originally from the Greek island of Samothrace but settled in Alexandria at a young age and went on to become the director of the Library of Alexandria. He is believed to have sought asylum on the island of Cyprus after fleeing Alexandria during Ptolemy VIII's purge of 145 BC. He died there soon after.

[143] Apollodorus eventually settled in Athens after fleeing Alexandria as a result of Ptolemy VIII's purge of 145 BC.

the winter. Previously, trade between the Mediterranean and India had been dependent on Arabian intermediaries. Greek and Indian sailors met each other halfway and exchanged goods with each other at Arabian ports, including what is now Aden (in Yemen), and the Arabians also controlled the caravan routes that carried goods from these ports to the Mediterranean coast via the Arabian desert. Even though their Indian counterparts had long used the monsoon winds to reach Arabia by ship, Greek navigators rarely attempted to sail beyond Aden due to it involving a long and arduous journey along a dangerous and rocky coastline. Therefore, it was only after Greek sailors acquired the expertise of Indian navigators that they were able to bypass the Arabian ports in the Gulf of Aden and Persian Gulf and establish direct commercial links with India.

According to the Greek scholar Poseidonius, the possibility of direct seaborne trade with India (without third party involvement) was brought to Ptolemy VIII's attention by an unnamed Indian sailor, who had been shipwrecked in the Red Sea and taken to the Ptolemaic court in Alexandria after being rescued. The sailor offered to guide Greek navigators to India via the Red Sea and Indian Ocean and Ptolemy gladly accepted the proposal. The Ptolemaic king appointed a Greek navigator and sailor named Eudoxus of Cyzicus to lead the first voyage (with the Indian sailor's assistance), which reportedly took place in 118 BC. Eudoxus returned to Egypt with a lucrative cargo of aromatics and precious stones and was so encouraged by its success that he decided to embark on a second voyage to India in 116 BC. Now he had been shown the route, he felt confident enough to set sail without a guide to assist him, but ended up being blown off course when the wind forced his ship south of the Gulf of Aden and down the coast of East Africa. Eventually he happened across a shipwreck that he believed had originated from Gades (present-day Cádiz, Spain) and caused him to come to the conclusion that it must have sailed all along the western and southern coast of Africa. This inspired him to attempt to circumnavigate Africa, but the undertaking was too difficult to accomplish and he reluctantly returned to Egypt.

The voyages of Eudoxus and other Greek sailors at this time marked the beginning of the Indian Ocean trade, which became a key factor in exchanges between the eastern and western world for many centuries to come, all the way to the age of European colonialism. More importantly for the Ptolemaic Kingdom, it enabled trade relations between Egypt and India to become closer in the decades that followed.[144]

---

[144] Over time, this inevitably prompted intervention by the Nabataeans, who had been made redundant as middlemen in east-west trade and reacted by launching a series of plundering

*

Ptolemy VIII died at about 68 years of age on 28 June 116 BC. He was succeeded by his eldest surviving son, Ptolemy IX, while Cleopatra II and Cleopatra III continued to serve as co-regents.[145]

Most accounts have few good words for Ptolemy VIII, and focus on comparing his faults to the virtues of his older brother. Criticised as a repulsive morbidly obese tyrant, his reign was a disaster on several counts. At home, Egypt was torn apart by civil war and suffered from a declining economy, while overseas its international reputation was significantly diminished. By banishing scores of academics from Alexandria, he undermined the Egyptian capital's position as the leading academic centre in the Mediterranean, and by marrying his niece he sowed further discord within the royal family. Most notably of all, his reliance on Egypt's native population to maintain his hold on power is a clear sign of the declining power of the Ptolemaic monarchy, which was a far cry from its state under the first three Ptolemies. Admittedly, the events of the civil war against Cleopatra II reveal he was successful in gaining and maintaining the support of the native Egyptian population, and the amnesty decrees that followed show he made some effort to bring harmony, stability and good government to his kingdom. But even these things were ultimately motivated by his desire to cling onto power, and therefore he is deserving of his reputation as one of the Ptolemaic dynasty's worst 'bad' kings.

---

campaigns into Ptolemaic and Seleucid territories during the reign of Aretas II (c. 120-96 BC).
[145] Ptolemy IX was the eldest child of Ptolemy VIII and Cleopatra III.

Ptolemy IX and Ptolemy X: The Warring Siblings Part 2

Ptolemy VIII was succeeded by his eldest surviving legitimate son, Ptolemy IX Soter, in 116 BC, while the new king's mother (Cleopatra III) and grandmother (Cleopatra II) continued to serve as co-regents.[146]

The precise date of Ptolemy IX's birth is unclear and continues to be debated by historians. When he became pharaoh he adopted the Horus name 'Distinguished through his birth together with the living Apis; twin in his birthplace with the son of Isis', which suggests he was born in the same year as the most recent Apis bull (in 143/142 BC). Because this would mean he was born before Ptolemy VIII and Cleopatra III got married (in c. 142-140 BC), some historians argue it is more likely that he born in 140 or 139 BC.

No matter which theory is correct, at the time of his birth the heir to the throne was his half-brother, Ptolemy Memphites. It was only after Ptolemy Memphites was murdered by his father in 130 BC that the future Ptolemy IX became heir apparent, although the fact that he had previously had the honour of serving as the priest of Alexander the Great (in 134/133 BC) reveals he was being groomed for a life of leadership from a very young age.[147]

In about 119 or 118 BC, Ptolemy IX was married to his younger sister, Cleopatra IV. Shortly after this, in about 117 BC, he gained some important political experience when his mother sent him to Cyprus to serve as the island's governor. During his time on the island, his wife may have borne him two sons – the future Ptolemy XII in about 117 BC and the future king of Cyprus (also named Ptolemy) in about 116 BC. It is generally believed that the mother of these two sons was actually a concubine rather than Cleopatra IV, meaning both sons were illegitimate. However, some scholars promote the alternative theory that Ptolemy XII and Ptolemy of Cyprus were sons of Cleopatra IV, but were considered illegitimate because it was not acceptable for a Ptolemaic prince to marry one of their siblings before their ascension to the throne.[148]

*

---

[146] Ptolemy IX's epithet Soter means 'Saviour'. He was also nicknamed Lathyros ('chickpea').
[147] The chief priest of Alexander the Great's cult served one-year terms.
[148] This may have resulted in the marriage between Ptolemy IX and Cleopatra IV being regarded as morganatic (a marriage between people of unequal social rank).

Shortly before his death on 28 June 116 BC, Ptolemy VIII allegedly left his second wife, Cleopatra III, in charge of Egypt and Cyprus and allowed her to choose which of their sons would become her co-regent. This is a clear sign of Cleopatra III's influence, as it went against the custom of the throne being inherited by the deceased monarch's eldest son. According to some accounts, Cleopatra III loathed her eldest son (Ptolemy IX) and doted on her younger son (Ptolemy X), who she wanted to make co-regent, but was compelled to select her elder son when the people of Alexandria (supported by Cleopatra II) rioted in his favour. If this is true, then her decision to have Ptolemy IX, appointed governor of Cyprus in 117 BC may have been an attempt to keep him out of the way while she made preparations for Ptolemy X to succeed his father. However, some historians believe this story is false and was fabricated at a later date, after Cleopatra III had deposed her eldest son and replaced him with her younger son. It is also doubtful that Cleopatra III really was given sole control over naming the next king, given that her mother and co-regent, Cleopatra II, was still alive at the time. And in reality it was the people of Alexandria who had the final say on who became their new king.

In order to keep the Alexandrians happy, Ptolemy IX was chosen as his father's successor and recalled to the Egyptian capital from Cyprus to take up the position. Cleopatra II and Cleopatra III continued to serve as co-regents alongside him, as they had done under Ptolemy VIII, although Cleopatra II disappeared from historical records in October 116 BC, which suggests she died soon after her grandson became pharaoh (in either late 116 BC or early 115 BC).[149]

Another alleged beneficiary of Ptolemy VIII's will was his illegitimate son, Ptolemy Apion, who was supposed to receive Cyrenaica to rule as an independent kingdom. In reality, this remained under Ptolemy IX's control for many years, and Ptolemy Apion did not secure this inheritance and become king of Cyrene until around 100 BC. This has led some historians to suggest that Ptolemy Apion fraudulently claimed Cyrenaica had been left to him by his father to justify his rule there.

Meanwhile, Ptolemy X was dispatched to Cyprus to replace his elder brother as its governor (*strategos*) – perhaps to keep him out of the way, if his mother really had attempted to make him king.[150]

---

[149] Ptolemy IX was also Cleopatra II's stepson.
[150] A former *strategos* of Cyprus, Helenus of Cyrene, became Ptolemy X's *tropheus* ('helper') and essentially governed the island on the prince's behalf. Helenus had been appointed *strategos* of Cyprus by Ptolemy VIII in 218 BC, before being replaced by the future Ptolemy IX

When Ptolemy IX was proclaimed pharaoh, he received the same epithet Cleopatra II had held during the civil war against her husband: *Philometor Soter* ('Mother-loving Saviour'). This hints that his grandmother played a key role in his government when he first came to the throne, although his mother (Cleopatra III) certainly became the dominant force in government after her death.

Soon after Ptolemy IX's accession to the throne, his mother (Cleopatra III) and sister-wife (Cleopatra IV) came into conflict with each other. Cleopatra III was determined to maintain her pre-eminence in government and found Cleopatra IV far too strong-willed for her liking. In order to neutralise this potential threat to her authority, she forced Ptolemy IX to divorce his wife at some point in 115 BC, and Cleopatra IV reacted by going into exile.

In the same year as his divorce, Ptolemy IX's mother arranged for him to be remarried to his younger sister, Cleopatra Selene, who was more pliable than her elder sister (Cleopatra IV). This was a further attempt by Cleopatra III to consolidate her hold on power and is evidenced by the fact that – in a break with tradition – Cleopatra Selene did not become her husband's co-regent. Instead, Egypt's rulers remained Ptolemy IX and his mother Cleopatra III, who were officially incorporated into the Ptolemaic dynasty's cult as the *Theoi Philometores Soteres* ('The Mother-loving Saviour Gods').

Soon after their marriage (in late 115 or early 114 BC), Cleopatra Selene bore Ptolemy IX a daughter – the future Berenice III. Some scholars support an alternative argument that Berenice III's mother was actually Cleopatra IV. However, on the basis that the legitimacy of Berenice III was not questioned by any ancient sources, it is far more likely that she was born as a result of Ptolemy IX's legitimate marriage to Cleopatra Selene rather than from his marriage to Cleopatra IV (which was considered illegitimate).

*

After fleeing Alexandria, Cleopatra IV travelled to Cyprus, where she attempted to marry her younger brother, Ptolemy X, but failed. Nevertheless, she did manage to recruit an army and seize control of the Cypriot fleet while she was on the island, which she used as a dowry when she moved onto Syria and agreed to marry the Seleucid king Antiochus IX.[151]

---

in 216 BC. He served in the position a second time (between 114 and 106 BC) when Ptolemy X declared himself king of Cyprus.

Antiochus' mother was Cleopatra III's sister, Cleopatra Thea, which meant his bride was also his cousin. To complicate things further, at the time of their marriage Antiochus was fighting a civil war against his half-brother Antiochus VIII, who was married to Cleopatra IV's elder sister Tryphaena.[152]

The military support Cleopatra IV brought from Cyprus gave her new husband some much-needed manpower in the ongoing civil war. However, it did not prevent Antiochus VIII from capturing the Seleucid capital (Antioch) in 112 BC, nor did it protect Cleopatra IV when she fled to the nearby suburb of Daphne and sought refuge in the temple of Apollo. As a rival Seleucid queen, Tryphaena hated her sister and was determined to have her put to death. She accused Cleopatra of remarrying without their mother's permission and of bringing foreign armies into the Seleucid Empire to give additional fuel to the dispute between their warring husbands. Antiochus VIII tried to persuade his wife to spare Cleopatra's life by arguing that his ancestors would not have acted with such ruthlessness towards a defenceless woman, but Tryphaena's mind was already made up. Defying her husband's wishes, she ordered several soldiers to break into the temple and murder her sister, although Cleopatra had enough time to curse her killers before she died.

Tryphaena soon got her comeuppance when she was taken prisoner by Antiochus IX (in 111 BC), who avenged his late wife by giving orders for her to be executed and sacrificed to the manes of her murdered sister. Nevertheless, the war between Antiochus VIII and Antiochus IX remained unresolved and dragged on for nearly two decades.

In the years that followed, Antiochus IX continued to receive support off Ptolemy IX, who favoured his side in the civil war. This included him sending reinforcements to the Seleucid king in about 109/108 BC to assist him in a campaign against the Jewish leader (of the Hasmonean dynasty) John Hyrcanus. However, not long after this Ptolemy found himself being distracted by a threat to his own throne.

---

[151] Ptolemy X openly rejected his elder brother's authority in 114 or 113 BC by having himself proclaimed 'king of Cyprus'.
[152] Antiochus VIII (a son of Demetrius II and Cleopatra Thea) had secured the Seleucid throne for himself after defeating the usurper king Alexander II in 123 BC. However, in 116 BC Antiochus IX (a son of Antiochus VII and Cleopatra Thea) decided to challenge his claim to the throne. This led to twenty years of civil war in the Seleucid Empire, which ended in 96 BC when Antiochus VIII was assassinated and Antiochus IX was subsequently killed in battle by Antiochus VIII's son Seleucus VI.

In the autumn of 107 BC, Ptolemy IX had a quarrel with his mother, causing the already tense relationship between the two co-regents to completely break down. Cleopatra III was now determined to replace Ptolemy IX on the throne with her younger son, Ptolemy X. In order to achieve this, she injured some of her own eunuch servants and presented them before the people of Alexandria, claiming Ptolemy IX had attempted to have her assassinated. As she had hoped, the Alexandrians reacted by rioting and forced her son into exile.

At the same time as this, Cleopatra III invited Ptolemy X to become her new co-regent.[153] He did not hesitate to accept the offer and travelled from Cyprus to Pelusium to meet his mother, who escorted him to Alexandria.

Cleopatra III's dominance in the Ptolemaic government became even stronger after Ptolemy IX's deposition. Officially, the newly proclaimed Ptolemy X received the same epithet his elder brother had held as co-regent: *Philometor Soter* ('Mother-loving Saviour'). He also took Ptolemy IX's place in the Ptolemaic cult, in which he was worshipped alongside his mother as the *Theoi Philometores Soteres* ('Mother-loving Saviour Gods'). However, at an informal level he also earned some far from complimentary nicknames. One of these was *ho Cocces* ('the son of Cocce'), which appears to be a reference to Ptolemy X's subordination to Cleopatra III (who remained the senior ruler), although the precise meaning of the name 'Cocce' is unclear. According to one interpretation, it means 'cuckoo' and refers to the way in which Cleopatra III made her younger son king, whereas other scholars have speculated that it has an even more derogatory meaning: translating to 'son of a cunt' or 'son of a scarlet lady'. If this wasn't bad enough, Ptolemy X earned a second derisory nickname after becoming king. This was 'Pareisactus' ('smuggled in'), which recalled the means by which he came to the throne.

When Ptolemy IX fled the Egyptian capital, he left his two sons, Ptolemy XII and Ptolemy of Cyprus, behind, as well as his wife, Cleopatra Selene. While the two boys became wards of their grandmother, Cleopatra III, Cleopatra Selene divorced Ptolemy IX so she could marry the newly-proclaimed Ptolemy X instead.

The Egyptian crown and a royal wife were not the only things Ptolemy X inherited off his brother. From the year of his accession (116 BC) until his deposition (in 107 BC) Ptolemy IX had held the prestigious position of Priest of Alexander every year to

---

[153] Ptolemy X's birth name was probably Alexander.

establish himself as the kingdom's leading religious figure. He was then replaced by Ptolemy X, who held the position for two consecutive terms (in 107/106 BC and 106/105 BC), while Cleopatra III flouted tradition by becoming the chief priest of Alexander the Great's cult for 105/104 BC. Until then the position had been reserved for men, and therefore this move highlights Cleopatra III's ambition and lust for power.

With the benefit of hindsight though, she would have been wise to rein it in. Her years in power better have been worth it, because in the near future her insatiable ambition would come at a highest possible price – her life.

*

After being banished from Alexandria, Ptolemy IX travelled to Cyprus, seeking refuge and support. However, the island was loyal to Cleopatra III and Ptolemy X, and he was forced to retreat to Seleucia Pieria (in present-day Turkey).

This initial setback did not deter Ptolemy IX, who led a successful conquest of Cyprus in 106 BC and also remained in control of Cyrenaica (until it was taken over by his half-brother Ptolemy Apion at some point between 105 and 100 BC). According to the Roman historian Justin, Ptolemy VIII had left Cyrenaica to his illegitimate son Ptolemy Apion in his will, although it is unclear if he really did or if it was fabricated to justify Ptolemy Apion's rule there after he had seized control of the territory. The fact that Ptolemy Apion left Cyrenaica to Rome in his will in the event of him dying without an heir suggests he was not allied with Ptolemy IX or Ptolemy X and was completely independent.[154] However, it is possible that he gained control of Cyrenaica with Cleopatra III's support, who sought to remove the territory from Ptolemy IX's sphere of influence.

As things turned out, Ptolemy Apion never married and died childless (in 96 BC). Consequently, Cyrenaica was inherited by Rome and the Ptolemaic Kingdom permanently lost this territory, which was severely detrimental to Egypt's economy, security and prestige. It resulted in the loss of Cyrenaica's many lucrative trade connections and allowed Rome's empire to reach the Egyptian border. Perhaps even

---

[154] Ptolemy Apion sought to prevent the independence of his newly-created kingdom from being undermined and to deter rivals from attempting to assassinate him by leaving Cyrenaica to the Roman Republic in his will in the event that he died without an heir. This was a common practice amongst Hellenistic monarchs, but was a risky policy that gambled the future of their dynasties.

more importantly, the loss of the Ptolemaic Kingdom's oldest foreign territory meant its only remaining overseas possession was Cyprus – a clear sign of the declining power and influence of the Ptolemies.

In 103 BC, Ptolemy IX received an appeal for assistance off the city of Ptolemais in Phoenicia, which was being besieged by the Hasmonean king of Judea, Alexander Jannaeus. Ptolemy saw this as an opportunity to gain control of the Judean coast, which he would be able to use as a springboard for a seaborne invasion of Egypt, so answered the city's call for help by sailing from Cyprus to Ptolemais with an army.

Unfortunately for Ptolemy, by the time his forces arrived the people of Ptolemais were having second thoughts about the wisdom of seeking his support. An individual named Demaenetus warned his fellow citizens that if they allied themselves with Ptolemy they would be effectively declaring war on Cleopatra III and Egypt, so they refused to allow the former Ptolemaic king and his troops to enter the city.

Meanwhile, Alexander Jannaeus was just as eager to avoid being drawn into a war between Ptolemy IX and Cleopatra III. For this reason, he abandoned his siege of Ptolemais and headed back to Jerusalem, but soon changed his mind and decided to sign a peace treaty with Ptolemy. This enabled the Judean king to resume his conquests in the region. The coastal cities of Dora and Straton's Tower both fell to Hasmonean forces, although his campaign was jeopardised when it came to Ptolemy's attention that Alexander had been secretly negotiating an alliance with Cleopatra III.

When Ptolemy learned of the Judean king's treachery, he delegated the task of besieging Ptolemais to his generals and set off in pursuit of the Judean army. His troops caused a great deal of destruction in Galilee, where they captured Asochis (taking 10,000 prisoners in the process) and launched an unsuccessful attack on Sepphoris. The war in Galilee came to a head when the armies of Ptolemy and Alexander fought a battle at Asophon. At the start of the battle the two armies were on opposite sides of the River Jordan. One of Ptolemy's commanders – Philostephanus – launched the initial attack by crossing the river with his troops. Technically the Hasmoneans had the advantage, but when Philostephanus held back some of his men they mistook them for a large number of reinforcements, causing a significant portion of the Judean army to panic and flee. Hasmonean soldiers were killed in their thousands in the chaotic retreat that followed and Alexander was decisively defeated.

After his victory at Asophon, Ptolemy proceeded to conquer a large portion of the Hasmonean kingdom, including northern Judea. Hoping to instil fear in his enemies, Ptolemy presided over a brutal campaign – allowing his troops to pillage settlements and cannibalise women and children.

The success of Ptolemy IX's campaign in Judea alarmed Cleopatra III and Ptolemy X, who feared he intended to use Judea as a base to invade Egypt from. To prevent this from happening, they launched their own invasion of Judea. Dividing their army into two forces, Ptolemy X sailed with a fleet to invade Phoenicia by sea in the summer of 103 BC and marched inland to Damascus, while Cleopatra III travelled overland with an army to Ptolemais. By the time Cleopatra arrived at Ptolemais (in about September 103 BC) it had fallen to Ptolemy IX, so she used her troops to lay siege to the city.[155]

While Cleopatra III and Ptolemy X were busy with their campaign, Ptolemy IX tried to sneak past them and attack Egypt in the autumn of 103 BC, but his plans were thwarted when Ptolemy X hurried back and blocked him from advancing on Pelusium. Ptolemy IX spent the winter of 103/102 BC with his army at Gaza, but concluded that his conquests were impossible to defend and opted to return to Cyprus. This brought the war to a sudden conclusion and marked the end of Ptolemy IX's attempts to regain his throne for the foreseeable future.

For the next 14 years he was reduced to a life of obscurity. Little is known about his activities during this time and it was not until 88 BC that he was thrust back into the spotlight.

*

When Ptolemy IX withdrew to Cyprus and the city of Ptolemais in Phoenicia surrendered to Cleopatra III's troops in early 102 BC, Cleopatra's advisors urged her to annex Judea (which was part of the lost Ptolemaic territory of Coele-Syria). The prospect of doing so must have been extraordinarily tempting, but she decided against it after being reminded by one of her commanders – a Jew named Ananias – that the Egyptian Jews were amongst the main supporters of her regime. Instead, when Alexander Jannaeus went to Ptolemais to pay homage to the Egyptian queen, she allowed him to keep his throne, in exchange for him agreeing to suspend his military

---

[155] Cleopatra III appointed two Jewish generals named Ananias and Chelkias (both sons of Onias IV) to command her forces during this campaign.

campaigns. Part of the reason for this decision might have been Cleopatra's reluctance to anger Rome, which had formed an alliance with Judea in 161 BC.

At the same time as the war in Judea, Cleopatra III and Ptolemy X had allied themselves with the Seleucid ruler Antiochus VIII. This made sense given that the Seleucid king was still engaged in a civil war with a rival claimant to the Seleucid throne, Antiochus IX, who had previously received support from Ptolemy IX. To cement this alliance, Cleopatra III forced Ptolemy X to divorce Cleopatra Selene and arranged for her to be married to Antiochus VIII (in 103 or 102 BC).[156]

Not long after this, in September 101 BC, Cleopatra III's dominance came to an end when she died, leaving Ptolemy X as Egypt's sole ruler. It is commonly believed that Ptolemy X had his mother murdered, either to gain complete control over the kingdom or because he suspected she intended to kill him. In any event, Cleopatra III's death paved the way for a reconciliation between Ptolemy IX and Ptolemy X. This was sealed when Ptolemy X married his elder brother's daughter, Berenice III, in October 101 BC, and named her co-regent in his deceased mother's place. To mark the beginning of this new era, Ptolemy X changed his epithet to *Philadelphus* ('Sibling-lover') and the new royal couple were incorporated into the Ptolemaic cult as the *Theoi Philadelphoi* ('Sibling-loving gods').

Ptolemy X's reign as senior monarch was plagued by repeated popular rebellions against his rule. A native Egyptian uprising in 91 BC resulted in him losing control of southern Egypt, including Thebes (where the rebels enjoyed the support of the city's

---

[156] When Antiochus VIII was assassinated in 96 BC, Cleopatra Selene married her late husband's brother and rival, Antiochus IX, in the same year (probably because she didn't trust Antiochus VIII's sons by his previous marriage to Tryphaena). Unfortunately she was widowed again soon thereafter when her new husband was killed in battle against Seleucus VI (the eldest son of Antiochus VIII and Tryphaena) in 96 or 95 BC. Not long after this she married her fourth and final husband, Antiochus X (Antiochus IX's son), who is presumed to have died in about 92 BC.
After the death of her final husband, Cleopatra Selene probably fled to Ptolemais in Phoenicia, which she remained in control of until her death. She spent the rest of her life trying to promote her son's (Antiochus XIII) claim to the Seleucid throne and was captured and executed in 69 BC after the Armenian king Tigranes II successfully besieged Ptolemais.
There is disagreement amongst historians over whether Cleopatra Selene was used as a pawn all her life by ambitious men or if she eventually evolved into a political schemer in her own right. Either way, the fact that she became a ruler in her own right, as well as being the wife of three successive Seleucid kings and the mother of another, turned her into a powerful symbol of continuity in the Seleucid Empire.

priests). The loss of southern Egypt cut off the Triacontaschoenus region (Lower Nubia) from the rest of the Ptolemaic Kingdom and enabled the Kingdom of Kush to seize control of it. Other than these basic facts, very little is known about the rebellion. Even the name and identity of its leader (or if they had themselves proclaimed pharaoh, as previous Egyptian rebels had) is a mystery.

In the spring of 88 BC, the Ptolemaic army and the people of Alexandria revolted against Ptolemy X and forced him into exile. They then invited Ptolemy IX to return to Egypt from Cyprus and retake the throne, after spending nearly two decades in exile. The supposed reasons for the rebellion against Ptolemy X vary depending on the source. The philosopher Porphyry of Tyre claimed Ptolemy X's friendly relations with the Jews had angered the army and Alexandrians, while the Greek historian Strabo reported they were enraged by his decision to have Alexander the Great's golden sarcophagus melted down and replaced with a new one made out of glass.

The most commonly recited version of events is a combination of the two. Ptolemy appears to have been forced into exile by the army at some point in 89 BC and was restored to the throne the following year when he returned to Alexandria with an army of mercenaries he had gathered in Syria and Palestine. However, he was swiftly overthrown once again when he enraged the Alexandrians by plundering the tomb of Alexander the Great to pay his mercenary soldiers.

Ptolemy IX's second reign officially began when he was re-crowned pharaoh at Memphis in November 88 BC. Due to the central role his mother had played in his deposition, he shortened the epithet he had used in his first reign – *Philometor Soter* ('Mother-loving Saviour') – to *Soter* ('Saviour'). He also got his own back on his mother and brother by having their cults and all memory of their rule suppressed.

Unfortunately for Ptolemy, he did not return to a country that was united or at peace. Since 91 BC southern Egypt had been controlled by native Egyptian rebels. In order to bring this area back under government control, Ptolemy IX sent a large army there in November 88 BC. The army was commanded by the general Hierax, who rapidly regained control of Thebes and punished its inhabitants by allowing his troops to sack the city. His military expedition ultimately brought all of the country as far south as Philae back under Ptolemaic control, although the majority of Lower Nubia (which had been seized by the Kingdom of Kush during the revolt) remained in Kushite hands.

Meanwhile, Ptolemy IX's brother (Ptolemy X) and daughter (Berenice III) had gathered a naval force and attempted to regain control of the kingdom after being expelled from Alexandria, but were defeated in a sea battle. After this setback, they recruited a new naval force at Myra (in Asia Minor) and tried to capture Cyprus. Ptolemy X was killed in the attempt, ending the threat he had posed to Ptolemy IX's newly restored regime, although it wasn't all good news. In order to finance his failed invasion of Cyprus, Ptolemy X had taken out a hefty loan from the Roman Republic. As collateral for this loan he had been compelled to leave the Ptolemaic Kingdom to the Romans in his will in the event that he died without an heir.[157] On this occasion the Romans did not attempt to claim their inheritance, but they did not reject it either and the mere possibility of Roman intervention forced Ptolemy IX and his successors to walk on eggshells around the Romans. When a Roman embassy (headed by the senator Lucius Memmius) had visited Egypt in 112 BC, the Ptolemaic government had rolled out the red carpet for them. The delegation was taken on a tour of the Fayum region and treated with the utmost respect, as well as being given the best possible hospitality by government officials wherever they went. Such instances reveal the Ptolemies had accepted the reality that Rome was now the dominant power in the Mediterranean and provides clear evidence of their desire to stay in the Roman Republic's good books. Given that Memmius was treated to a sightseeing tour that included visiting the so-called Labyrinth of Egypt (near the foot of the Pyramid of Amenemhat III at Hawara) and the opportunity to feed the crocodile god Petesuchos, it is also one of the earliest examples of Roman tourism in Egypt, which became incredibly popular after the Roman conquest of the Ptolemaic Kingdom.[158]

Two and a half decades later, in 86 BC, a Roman fleet sailed to Alexandria. Its commander, Lucius Licinius Lucullus, had come to request financial and military support off Ptolemy in the ongoing First Mithridatic War between Rome and Mithridates VI of Pontus.[159] The visit put the Ptolemaic king in an awkward position and he proceeded with caution. Rome's status as the dominant power in the Mediterranean and his late brother's will meant he could not afford to offend the

---

[157] Ptolemy X had one legitimate son by his sister-wife Cleopatra Selene – Ptolemy XI.
[158] The oldest known Latin inscription in Egypt can be found on the wall of the temple of Isis at Philae, where a group of Roman visitors carved their names on the temple wall in 116 BC.
[159] The First Mithridatic War lasted from 89-85 BC and was the first of three wars between the Roman Republic and Mithridates VI of Pontus. The immediate cause of the war was the Asiatic Vespers of 88 BC: a series of massacres of Romans and other Latin-speaking peoples in western Anatolia, perpetrated by supporters of Mithridates VI of Pontus, who desired to put an end to Roman expansionism in the region.

Romans. For the time being though, it was uncertain who Rome was. While Lucullus represented the leader of the Roman war effort (Sulla), back in Rome two of Sulla's opponents – Marius and Cinna – had presided over a reign of terror that left many of his supporters dead, and it remained uncertain which side would prevail. The situation was complicated further by the fact that Mithridates VI had captured Ptolemy's own sons – the future Ptolemy XII and Ptolemy of Cyprus (who had resided on the Greek island of Kos since 103 BC) – and therefore the Ptolemaic king could not risk angering the Pontic ruler by directly supporting the Roman campaign against him. After taking all of these factors into consideration, Ptolemy greeted Lucullus warmly and treated him to magnificent hospitality during his stay – providing him with accommodation in the royal palace and inviting him to dine on the royal table. However, he did not provide him with ships or any other practical support for his war against Mithridates.[160]

At some point between the death of her husband (in 88 BC) and 81 BC, Berenice III was reconciled with her father, who promoted her to the rank of co-regent on 5 August 81 BC. A few months later (probably in December 81 BC) Ptolemy IX died and was succeeded by Berenice III. Although Ptolemy IX is known to have had at least two sons (Ptolemy XII and Ptolemy of Cyprus), they are widely believed to have been illegitimate offspring, which would explain why his daughter succeeded him instead.

Like his predecessors, Ptolemy IX fulfilled the duties of a traditional Egyptian pharaoh during his lifetime. Construction and decorative work may have been carried out at various religious sites during the reigns of both Ptolemy IX and his brother Ptolemy X, including at the Temple of Edfu, the temple of Isis in Contra Latopolis, the temple of Haroeris and Heqet at Qus, the small temple of Medinet Habu, and the Dendera Temple complex. There is also evidence that he visited the island of Elephantine in August 115 BC to attend a festival being held in honour of the 'Great God of the Nile'. During this festival he presided over a ritual to give thanks to the god for that year's inundation of the Nile and ensure the success of the next, as well as granting privileges to the priests of Khnum. The fact that Ptolemy carried out this traditional pharaonic duty himself rather than delegating the task to a local priest reveals the extent to which he embraced his role as pharaoh.

*

---

[160] After Athens was sacked by the Romans in 86 BC as part of the First Mithridatic War, the Ptolemies helped to rebuild the city. The Athenians showed their gratitude for this generosity by erecting commemorative statues of the Ptolemaic rulers.

The era of Cleopatra III, Ptolemy IX and Ptolemy X was a time of internal conflict, as demonstrated by the fate of its rulers. Cleopatra III was most likely murdered by her younger son, Ptolemy X was killed in a botched attempt at reclaiming his throne, and Ptolemy IX spent nearly two decades in exile between his two reigns. Some semblance of stability was imposed when Ptolemy IX secured his position as sole ruler in 88 BC and he continued to strengthen his kingdom's trading links with the East throughout his reign. However, the many decades of division and rivalry within the Ptolemaic dynasty had left a deep and lasting mark on social and economic life in Egypt. And most significantly of all, Ptolemy IX had to maintain the delicate balance between avoiding conflict with the increasingly powerful Roman Republic and preventing it from undermining the Ptolemaic Kingdom's autonomy.

Berenice III, Ptolemy XI, and Ptolemy XII: Continued Decline

When Berenice III's father died in 81 BC she became Egypt's sole ruler and had herself reincorporated into the Ptolemaic cult under the revised epithet *Thea Philopator* ('Father-loving God') to highlight her right to the throne. However, it was not customary for women to rule by themselves in Ptolemaic Egypt, so within a few months of her accession to the throne she married her cousin, former stepson and possible half-brother Ptolemy XI, who became her co-regent.[161]

Ptolemy XI travelled to Alexandria from Rome to accept his elevation to the throne. His appointment as Berenice III's co-regent is said to have resulted from interference by the Roman dictator Sulla, who was eager to install a compliant pro-Roman ruler on the Egyptian throne. Sulla justified his interference in Egyptian affairs by citing Ptolemy X's will, which had left all his territories to Rome in the event that he died without heirs.

In 103 BC, Ptolemy XI's grandmother (Cleopatra III) had sent him to Kos to keep him safe during her anticipated campaign in Syria. He was accompanied by his cousins Ptolemy XII and Ptolemy of Cyprus and a substantial amount of treasure, and they remained on the island until 88 BC, when they were captured by the king of Pontus (Mithradates VI), who had taken over Kos after a military victory against the Romans.

Despite being treated well by his captor (and even provided with an education), Ptolemy XI seized the opportunity to flee Mithradates' custody during a battle between Pontus and Rome in 84 BC. He was taken back to Rome by the future Roman dictator Sulla, who understood the Ptolemaic prince's political value and established an amicable relationship with him. Sulla kept Ptolemy XI in the city as a hostage until Ptolemy IX's death 81 BC, at which point he sent him to Alexandria to marry Egypt's new ruler, Berenice III.

The union between Berenice III and Ptolemy XI could hardly have been shorter or more disastrous. Ptolemy XI was significantly younger than Berenice III. He felt no affection for his wife and had married her for the sole purpose of acceding to the

---

[161] Ptolemy XI was a son of Ptolemy X. His mother was probably Cleopatra Selene, and if this was indeed the case then he would have been Berenice III's half-brother, in addition to being her cousin and former stepson.

throne. Consequently, after about 19 days of joint rule, Ptolemy XI murdered his wife so he could take full control of the kingdom.[162] However, by doing this he had overplayed his hand and seriously underestimated the reaction of the Alexandrians. Berenice III had been a popular figure in the Egyptian capital and the city's residents were enraged by her murder.

On 22 April the people of Alexandria rioted against Ptolemy XI and brought his reign to a swift end when a mob dragged him from the royal palace to the gymnasium and cut him to pieces.[163]

Once Ptolemy XI had been disposed of, the Alexandrians hastily selected a new king to keep the Ptolemaic dynasty alive – fearing the Romans would use Ptolemy X's will and the absence of legitimate heirs as an excuse to intervene. Only one legitimate member of the Ptolemaic family remained, and this was Cleopatra Selene (the widow of the Seleucid king Antiochus X, who was living in Cilicia at the time). In these desperate circumstances, the Alexandrians selected the eldest surviving son of Ptolemy IX, Ptolemy XII, as their new ruler.

While there is a general consensus amongst historians that Ptolemy XII was an illegitimate son of Ptolemy IX, the identity of his mother remains uncertain. The Gallo-Roman historian Gnaeus Pompeius Trogus stressed Ptolemy XII's illegitimacy by calling him a *nothos* ('bastard'). However, although it is highly likely that Ptolemy XII's mother was a concubine, some scholars have argued that his mother was actually Cleopatra IV and that her marriage to Ptolemy IX was considered illegitimate because she married her brother before he became king and never served as his co-regent.[164]

Ptolemy XII had a younger full brother (Ptolemy of Cyprus) and at least one half-sibling (Berenice III). When his father had been removed from power in 107 BC, the future Ptolemy XII had remained in Alexandria. However, when Ptolemy IX invaded Judea in 103 BC as part of a plan to regain control of Egypt, Ptolemy XII's grandmother Cleopatra III sent him to the island of Kos (along with his younger

---

[162] Ptolemy XI's coronation as Berenice III's co-regent is reported to have taken place on 3 April 80 BC.

[163] If the widely held belief that Ptolemy XII was illegitimate is true, then Ptolemy XI was the last legitimate Ptolemaic ruler.

[164] Cleopatra IV's role was limited in Ptolemy IX's government due to the dominance of his mother, Cleopatra III.

brother Ptolemy of Cyprus, his cousin Ptolemy XI, and a large quantity of treasure) to keep him safe. As mentioned earlier in this chapter, the three Ptolemaic princes lived here in relative safety for the next decade and a half, before being taken prisoner by Mithridates VI of Pontus when he captured Kos in 88 BC (during the early stages of the First Mithridatic War).[165]

During their captivity, Ptolemy XI managed to escape to Rome, but Ptolemy XII and Ptolemy of Cyprus remained in Mithridates' custody and were eventually engaged to the Pontic king's daughters Mithridatis and Nyssa. The engagements probably took place in 81 or 80 BC and it is likely that Mithridates did this in the hope of eventually gaining Ptolemaic support for his anti-Roman policy.

Shortly after this, in April 80 BC, Ptolemy XII and Ptolemy of Cyprus were finally released from Mithridates' custody when they were invited to become the kings of Egypt and Cyprus respectively, following the deaths of the last two fully legitimate members of the Ptolemaic royal family – Berenice III and Ptolemy XI. By formally separating Cyprus from Egypt, the Alexandrians may have hoped to appease the Romans and make them more willing to accept their choice of successor.

Ptolemy XI was the only legitimate son of Ptolemy X, who had left the Ptolemaic Kingdom to Rome in the event of his death without an heir. Consequently, the Roman Republic now had sound legal grounds to take over Egypt. However, many Roman aristocrats were concerned that whichever Senator was placed in charge of an Egyptian province would become too powerful and upset the delicate balance of power in the Republic. For this reason, they agreed to the division of the Ptolemaic Kingdom between Ptolemy IX's two illegitimate sons, which they knew would further weaken their dynasty.

In the year after Ptolemy XII's accession to the Egyptian throne (79 BC), he married Cleopatra V, who was probably his sister or cousin. His wife also became his co-regent and the royal couple were added to the Ptolemaic dynastic cult as the Theoi Philopatores kai Philadelphoi ('Father-loving and Sibling-loving Gods').[166] By adopting this title, Ptolemy probably hoped to emphasise his ties to his father and promote his right to rule, while downplaying his illegitimacy on his mother's side.

---

[165] Ironically, Ptolemy XII's father had regained the Egyptian throne at around the same time as he was taken prisoner.
[166] Cleopatra V is the only confirmed wife of Ptolemy XII.

There is very little surviving evidence for Cleopatra V, making her an extremely obscure member of the Ptolemaic dynasty. There is no record of who her parents were, but she might have been a daughter of Ptolemy IX or Ptolemy X, which would have made her a sister or cousin of her husband Ptolemy XII. In ancient sources, she is referred to with the byname Tryphaena. It is possible that this was her name before her marriage to Ptolemy XII and that she only adopted the traditional royal name 'Cleopatra' after her accession to the throne.

Ptolemy XII and Cleopatra V had at least one child together during their marriage – a daughter called Berenice IV (c. 77 BC). There is a great deal of uncertainty over the identity of Cleopatra VI, who was either the second daughter of Ptolemy XII and Cleopatra V, or was the same person as Cleopatra V. If the latter theory is correct, then Ptolemy XII's second child was Cleopatra VII (who was born in 70/69 BC and went on to become the Ptolemaic dynasty's most famous ruler). Cleopatra VII's mother is unknown, but on the basis that she was born shortly before Cleopatra V disappears from historical records, it is likely that Cleopatra V was her mother. Another piece of evidence that supports this theory is the fact that despite the many attacks made against Cleopatra VII by her Roman enemies, none of them involved accusing her of being illegitimate (which would have been the case if she hadn't been born to Ptolemy XII's queen).

Due to the sudden disappearance of Cleopatra V, Ptolemy XII's three youngest children – Arsinoe IV (c. 68-63 BC), Ptolemy XIII (c. 61 BC) and Ptolemy XIV (c. 59 BC) – are believed to have had a different mother (whose identity is unknown). Some historians have gone as far as arguing that *all* of Ptolemy XII's children were borne by Cleopatra V, although it is far less likely that Arsinoe IV, Ptolemy XIII and Ptolemy XIV were her children than Cleopatra VII.

*

When the High Priest of Ptah, Pedubast III, died in 76 BC, Ptolemy visited Memphis to officially appoint the late high priest's teenage son, Pasherienptah III, as his successor.[167] The new high priest crowned Ptolemy pharaoh and they both then returned to Alexandria, where Ptolemy selected Pasherienptah III to serve as his 'prophet'. This reflects the close relationship that had been formed between the Ptolemaic monarchy and the priesthood of Memphis.

---

[167] Pasherienptah III was 14 or 15 years old at the time he became High Priest.

From August 69 BC Cleopatra V's name disappears from monuments and papyri and she is no longer mentioned as Ptolemy's co-regent. Because of this (and the fact that engravings of her on the main pylon of the Temple of Edfu were erased at around this time), historians have assumed that Ptolemy divorced his wife. Alternatively, Cleopatra V may have died at around this time, but this is contradicted by an inscription at the Temple of Edfu (dated 5 December 57 BC), which reads: 'Ptolemy, Young Osiris, with his Sister, queen Cleopatra, surnamed Tryphaena.' This is clearly referring to Ptolemy XII's wife rather than a daughter, and it is highly unlikely that her name would have been included if she had died over a decade earlier.

In any case, after Cleopatra V had disappeared from the scene Ptolemy took the new epithet *Neos Dionysos* ('New Dionysus').[168] In the years that both preceded and followed the removal of Cleopatra V, Ptolemy earned a reputation as an aloof ruler who enjoyed living in luxury, and so it is unsurprising that he was unpopular with his subjects. To make matters worse, throughout his reign the threat of Roman annexation hung over his kingdom. This was due to Ptolemy X leaving his domains to Rome in his will in the event of him dying without an heir, but also more generally because of Rome's growing dominance in the Mediterranean world and the Ptolemaic Kingdom's long-term decline.

To prevent Egypt from being absorbed into the Roman Republic's growing empire, Ptolemy continued the pro-Roman policies of his predecessors. In the face of the Romans, who were ruthless, well-armed and determined to extend their frontiers, all independent states in the Mediterranean faced the same dilemma: resist and be conquered, or collaborate and at least maintain some semblance of autonomy. In Egypt's case, the Romans were well aware it was the richest country in the region and did not hesitate to use Ptolemy X's will as an excuse to extort vast sums of money from its coffers.

Unfortunately for Ptolemy XII, even his compliance was not enough to guarantee his kingdom's autonomy. Rome's hunger for power and territory was simply insatiable, and this danger was highlighted in 65 BC when the Roman statesman Marcus Licinius Crassus tried to convince the Senate to annex Egypt.[169] Many members of the Senate

---

[168] Alternatively, Ptolemy XII was known as the 'young Osiris' to his native Egyptian subjects.
[169] Crassus was a member of the First Triumvirate (formed in 60 BC), alongside Pompey and Julius Caesar. Famously referred to as 'the richest man in Rome', he was defeated at the Battle of Carrhae (53 BC) by the Parthians, who are said to have mocked his thirst wealth by pouring molten gold into his mouth.

(including Quintus Lutatius Catulus and Cicero) were wary about this proposal, because whoever became governor of a Roman province of Egypt might become too wealthy and upset the delicate balance of power in the Republic. For this reason, Crassus' calls for Egypt to be absorbed into the empire were rejected, although it didn't prevent the issue from resurfacing in the future and many ambitious Roman aristocrats remained tempted by Egypt's seemingly boundless wealth.

In a desperate attempt at maintaining the support of Rome's ruling elite, Ptolemy resorted to bribing powerful Roman statesmen. One of the main beneficiaries of such bribes was the renowned general Pompey, who Ptolemy gifted with a golden crown after his decisive victory over the Kingdom of Pontus in the Third Mithridatic War (73-63 BC) and gave the necessary funds to maintain a force of 8,000 cavalry during his military campaign against Judea.

While it is true that Egypt was in no position to confront Rome militarily, this conciliatory policy was incredibly expensive and created as many dangers as it averted – wreaking havoc on the economy and stirring up domestic unrest. In order to fund such hefty bribes, Ptolemy raised taxes to unsustainable levels and cut back on administrative costs, which caused conditions to deteriorate even further for Egypt's working population and alienated his subjects against him. A papyrus document dated to 61/60 BC records a strike by farmers who worked on royal land in a village of the Middle Egyptian nome of Herakleopolis, which reflects the discontent people all over Egypt felt towards the high levels of taxation being imposed on them. Ironically, when the tax rises sparked a revolt, Pompey declined Ptolemy's request for assistance, maybe because he judged intervening in Egypt would have serious consequences in Rome and undermine his attempt to gain official recognition for his military accomplishments elsewhere in the East.

In addition to taxation, Ptolemy became increasingly dependent on loans from Roman bankers (most notably Gaius Rabirius Postumus) to keep his finances afloat. By doing so, he was only digging himself into a deeper hole, because it made him even more reliant on Rome and enabled the Romans to exert greater influence over his kingdom. As the Ptolemaic Kingdom became increasingly indebted to its so-called 'protector', the Egyptian people naturally developed an intense hatred for the Romans, who they regarded as bullies and a threat to their independence.

In 60 BC Ptolemy visited Rome, where an unofficial political alliance between Pompey, Crassus and Julius Caesar (known to posterity as the First Triumvirate) had recently taken control of the Republic. By paying Pompey and Caesar 6,000 talents (an enormous sum of money that was equivalent to Egypt's annual revenue), Ptolemy managed to secure official recognition off the Senate as king of Egypt and was also declared a friend and ally of the Roman people in 59 BC. Ptolemy did this in response to rumours that Caesar (one of the consuls for 59 BC) was planning to include the annexation of Egypt on his political agenda, on the basis that Ptolemy XII was illegitimate and therefore had no right to rule. Nevertheless, the bribe was money not well spent. It did not secure his hold on power in Egypt and failed to deter Rome from annexing Cyprus the following year (58 BC).

The decision to seize Cyprus was partly motivated by an event that had taken place almost a decade earlier. In 67 BC the Roman politician Publius Clodius Pulcher had been captured by pirates. Clodius reassured his captors that they would receive a substantial reward if they agreed to release him, but when the pirates went to the Roman ally Ptolemy of Cyprus to negotiate a ransom the Cypriot king was only willing to pay a paltry sum. Clearly Clodius had significantly overestimated his worth and the pirates were so amused that they released the humiliated Roman free of charge.

Ever since his release, Clodius had been thirsting for revenge against Ptolemy of Cyprus for his insulting behaviour. He eventually achieved this in 58 BC when he secured the support of the Triumvirate to pass a bill that stripped Ptolemy of Cyprus of his kingship and declared Cyprus to be a territory of the Roman Republic, on the premise that the Cypriot king had been colluding with pirates.

The task of enforcing this bill was given to Cato the Younger, who led the Roman invasion of the island and became its governor.[170] Even though Cato was willing to be merciful towards the Cypriot king and offered him the distinguished position of High Priest at the Sanctuary of Aphrodite in Paphos, Ptolemy of Cyprus decided to commit suicide rather than suffer the indignity of losing his throne.

Back in Alexandria, Ptolemy XII refused to take action against Rome for the death of his brother and the seizure of an important and longstanding Ptolemaic territory.[171]

---

[170] Cato was a potential opponent of both Clodius and the Triumvirate. By appointing him to lead the expedition to Cyprus, they hoped to keep him out of Rome for some time, while also appeasing him with the prestige and financial gain the opportunity offered.

[171] Cyprus remained under Roman control until it was returned to the Ptolemaic Kingdom by Julius Caesar in 48 BC.

This proved to be the last straw for his subjects. Already enraged by the heavy tax burden, it confirmed in their minds that Ptolemy's submissive approach towards Rome had failed to protect Egypt from Roman expansionism, and the Alexandrians reacted by deposing their king (sometime in the late summer of 58 BC), who fled to Rome to request military support.

In Ptolemy's absence, the people of Alexandria replaced him on the throne with his eldest daughter, Berenice IV, and Cleopatra Tryphaena.[172]

The identity of Berenice's co-regent, Cleopatra Tryphaena, is ambiguous. Limited, fragmentary and contradictory source material has made it incredibly challenging to reconstruct the Ptolemaic family tree during its later generations, although the available evidence has allowed her identity to be narrowed down to two main candidates. If Cleopatra V really did die around 69 BC, then the Cleopatra Tryphaena who briefly ruled alongside Berenice IV was probably a daughter of Cleopatra V and Ptolemy XII (and has therefore been numbered Cleopatra VI by some historians).[173] However, there are other scholars who believe Cleopatra V was still alive in 58 BC and therefore regard Cleopatra V and Cleopatra VI as being the same person. This theory fits in with Strabo's account, which reported that Ptolemy XII had three daughters. Given that Berenice IV, Cleopatra VII and Arsinoe IV have all been confirmed as daughters of Ptolemy XII, this would imply the so-called Cleopatra VI was not his daughter. One possible explanation that has been put forward for this is that Cleopatra V disappeared from records in 69 BC not because she had died but because she had fallen out of favour with Ptolemy XII and was stripped of her position as co-regent.

Whoever she was, Cleopatra Tryphaena died of unknown causes in 57 BC, after about a year on the throne.

Berenice IV spent the next two years (57-56 BC) as Egypt's sole ruler. However, it wasn't customary for a woman to rule the kingdom by herself, so she was expected to find a husband to serve as her co-regent.

Initially, her advisors considered two Seleucid princes for her hand in marriage, but both attempts fell through – with one of the princes dying during the negotiations and

---

[172] Tryphaena means 'opulent'.
[173] The account of the third century AD philosopher Porphyry is the only surviving source that states Cleopatra Tryphaena was a daughter of Ptolemy XII.

the other being forbidden from accepting the offer by the Roman governor of Syria, Aulus Gabinius. In the end, the Alexandrians arranged for Berenice to marry another Seleucid prince named Seleucus, who travelled to the Egyptian capital. This union was as short and disastrous as the one between Berenice III and Ptolemy XI. Both Berenice and her subjects were appalled by Seleucus' bad manners and vulgar appearance. The Alexandrians gave him the derisive nickname Kybiosaktes ('Salt-fish-monger') and it quickly became apparent that he was not capable of earning the respect of the populace.

Within a few days of her wedding, Berenice proved herself to be just as ruthless and bloodthirsty as her ancestors when she had her husband strangled to death. However, that meant she was now in need of a new male co-regent to legitimise her rule in a misogynistic world. This was swiftly resolved when she was remarried to a Greek nobleman and priest called Archelaus the following year.

Archelaus claimed to be a son of King Mithridates VI of Pontus, although according to Strabo his father was actually a prominent general who served under Mithridates VI – also named Archelaus.[174] The first scenario is highly unlikely and the second scenario is widely believed to be the legitimate one, but his mother is unknown so it is still possible that Archelaus was related to Mithridates. In any event, his family would have been active at the Pontic court, and he became a ruler in his own right in 63 BC when the Roman general Pompey appointed him to the position of High Priest in the Cappadocian temple-city of Comana. The city was governed directly by its priest and was a Roman client state, which was symbolised by its temple being rededicated to Bellona (the Roman goddess of war).

In his capacity as a Roman client ruler, Archelaus travelled to Syria in 56 BC to offer his services to the governor of Roman Syria, Aulus Gabinius, who was planning a military campaign against the Parthians. This show of support backfired when Gabinius became suspicious of his associations with the Egyptians and had him arrested. Fortunately for Archelaus, his imprisonment was only brief. He soon managed to persuade Gabinius that he did not pose a threat and may have facilitated his release by paying a bribe.

---

[174] Archelaus' father (also named Archelaus) was Mithridates VI's favourite general during the First Mithridatic War. He was sent by Mithridates to conduct peace negotiations with the Roman general Sulla, but fell out of favour with his king when Mithridates concluded he had made too many concessions to the Romans. Archelaus subsequently defected to the Romans, who he assisted in the Second and Third Mithridatic Wars.

Once Archelaus was at liberty, he travelled to Egypt in the winter of 56/55 BC to accept the invitation he had received to become Berenice's husband and co-regent. He wooed his bride by showcasing his military talents and showering her with gifts, and proved to be a much better match for Berenice than her first husband.

Unfortunately, their union was also tragically brief. Within six months of their marriage, both died violent deaths.

*

After being deposed, Ptolemy XII travelled to Rome (probably accompanied by his 11-year-old daughter, Cleopatra VII), where he hoped to gain the necessary support to retake his throne by force. On the way to Rome he stopped off at the island of Rhodes, where he had a particularly humiliating audience with the Roman senator Cato the Younger. When he was brought before Cato, the senator had just received a particularly effective dose of laxative and was sitting on the lavatory. To compliment this openly disrespectful behaviour, he proceeded to scold Ptolemy for losing his kingdom, although he did also provide him with some helpful advice on how to deal with members of the Roman aristocracy. Cato was at odds with the Triumvirate and Rome's leading men at the time, so when Ptolemy informed him of his intention to go to Rome, the senator warned him that the greedy and corrupt Roman aristocracy's primary interest in Egypt was to exploit its wealth.

Nevertheless, this did not deter Ptolemy, who continued his journey to Rome via Athens.

When Ptolemy arrived in Rome, his ally Pompey provided him with lodgings in his villa in the Alban hills, where he resided from 58 BC until the end of 57 BC. During this time, Pompey tried to persuade the Senate to provide Ptolemy with assistance to regain the Egyptian throne. Meanwhile, Ptolemy complimented these efforts by distributing bribes to numerous senators, although doing so forced him even deeper into debt with Roman moneylenders. The one good thing about the vast sums of money he owed was that it ensured the various Roman creditors who had loaned him money would support his cause, given that it was unlikely they would receive the repayments they were owed unless he was restored to power.

While Ptolemy was working hard to gain the support of the Roman people, Berenice IV and the people of Alexandria had dispatched an embassy of their own to Rome. Its delegates were tasked with persuading the Senate to recognise Berenice as the rightful ruler of Egypt and deterring them from helping the deposed king to regain his throne by presenting charges of his misrule. Unfortunately for them though, Ptolemy had no intention of allowing them to go about their work, and neutralised the threat they posed in the most extreme way possible when he arranged for the leader of the embassy (the philosopher Dio of Alexandria) and many of its members to be assassinated. Although this ruthless measure could have backfired and caused a serious scandal, the crime was covered up with assistance from his powerful Roman supporters. It was not until after Ptolemy had departed Rome that anyone was put on trial on suspicion of committing the murders and even then the prosecution failed to secure a conviction.[175]

Meanwhile, the Senate continued to procrastinate over how to respond to the situation in Egypt. They delayed their answer to Ptolemy's appeal for support for many months and it was not until late 57 BC that they finally agreed to back his claim to the throne, after facing pressure from many prominent members of the Roman public. However, this was a hollow victory. Some senators still opposed the move and the Senate's decision fell short of providing Ptolemy with the military support he would need to regain his throne, due to an oracle being found in the *Sibylline Books* that prohibited the use of an army to restore the deposed king to power.

When he received this disappointing verdict, Ptolemy realised he would be wasting his time by staying in Rome any longer. He left the city empty-handed in late 57 BC and travelled to Ephesus (in Asia Minor), where he took up residence in the Temple of Artemis and continued his search for an army.

*

It was not until the spring of 55 BC that Ptolemy finally secured the financial and military support he needed to recover his throne. He achieved this by bribing the Roman governor of Syria Aulus Gabinius 10,000 talents to invade Egypt and remove his daughter from power.

---

[175] Dio of Alexandria is believed to have been poisoned in the home of his Roman host. The prime suspect was the politician Marcus Caelius Rufus, who was prosecuted in early 56 BC for *vis* ('violence'). This charge included the murder of Dio, although he was successfully defended by both Crassus and Cicero in the trial that followed. Cicero's defence speech, delivered on 4 April 56 BC and known as *Pro Caelio*, is considered to be one of the greatest orations in Roman history.

In addition to the financial incentive, Gabinius was encouraged to take this action by Pompey. The war was technically illegal, on the basis that he hadn't received consent off the Senate, but that did not deter him and he led a brutally efficient campaign.

Gabinius launched his invasion of Egypt via Judea, where the Hasmonean ruler Hyrcanus II and Antipater the Idumaean (Herod the Great's father) provided his army with supplies. He started his campaign by seizing control of the frontier city of Pelusium. Possession of this key fortress opened the gates to Egypt and his army marched on Alexandria, which quickly fell to his forces in April 55 BC.

One of Gabinius' subordinates during this campaign was a young cavalry officer named Mark Antony. He went on to become one of the most famous generals in Roman history (and a key player in the fall of the Ptolemaic Kingdom), but for the time being distinguished himself in the invasion by conducting himself with considerable honour. When Pelusium was captured, he stopped Ptolemy from massacring the city's inhabitants in a fit of vengeful wrath, and after Archelaus was slain in battle he acted against Ptolemy's wishes by ensuring his body was given a proper royal burial.[176]

Even though the campaign was both brief and successful, it had serious consequences for Gabinius, who was eventually held accountable by the Senate for waging war without its consent. During his absence from Syria, the province had been plagued by disorder. As soon as Ptolemy XII was back in control of Egypt, Gabinius returned to Syria and restored order, but it was too little, too late. The Roman *equites* (knights) in his province had suffered heavy financial losses as a result of the disorder (in their capacity as tax collectors) and blamed this on their governor's dereliction of duty. Consequently, when Gabinius' governorship came to an end and he returned to Rome in the autumn of 54 BC, he was put on trial and faced three charges. The first and most serious charge was *maiestas* (high treason), which was incurred for his decision to abandon his province and wage war in Egypt without the Senate's permission (and in defiance of the *Sibylline Books*). Thanks to the intervention of his powerful ally Pompey (and probably a bribe paid to the judges) he was acquitted of this charge. However, he had no such luck with the second charge, which accused him of *repetundae* (extortion during the administration of his province). Despite being defended by one of the most eloquent orators of the age – Cicero – and having

---

[176] Archelaus was succeeded as High Priest at Comana by his son of the same name. This child was borne by his first wife, who had died sometime before his marriage to Berenice IV.

evidence presented in his favour by Pompey and numerous witnesses from Alexandria, there was no hiding from the fact that he had accepted a bribe of 10,000 talents off Ptolemy and he was found guilty.[177] The third and final charge brought against him – for *ambitus* (resorting to illegal practices when running for the consulship) – was dropped, but by now this was irrelevant to the outcome of the trial. For the guilty verdict on the second charge, Gabinius' property was confiscated and he was sent into exile.

*

When Ptolemy XII was restored to the throne (at some point during the spring of 55 BC) he was no mood for reconciliation. One of his first acts of his second reign was to have his rebellious daughter, Berenice IV, executed, along with her supporters.

To help the unpopular king maintain his hold on power in the turbulent Egyptian capital, Gabinius left behind a force of approximately 2,000 Roman soldiers and 500 Gallic and German cavalry (known collectively as the Gabiniani). By keeping a military presence in Egypt, the Romans sought to prevent Ptolemy from being overthrown by his subjects and to ensure he continued to govern his kingdom in accordance with the interests of the Roman Republic. However, the Gabiniani quickly became comfortable with their lives in Egypt. They embraced the comfortable and luxurious Alexandrian way of life and neglected Roman discipline. Many even married Egyptian women, and it wasn't long before they switched their allegiance from Rome to the Ptolemaic monarchy.

As soon as Ptolemy was back in power, the Roman creditors he had borrowed money from demanded the repayment of their loans. Unfortunately, there wasn't enough money in the royal treasury to pay off his debts, so he addressed the situation by appointing his primary creditor – the Roman banker Gaius Rabirius Postumus – as his *dioiketes* (finance minister). This gave Rabirius the authority to raise money to pay off Ptolemy's debts and he did not hesitate to take advantage of his new position: exploiting Egypt's wealth to the full and draining the country of its resources. In addition to getting his creditors off his back, Ptolemy may have hoped that it would help to redirect his subjects' anger about the tax rises from himself to the Roman banker, but the arrangement didn't last long.

---

[177] Cicero was an opponent of Gabinius, so it is generally believed that he defended him as a favour to Pompey. It has also led to claims that Gabinius ended up being convicted as a result of Cicero giving a half-hearted defence.

Unsurprisingly, Rabirius quickly earned the hatred of the Egyptian people for his exploitative practices. The citizens of Alexandria became so enraged that they rioted against the finance minister and Ptolemy was forced to imprison Rabirius for his own protection.

By late 54 BC Ptolemy had sent Rabirius back to Rome, where he was put on trial for his activities in Egypt. The charges brought against Rabirius included extortion and complicity with Aulus Gabinius' unsanctioned military campaign, but he was successfully defended by Cicero, who secured him an acquittal on a technicality.

Another measure Ptolemy took as part of his efforts to repay his mounting debts and stabilise the economy was to permit the debasing of coinage. This was carried out so extensively that by the end of his life the value of coinage had dropped by approximately 50 percent since the start of his first reign. However, it did not resolve his financial woes and further debasing had to take place during the reign of his daughter and successor – Cleopatra VII.

Ptolemy also attempted to secure his tenuous position by financing major religious construction projects. This included decorative work on the temple of Montu at Medamud, the construction of a birth house at the temple of Repyt in Athribis, the completion of the Temple of Edfu, and founding a new temple dedicated to the goddess Hathor at the Dendera Temple complex. The foundation stone of the Temple of Hathor at Dendera was laid on 16 July 54 BC and at around this time Ptolemy also fulfilled his traditional pharaonic duties by going on an official visit to Memphis, accompanied by the most prominent member of the city's priesthood – the High Priest of Ptah, Pasherienptah III. By doing these things, he hoped to win over the Egyptian priesthood, as well as the native population in general, and he took a further step to secure his dynasty in 52 BC by promoting his eldest surviving daughter, Cleopatra VII, to co-regent.[178]

Just a few months after this, in early 51 BC, Ptolemy XII died and was succeeded by his eldest surviving daughter (Cleopatra VII) and eldest son (Ptolemy XIII), in accordance with his will. To ensure his wishes were respected (and as a sign of the extensive influence the Roman Republic now exerted over the Ptolemaic Kingdom), he had named Rome as the executor of his will. While the original will was kept in Alexandria, a copy of it was sent to Ptolemy's ally, Pompey, in Rome. Pompey was

---

[178] An inscription in the Temple of Hathor at Dendera indicates that this promotion took place on 31 May 52 BC.

happy to maintain the status quo and approved its contents, not knowing that his alliance with the Ptolemies would one day cost him his life.

*

Ptolemy XII is generally regarded as a weak ruler who presided over the continued decline of Ptolemaic power. He was described as a self-indulgent individual who drank excessively and had a passion for music. This resulted in many of his subjects referring to him by the derisive nickname *Auletes* ('the Flautist'), which ridiculed him for his passion for playing the flute, particularly during Dionysian festivals.[179] According to the Greek historian Strabo: 'Now all of the kings after the third Ptolemy, being corrupted by luxurious living, administered the affairs of government badly, but worst of all were the fourth, seventh, and the last, Auletes, who, apart from his general licentiousness, practised the accompaniment of choruses with the flute, and upon this he prided himself so much that he would not hesitate to celebrate contests in the royal palace, and at these contests would come forward to vie with the opposing contestants.'

On a positive note, intellectual life in Alexandria experienced something of a renaissance under the twelfth Ptolemy. Several new philosophical schools were established in Alexandria during the first century BC and the physician Apollonios of Kition dedicated his study of the teachings of Hippocrates – *Peri Arthron* (On Joints) – to Ptolemy's brother, Ptolemy of Cyprus.

It should also be acknowledged that Ptolemy achieved his primary aim of holding onto his throne and passing it onto his children, but this came at a high price. His questionable legitimacy made him heavily dependent on Rome to maintain his hold on power and the Ptolemaic Kingdom essentially became a client kingdom of the Roman Republic in all but name during his reign. In order to maintain the support of prominent Romans and in turn preserve his dynasty, he was forced to resort to extensive bribery, which he funded by stripping his kingdom of its wealth. This left Egypt in deep financial trouble that was inherited by his successors.

---

[179] Officially, Ptolemy XII's full name was 'Ptolemy Theos Philopator Philadelphos Neos Dionysos'.

Cleopatra VII: Depraved Seductress or Masterful Politician?

The last active ruler of Ptolemaic Egypt, Cleopatra VII Thea Philopator, is one of the most memorable figures in ancient Egyptian history and also one of the most famous women in history as a whole.[180][181][182] During her time on the throne she reasserted Ptolemaic power and rebuilt her ancestors' lost empire, only for it all to come crashing down in dramatic fashion when she overplayed her hand. Her defeat and suicide in 30 BC brought three millennia of pharaonic rule to an end and resulted in Egypt being absorbed into the Roman Empire – the exact eventuality she and her predecessors had been seeking to avoid, but one that had seemed inevitable nonetheless. More broadly, the demise of the Ptolemaic Kingdom marked the end of the Hellenistic Period, as Ptolemaic Egypt had been the last major Hellenistic state left standing.[183]

Cleopatra was born in late 70 or early 69 BC to the reigning pharaoh, Ptolemy XII. It is uncertain who her mother was, but it was probably her father's wife and queen, Cleopatra V, who disappeared from records a few months after her birth.

Little is known about Cleopatra's early life, but it is safe to say that she received a first-rate education. As a young girl, Cleopatra benefitted enormously from the academia and scholarship sponsored by her ancestors. Born and raised just a stone's throw away from the Musaeum and Library of Alexandria (which was situated in the city's royal quarter), she presumably studied there. Her schooling was primarily Hellenistic-Greek and she was tutored by a scholar named Philostratus during her childhood, who ensured she was thoroughly educated in the Greek arts of philosophy and oratory.

---

[180] Cleopatra VII's epithet was Thea Philopator ('Father-loving Goddess'). Ptolemy XIII''s epithet was the male equivalent: Theos Philopator ('Father-loving God').
[181] Cleopatra is an Ancient Greek name which means 'glory of her father'. The Ptolemies started using the name after Ptolemy V married the Seleucid princess Cleopatra I Syra.
In addition to the many members of the Ptolemaic dynasty who were named Cleopatra, other famous figures who were given the name include Cleopatra of Macedonia (Alexander the Great's sister) and Cleopatra Alcyone (the wife of the hero Meleager in Greek mythology).
[182] Technically Cleopatra VII was succeeded by her son, Caesarion, after her death, but he never had the chance to exercise his authority as pharaoh and was executed soon after.
[183] The Ptolemaic Kingdom's two main Hellenistic rivals, the Kingdom of Macedonia and the Seleucid Empire, had been defeated by the Romans in 168 BC and 64 BC respectively.

Cleopatra's superb education was complimented by her passion for academia. Like her Ptolemaic kin, her first language was Koine Greek, but she mastered many other languages too and is believed to have been the only Ptolemaic ruler who bothered to learn the language of her native Egyptian subjects. In addition to Greek and Egyptian, Plutarch claims she was able to speak Ethiopian, Arabic, Median, Parthian, Hebrew (or Aramaic), the Syrian language (perhaps Syriac), and the language of the Troglodytes. She is also believed to have been proficient in Latin, although she tended to speak to Romans in her native Greek tongue.

Cleopatra's knowledge of languages other than the obvious ones – Greek and Egyptian (the dominant languages in Egypt) and Latin (the language of the leading power in the Mediterranean) – reflected her desire to rebuild the Ptolemaic Kingdom's empire in north Africa and western Asia that had been gained and lost by her ancestors. Knowing the language of the armies she was leading into battle was an extremely important asset, and being fluent in the language of the Egyptian people helped boost her legitimacy and improve relations with her subjects.

*

When Cleopatra's father was deposed in 58 BC, she probably accompanied him into exile. During Gabinius' campaign to restore Ptolemy XII to power (in 55 BC), Cleopatra – then just 14 years old – is reported to have met her future lover, Mark Antony, for the first time, although this is unlikely. It is far more likely that she first encountered Antony at some point between 46 and 44 BC, when she was residing in Rome and Antony became Julius Caesar's right-hand man.

After the execution of her elder sister, Berenice IV, Cleopatra became the heir to the throne and was named her father's co-regent three years later. Not long after this, in early 51 BC, Cleopatra VII acceded to the throne in her own right at just 17 years of age, following the death of Ptolemy XII. In accordance with the late king's will she ruled alongside her younger brother, Ptolemy XIII, who was about 10 or 11 years old. The royal couple were required to get married in the terms of their father's will (although this may not have happened) and they also inherited their father's staggering debts to the Roman Republic along with his throne.

Soon after becoming queen, Cleopatra sailed up the Nile to Hermonthis (south of Thebes) to preside over the installation of a new Buchis bull, which took place on 22 March 51 BC. The Buchis bull was one of a number of sacred bulls throughout Egypt and was regarded as being a living manifestation of the Egyptian war god Montu. By taking part in its induction ceremony she was performing a traditional pharaonic duty and honouring Egyptian religious customs, which she hoped would help her to gain legitimacy in the eyes of her native subjects.

Initially, Cleopatra emerged as Egypt's senior ruler and successfully sidelined her brother. By the end of August 51 BC Cleopatra's name had started appearing by itself in official documents, which suggests she had rejected her brother's position as co-regent. However, attempting to become Egypt's sole ruler was easier said than done. Although Ptolemy XIII was only a young boy, he had powerful allies at the royal court who were determined to protect his interests. The most notable of these were his three guardians: the eunuch Pothinus (who served as his regent and tutor), Achillas (the commander of his army), and Theodotus of Chios (his rhetoric tutor).

Cleopatra managed to maintain her dominance for about 18 months, but her hold on power was undermined by a series of disasters – some natural, some political; some unavoidable, others of her own creation. One of the most serious of these issues was the crop failure and severe food shortages that followed an unusually low inundation of the Nile in the summer of 50 BC. Many of her subjects would have interpreted this concerning development as a sign that the gods had already deserted their queen and compelled Cleopatra to work with her co-regent to pass emergency legislation in October 50 BC. This legislation provided relief to her subjects and prevented famine by ordering the royal granaries to provide food to the starving population. It also required anyone in Middle Egypt selling grain or legumes to send their produce to Alexandria, on pain of death, to prevent hunger riots in the capital. This benefited Ptolemy XIII's support base (in Alexandria) at the expense of Cleopatra's main support base (in rural Egypt) and is a clear indicator of Cleopatra's weakening position at the royal court. The fact that Ptolemy XIII's name not only reappeared on official documents from this point onwards but preceded Cleopatra's hints the balance of power had shifted in his favour by the autumn of 50 BC – with the young king serving as senior ruler and his regent Pothinus acting as the power behind the throne.

Admittedly, the devastation inflicted by the famine was out of Cleopatra's control, but her growing unpopularity was made worse by her own actions. She mishandled a number of other serious issues during her initial 18 months of dominance, including the lawless behaviour of the Gabiniani, who had renounced their allegiance to Rome and become assimilated to life in Egypt by the time she acceded to the throne.

In 50 BC, the Roman governor of Syria, Marcus Calpurnius Bibulus, sent his two eldest sons to Egypt with instructions to recruit the Gabiniani to help defend his province against the Parthians. However, the Gabiniani were happy with their new lives in Egypt and had no intention of returning to Roman service, so they responded to the request by torturing and murdering both sons. Eager not to bring the wrath of Rome down on her recently-established regime, Cleopatra had the culprits arrested and sent to Bibulus to be punished as he saw fit, but this gesture backfired twice.[184] Far from being grateful, Bibulus sent the prisoners back to Egypt and scolded Cleopatra, saying only the Senate had the authority to put them on trial (as they were still Roman citizens). Meanwhile, the Gabiniani were enraged by her actions and the Alexandrians saw the submissive gesture as evidence that their queen was little more than a Roman puppet. Consequently, both groups became hostile towards Cleopatra and threw their weight behind Ptolemy XIII.

*

At the same time as Cleopatra was struggling to maintain her supremacy in government, the Roman world was plunged into civil war. Known to posterity as Caesar's civil war, it was fought between the two surviving members of the First Triumvirate – Pompey (supported by the Senate) and Julius Caesar – and had broken out when Caesar and his army famously crossed the Rubicon on the night of 10/11 January 49 BC. It was illegal for Roman provincial governors to take their armies to Italy, so this action made Caesar an outlaw. However, Pompey and his allies had insufficient manpower to defend Rome against Caesar's advance, and they were compelled to withdraw to Greece where they intended to raise an army to bring Caesar to heel.

In the spring/summer of 49 BC, Gnaeus Pompeius (Pompey's eldest son) arrived in Alexandria, seeking Egyptian support for his father's cause in the ongoing civil war. Given that Pompey had been her father's most important Roman ally and seemed to have the best odds of coming out on the winning side, Cleopatra naturally favoured his side in the conflict. In what might have been their last joint decree, Cleopatra and Ptolemy XIII responded favourably to Gnaeus Pompeius' request by providing him with 500 Gallic and German cavalry of the Gabiniani and 50 warships to support his father. By doing so, they not only maintained friendly relations with the most

---

[184] Given that Bibulus claimed only the Senate could punish his sons' murderers, some historians believe he sent the culprits to Rome rather than back to Egypt.

powerful man in the Roman world but also managed to eliminate some of the enormous debt they owed to Rome from the reign of their father. However, with the benefit of hindsight, this alliance was of little benefit to Cleopatra in the short-term and did not protect her from her political enemies at the royal court or her growing unpopularity amongst her subjects.

Before the end of the summer of 49 BC, the power struggle between Cleopatra and Ptolemy XIII finally came to a head when her brother's ambitious guardians (supported by the people of Alexandria and the Gabiniani) forced Cleopatra into exile and proclaimed Ptolemy sole ruler. Unfortunately for them, Cleopatra had no intention of giving up her throne without a fight and their actions sparked a civil war.

After being banished from Alexandria, Cleopatra fled first to Upper Egypt and then to Roman Syria, where she raised an army. By the late summer of 48 BC she had marched on Egypt with her army. Her forces were prevented from crossing Egypt's eastern border and advancing on Alexandria by Ptolemy XIII's army, which was in control of the key border fortress of Pelusium. Despite the swiftness with which Cleopatra had managed to raise an army, Ptolemy remained in the stronger position. He enjoyed the support of the capital and had a superior army (bolstered by the Gabiniani, who Cleopatra had previously angered), forcing Cleopatra to camp outside Pelusium and engage in a lengthy standoff.

At the same time as Cleopatra and Ptolemy XIII were confronting each other at Pelusium, the civil war between Pompey and Caesar came to a head at the Battle of Pharsalus (in Greece). Fought on 9 August 48 BC, it led to the destruction of Pompey's army and a decisive victory for Caesar.

Hoping to live to fight another day, Pompey fled to Egypt. This seemed to be the obvious place to seek refuge, given the Ptolemaic Kingdom's immense wealth and the close relationship he had with its rulers. As a political ally of Ptolemy XIII's late father, he expected to receive a warm welcome at the Ptolemaic court and be provided with the money and troops he needed to rebuild his army and keep up the fight against Caesar. Little to his knowledge, however, Ptolemy's guardians were unwilling to get drawn into Rome's civil war or to anger Caesar, who they believed would be victorious in the conflict. At the same time though, they were reluctant to send Pompey away. Doing so would anger Pompey (turning him into a dangerous enemy in the future if his fortunes bounced back) and infuriate Caesar (who was eager to capture his rival and would not appreciate the Egyptians passing up on the opportunity to apprehend him).

After debating the issue, the Egyptian king's advisors decided to have Pompey killed. This was in accordance with a scheme devised by Theodotus, who counselled 'dead men don't bite' and argued Caesar would be grateful to have his rival eliminated without having to get any blood on his hands.

Pretending that all was well, Ptolemy's advisors sent a welcoming message to Pompey, but when he arrived off the coast of Pelusium in his ship he didn't even get the chance to set foot on Egyptian soil. As the veteran general was being rowed ashore he was stabbed to death by an officer named Lucius Septimius, who had previously served under him but was now in Ptolemy's service.[185] The murder took place on 28 September 48 BC in full view of his wife (who watched on in horror from the deck of the ship they had arrived on) and the young king and his army on the shore.

Caesar arrived off the coast of Egypt in pursuit of Pompey a few days after his assassination, in early October 48 BC. Because he had been in a hurry to catch up with Pompey, he had only brought a small fleet with him (carrying two small legions of approximately 3,200 infantry and 800 cavalry), and he received a gruesome welcome when Ptolemy's advisors sent him Pompey's severed and pickled head. They hoped this would help them gain the general's favour, but it did the complete opposite. Caesar was furious by the barbaric treatment of an esteemed Roman general, who had been both a consul and his own son-in-law in the past. He is said to have turned away in disgust and wept (although it is uncertain how genuine these tears were) and given orders for the rest of Pompey's body to be found and given a proper funeral.

Caesar had initially delayed landing in Alexandria due to the hostile reception his presence had received in the Egyptian capital, but this latest development prompted him to dock his ships. He then marched through the city, accompanied by his lictors in the manner of a consul visiting a subject territory, and occupied the royal palace with his troops. This imperious behaviour was regarded as an insult to the sovereignty of Egypt by the city's residents, who made no attempt to hide their anger at the Roman presence.

---

[185] Lucius Septimius was one of the Gabiniani. He was assisted in the murder of Pompey by another member of the Gabiniani – a centurion named Salvius.

At the time Ptolemy and Cleopatra were still engaged in their standoff at Pelusium, so Caesar ordered both of the royal siblings to disband their armies and come to Alexandria so he could mediate an end to their dispute, as well as demanding a payment of 10 million denarii towards their father's debts. A copy of Ptolemy XII's will had previously been held by Pompey, who had acted as its executor on behalf of Rome. Now he was dead though, the victorious Caesar claimed the authority to take on this responsibility.

Ptolemy returned to Alexandria with his guardians Pothinus and Theodotus, but did not comply with Caesar's order to disband his army. He left his third guardian – the general Achillas – behind at Pelusium to command his army and keep the Egyptian border secure, and this made it impossible for Cleopatra to travel to Alexandria safely.

With Ptolemy's army blocking the way, Cleopatra initially communicated with Caesar via messengers. However, when it was brought to her attention that the Roman general had a reputation for having affairs with aristocratic women she realised her young female body was the one trump card she had that her brother did not and became determined to meet Caesar in person. In order to do this, she had herself smuggled across the Egyptian border and into the royal palace in Alexandria. If Plutarch is to be believed, Cleopatra was carried past the guards and into Caesar's quarters by one of her attendants, cleverly hidden inside a rolled-up rug or bed sack.

The meeting that took place between Caesar and Cleopatra that evening is one of the most famous scenes in all of history. Now Caesar was the dominant figure in the Roman world, it was critical that Cleopatra gain his support for her claim to the throne before her brother's ministers persuaded him to do the opposite, and she pulled out all the stops to secure a favourable outcome. Cassius Dio claims she had attired herself as attractively as possible before her meeting with Caesar and seduced him with her wit. By exploiting her female charm to the full, she persuaded him to support her claim to the throne, and they slept together that very night. However, given that Caesar was 52 and an experienced womaniser, in comparison to Cleopatra, who was 21 and may not have even been in a sexual relationship before, it is far more likely that it was Caesar who did the seducing. Despite being commonly portrayed as a woman of extraordinary beauty in legend, it is generally believed that it was Cleopatra's charm, intelligence, charisma and boundless wealth that was alluring, not her physical appearance. And while it is certain that they started a love affair in the months that followed, it may not have begun as early as the night they first met.

On a less romantic note, both Cleopatra and Caesar were driven by practical considerations and intended to use each other. Cleopatra needed Roman support to regain her throne and Caesar needed a competent and compliant ruler on the Egyptian throne so he could ensure the debts Ptolemy XII had incurred were paid off in full.

When Ptolemy discovered his sister had managed to sneak into the palace and gain Caesar's support for her restoration as co-regent, he was furious. He was probably well aware that his sister (as a young woman) was already closer to Caesar than he could ever be (as a mere boy) and reacted by storming out of the palace in a childish tantrum. Standing before a large crowd, he threw his diadem on the ground. He shouted that he had been betrayed and encouraged the people of Alexandria to riot.

Caesar reacted rapidly to the situation before it got out of hand. He had the young king apprehended and then appeared on a balcony, from which he managed to calm the furious crowd with his oratorical skills.

As soon as this immediate danger had been defused, Caesar took Cleopatra and Ptolemy XIII to a meeting of the assembly of Alexandria. Here, he read out Ptolemy XII's will (which had been in Pompey's possession until his death) and asserted his right (as the most powerful man in Rome) to assert its terms and arrange for the warring royal siblings to be reconciled. Caesar announced that Cleopatra and Ptolemy XIII must resume ruling alongside each other (as stated in the will), although Ptolemy's councillors knew this would not be an even partnership and effectively amounted to a return to political dominance for Cleopatra. At the same time, Caesar tried to heal old wounds and pacify the hostile population of Alexandria by returning Cyprus to Ptolemaic control (which had been annexed by Rome in 58 BC). He named Ptolemy XII's two other children – Arsinoe IV and Ptolemy XIV – as the island's rulers, which had the additional benefit of removing two potential rival claimants to the Egyptian throne.

Unfortunately for Caesar, Ptolemy's guardians had no intention of sitting back and accepting Cleopatra's return to political dominance. They were encouraged by the knowledge that their army (which was composed of approximately 20,000 troops, including the Gabiniani) far outnumbered Caesar's Roman force (which numbered about 4,000 troops) and were determined to act while they still had the upper hand.

Hoping to neutralise the threat posed by Caesar and Cleopatra with military force, Pothinus gave secret instructions to Achillas to lead the Ptolemaic army from

Pelusium back to Alexandria. This plan was compromised when one of Caesar's slaves discovered the plot and warned his master, who had Pothinus put to death. However, the wheels had already been set in motion and Achillas proceeded with the plan: departing Pelusium and marching on Alexandria with 20,000 soldiers and 2,000 cavalry.

Caesar recognised his forces were significantly outnumbered, so dispatched ambassadors to conduct negotiations with Achillas.

With the advantages of numerical superiority and the support of the people of Alexandria, Achillas saw no need to negotiate and responded Caesar's call for parley with actions rather than words. He had the Roman ambassadors murdered and then moved in on Alexandria, where he occupied most of city and besieged the royal palace.

Eager to prevent his opponents from using the ships docked in the harbour to form a blockade and prevent supplies or reinforcements from reaching him by sea, Caesar gave orders for them to be set on fire. The blaze rapidly consumed the ships and soon spread to the city, damaging its famous library in the process.

Meanwhile, Cleopatra's younger sister, Arsinoe IV, managed to escape the palace – accompanied by her eunuch-tutor Ganymedes – and joined forces with Achillas. Arsinoe was declared queen by the besieging army (as a replacement for Ptolemy XIII's co-regent, Cleopatra VII), but a power struggle soon broke out that resulted in Ganymedes killing Achillas and usurping his position as commander of the army.

Initially, Ganymedes tried to force Caesar to surrender by tampering with his water supply. The Ptolemaic army had control of both the River Nile and the canals that supplied Alexandria with water, which enabled Ganymedes to fill the canals and cisterns that served the royal palace with salt water.

For a while, the plan seemed to be working. As the water supply became increasingly brackish, the Romans started to panic. However, Caesar was aware that Alexandria was built on limestone (which is porous) and countered his enemies' sabotage by ordering wells to be dug. This restored his water supply and calmed his troops, but was still insufficient for his long-term needs, so sent ships along the coast to search for additional sources of fresh water.

Two days after Ganymedes' scheme had been thwarted a fleet carrying the Thirty-Seventh Legion – along with supplies and artillery – arrived off the coast of Egypt. They were suffering from water shortages and contrary winds prevented them from landing in Alexandria, which prompted Caesar to set out with his own fleet to assist them.

During this mission, Caesar sent some of his sailors ashore to search for water, but they were captured by a Ptolemaic cavalry force, which discovered Caesar's location and passed the information on to Ganymedes. Sensing an opportunity to decisively defeat Caesar, Ganymedes gathered as many ships as he could and set off in pursuit of Caesar.

In the naval battle that followed, the Romans emerged victorious. This disheartened the people of Alexandria, but Ganymedes succeeded in gathering an even larger fleet to fight a further battle. Despite his confidence, Ganymedes suffered an even worse defeat at the hands of the Romans in this second engagement.

These setbacks convinced Ganymedes that a change of tactics was in order. He dedicated his attention to bombarding Caesar's forces, but neither side made any breakthroughs and a stalemate ensued.

Now Caesar had won naval supremacy, he attempted to seize the island of Pharos, which would enable him to control access to Alexandria's two harbours. He had already installed a small garrison on the north-eastern part of Pharos and now ordered an amphibious assault (composed of ten cohorts of legionaries, in addition to some cavalry and light infantry) to assist them in their struggle against Ptolemaic forces on the island. In the fierce fighting that followed, Caesar's forces successfully captured the island, although their subsequent effort to take control of the long bridge that connected Pharos with the mainland ended in disaster and almost cost Caesar his life.

The day after Pharos had fallen to the Romans, Caesar forced the Alexandrians off the bridge by sending several ships – carrying archers and artillery – to bombard it. As soon as the bridge had been cleared, Caesar landed on it along with three cohorts. They immediately set about building a rampart to secure their position, but suddenly faced a two-pronged counterattack by the Alexandrians, who launched a fierce assault by both land and sea. In the fighting that ensued, the Romans were caught in a pincer and outfought by their opponents, causing them to panic and withdraw to their ships in a mad rush. The vessel Caesar boarded became so swamped with troops that he was forced to abandon ship before it sank. To prevent himself from drowning (and avoid drawing enemy fire), he removed his armour and purple cloak and swam all the way to the shore. He was lucky to escape with his life, and it is all the more remarkable that he achieved it while holding his left hand above the water to prevent some important documents he had on his person from getting wet.

Caesar's failure to capture the bridge to Pharos was a key symbolic victory for Arsinoe IV and cost many Roman lives. Nevertheless, Caesar maintained his troops' morale and by now many of the Alexandrians had started to grow weary of the leadership of Arsinoe and Ganymedes. Desiring that their king lead them instead, they sent a delegation to Caesar to negotiate the release of Ptolemy XIII, who had been held prisoner by Caesar in the royal palace since the start of the war.

Caesar was eventually persuaded to release Ptolemy on the condition that he would act as an intermediary to bring the siege to an end. However, the boy king had no intention of doing any such thing and joined forces with his sister Arsinoe as soon as he was at liberty.

Caesar was no fool and had probably guessed this was Ptolemy's intention all along. His decision to set the boy free was most likely based on the assumption that it would be beneficial in any event. If Ptolemy kept his word, then the war would come to an end; and if he reneged on his promise by joining the rebellion, Caesar would have an excuse to eliminate him.

At some point between January and March 47 BC, Caesar was able to breathe a sigh of relief when the reinforcements he had called for finally arrived. Although trained in the Roman way, this force was not a Roman army. Rather, they were led by the Roman allies Mithridates of Pergamon (the future king of the Bosporan Kingdom) and Antipater the Idumaean (the father of the future king of Judea, Herod the Great), and also included a cavalry force from Petra (provided by the Nabataean king Malichus I).

After raising an army in Asia Minor, Mithridates had marched overland towards Egypt with his troops. He had been joined by Antipater's Jewish force of 3,000 troops on the way when he passed through Judea and the combined army had then advanced on the strategically important city of Pelusium, which was stormed and captured. Possession of Pelusium enabled them to march into Egypt and towards Alexandria.

The arrival of these reinforcements prompted Ptolemy and Arsinoe to abandon their siege of the royal palace and withdraw with their army to the Nile. Caesar set off in pursuit and joined forces with Mithridates and Antipater, which gave him the manpower needed to inflict a decisive defeat on the Ptolemaic army at the Battle of the Nile.

In the chaotic retreat that followed, Ptolemy attempted to escape by boat, but it became overloaded with panicking soldiers and capsized. Weighed down by the golden armour he was wearing, the boy king drowned in the River Nile. Ganymedes is also believed to have perished in the battle and Arsinoe was taken prisoner. Meanwhile, Ptolemy's last surviving guardian, Theodotus of Chios, managed to escape, but fate caught up with him in the end when he was captured and executed by Marcus Junius Brutus many years later (in 43 or 42 BC).

After the Battle of the Nile, Caesar made a triumphant return to Alexandria. He was conscious that it wasn't customary for a female monarch to rule alone in Egypt and was eager to prevent any further rebellions by the hostile local population. For this reason he arranged for Cleopatra to marry her other younger brother, Ptolemy XIV, who was then aged about 12 years old and replaced Ptolemy XIII as her co-regent.[186] Unlike his elder brother, Ptolemy XIV had no powerful councillors to protect his interests, so he was little more than a puppet. Cleopatra was the dominant partner in the co-regency, but it was Caesar who was ultimately in charge, given that it was his military muscle that had restored the Egyptian queen to power and was propping up her new regime.

To celebrate their victory, Cleopatra took Caesar on a cruise up the Nile in a luxurious barge. Although it is traditionally presented as a romantic pleasure cruise in which the two rulers were able to put their feet up after the stressful events of the past few years, take their love affair to the next level, and enjoy the scenery and monuments of Egypt, it had a clear political purpose. Now she was back in power, Cleopatra would have wanted to prevent any further attempts to undermine her authority by showing her subjects the awesome Roman military power that supported her regime, and Caesar would have been eager to do the same to ensure a stable pro-Roman government remained in control of Egypt. At the same time, Cleopatra was no doubt eager to wow her Roman guests by boasting her kingdom's wealth and abundance.

Throughout the cruise, the royal barge was accompanied by a large flotilla of support vessels. Caesar had a fascination with geography and is said to have desired to

---

[186] Cleopatra's marriage to one of Cyprus' co-regents (Ptolemy XIV) and the imprisonment of the other (Arsinoe IV) meant she was able to gain control of the island.

discover the source of the Nile (a feat that was not accomplished until the nineteenth century AD), but only made it as far as the First Cataract (near Aswan), where he was forced to return to Alexandria by his troops, who felt he was neglecting his duties and becoming too captivated by the Egyptian queen.

Caesar's extended stay in Egypt came to an end in about April 47 BC, when he departed Alexandria to bring Pharnaces II of Pontus to heel, who had taken advantage of Rome's civil war by invading part of Anatolia.[187] Cleopatra was also heavily pregnant by this time (allegedly with Caesar's child) and therefore some sources conclude that his departure was also motivated by his reluctance to be present when the Egyptian queen gave birth. At the time Caesar was married to a prominent Roman aristocrat named Calpurnia, so he would have been eager not to cause a scandal in Rome or to anger his powerful in-laws.

Before departing Egypt, Caesar stationed three Roman legions in the Nile Valley, which was later increased to four and placed under the command of a reliable officer named Rufio. The purpose of this Roman military presence in Egypt was twofold: to prevent Cleopatra's subjects from overthrowing her; and to ensure she remained loyal to Rome.[188] As Caesar reasoned in his own words, he 'thought it beneficial to the smooth running and renown of our empire that the king and queen [Ptolemy XIV and Cleopatra] should be protected by our troops, as long as they remained faithful to us; but if they were ungrateful, they could be brought back into line by those same troops.'

*

On 23 June 47 BC Cleopatra gave birth to a son. Eager to emphasise that the boy's father was none other than Julius Caesar, she named him Ptolemy Caesar – although today he is better known by his regnal name, Ptolemy XV, or the nickname Caesarion ('Little Caesar').

---

[187] In what turned out to be a swift and effective campaign, Caesar defeated Pharnaces at the Battle of Zela on 2 August 47 BC. After this victory, Caesar sent a letter to the Senate in which he is alleged to have summarised his campaign in three words: *'veni, vidi, vici'* ('I came, I saw, I conquered').

[188] Rufio was the son of a freedman. Caesar chose a man of his modest station to lead his forces in Egypt rather than a senator because he feared anyone from an aristocratic background might attempt to exploit Egypt's wealth and strategic position to make a bid for power, whereas Rufio did not have the necessary experience, influence or connections to do so.

To celebrate the birth of the royal prince, Cleopatra ordered the Cyprus mint to issue commemorative coins featuring the double cornucopia, which essentially proclaimed the abundance the Romano-Egyptian union promised to yield. She also ordered the construction of a 'birth house' at Hermonthis and the consecration of a roof shrine at the Temple of Hathor at Dendera (which was appropriate for the occasion given that Hathor was a mother goddess). During her reign, Cleopatra associated herself with the Egyptian goddess Isis and promoted her cult, so it was only natural that she now presented Caesarion as Horus (Isis' son and the god of kingship). This divine propaganda was intended to highlight that Cleopatra had secured the future of the dynasty by producing a successor who was destined to one day become king. However, that did not prevent many of her enemies from rejecting the claim that he was a child of Caesar, and Caesar himself was reluctant to talk about the child's parentage. In public, the Roman dictator did not make any attempt to confirm or deny he was Caesarion's father. His silence could be explained by the fact that his marriage to Calpurnia had not yet produced any children, as well as the knowledge that Caesarion could not be classed as a legitimate son or serve as his heir under Roman law (due to him being born outside of marriage and to a foreign mother).

Another high profile birth was celebrated in Egypt the following year (46 BC) when Taimhotep (the wife of the High Priest of Ptah, Pasherienptah III) gave birth to a son. This son was named Imhotep-Pedubast and would go on to succeed his father as High Priest of Ptah. His birth came as a considerable relief to his parents, given that the first 12 years of their marriage had produced three daughters, making it highly probable that he would end up dying without a successor. Every man in Egypt desired a male heir, and it was particularly important for Pasherienptah to secure one considering his family had held the title High Priest of Ptah for ten generations.

Before the birth of Imhotep-Pedubast, Taimhotep had desperately sought the help of the gods (in particular Imhotep) to procure a son. In his mortal life Imhotep had been an influential courtier during the reign of the Third dynasty pharaoh Netjerikhet (better known as Djoser). He served as the High Priest of Ra and is believed to have been the architect of the Step Pyramid of Djoser. In the 3,000 years that followed his death he was gradually deified and came to be worshipped throughout Egypt as a god of medicine, healing and wisdom. The divine powers he wielded, in addition to the fact that the centre of his cult was in Memphis and Taimhotep herself bore his name, made him the most obvious god for Taimhotep to pray to for a son, and when she did so her prayer was miraculously answered. Imhotep reportedly came to her in a dream and promised to give her the son she yearned for. In return, he expected her to arrange for his shrine in Memphis to be embellished. As her husband was the head of the Memphite priesthood, this work was carried out at a rapid pace, and they received their reward on 15 July 46 BC when Taimhotep gave birth to a male heir.

*

As soon as Caesar had stamped out the last flames of Pompeian opposition, he returned to Rome (in 46 BC) where a four-day triumph was held in his honour. Each day was dedicated to a different victory – in Gaul (against Vercingetorix and a coalition of Gallic tribes in 52 BC), Pontus (against Pharnaces II of Pontus in 47 BC), Africa (against his Pompeian opponents in 46 BC), and Egypt (against Ptolemy XIII and Arsinoe IV in 47 BC). The starring role in the Egyptian triumph was reserved for Arsinoe IV, who had been brought to Rome as a prisoner. During the procession she was paraded behind a burning effigy of the Lighthouse of Alexandria, which had once been a symbol of the teenage princess' victory over Caesar but was now a reminder of her defeat.

Arsinoe had a lot more to worry about than humiliation during the festivities due to it being customary for prominent prisoners to be strangled at the end of a Roman triumph. This is precisely what happened to the Gallic leader Vercingetorix and Caesar would have done the same thing to Arsinoe were it not for the people of Rome, who took pity on the teenage princess. While they had no issue with a battle-hardened man being publicly executed, they regarded Arsinoe as a young and helpless girl, which compelled Caesar to spare her life and send her into exile instead – to the Temple of Artemis at Ephesus.

Arsinoe may not have been the only member of the Egyptian royal family in Rome at the time of Caesar's triumph, because Cleopatra made two separate visits to the city, in 46 and 44 BC. Some historians have speculated this may have been a single extended stay rather than two separate visits, but this is unlikely as it would have been unwise for Cleopatra to be absent from her kingdom for such a long period of time. Her first visit was made with her co-regent Ptolemy XIV (but probably without Caesarion), whereas she is believed to have been accompanied by both Ptolemy XIV and Caesarion during her second visit.

Throughout her stay in Rome, Cleopatra resided in Caesar's villa across the Tiber (which was situated in one of two parks he owned, known collectively as the *Horti Caesaris* or 'Gardens of Caesar'), rather than in his main residence within the city walls (where his wife resided). Like their father before them, Cleopatra and Ptolemy XIV received formal recognition off the Senate as a 'friend and ally of the Roman people'. Cleopatra didn't venture beyond Caesar's estate much, but was visited in the villa by many prominent Romans, who were eager to obtain favours from the Egyptian queen (either in relation to her own kingdom or to ask her to intercede with Caesar on their behalf). The most notable of these visitors was the powerful senator and skilled orator Cicero, who found the Egyptian queen arrogant and became one of her principal opponents in the city.

Cleopatra wasn't the only person who was making a lot of enemies in Rome at this time. Despite his military success in the civil war, Caesar's behaviour became increasingly autocratic and he made a number of controversial decisions as dictator that convinced many Roman aristocrats he intended to overthrow the Republic and have himself proclaimed king. The presence of the Egyptian queen could hardly have helped quash these rumours (as she was a figurehead of female independence, effeminate eastern culture, and monarchy – all of which were anathema to the Romans) and Caesar made things worse by ordering a golden statue of Cleopatra to be erected inside the newly-established Temple of Venus Genetrix.[189] Installing a statue of a living woman was controversial enough, but the fact that she was a foreigner and that Caesar was using it to associate the mother of his child with the goddess Venus (who also happened to be the mother of the Romans) was a bitter pill to swallow for many Romans.

As a result of Caesar's disregard for the legislative process (making decisions and passing laws behind closed doors, without proper debate or consultation) even many beneficial reforms he pushed through faced fierce resistance. This included his decision to replace the inaccurate Roman calendar with a new one, which was modelled off the Egyptian calendar and was calculated with the assistance of a member of the Ptolemaic court who accompanied Cleopatra to Rome – the astronomer Sosigenes. Known as the 'Julian calendar' to posterity, it replaced the Roman lunar year with a year of 365 ¼ days. It was introduced on 1 January 45 BC and is still used by the Orthodox Church to this day. This was a beneficial reform as it kept the seasons in sync and prevented the calendar being manipulated for political reasons, namely adding extra months to a year (ostensibly to bring the calendar back in sync with the seasons, but really to extend someone's term in office).

---

[189] The Temple of Venus Genetrix was established by Julius Caesar in the newly created Forum of Caesar on 25 September 46 BC.

Although there is no hard evidence that Caesar intended to make himself a monarch, he was certainly seeking to gain political supremacy. He was also tone deaf to public opinion and did little to refute the rumours that he intended to overthrow the Republic. He started sitting in a golden throne and during the Lupercalia festival (on 15 February 44 BC) his right-hand man Mark Antony attempted to crown him with a royal diadem. Caesar rejected the offer (which had more than likely been staged at his request to assure the people he didn't desire to become king), but there were others who believed he did it to gauge the public reaction to such a move, and if there hadn't been such an uproar he would have gladly accepted the bestowal of kingship. Cicero, who was in attendance at the festival, attributed this brazen display of Hellenistic-style kingship to the influence of Cleopatra and made a subtle reference to the Egyptian queen when he mockingly asked where the diadem had come from.

Fears of Caesar's monarchical ambitions were further heightened when he had himself named 'dictator for life' (in January or February 44 BC), as well as by his plans to embark on a campaign against the Parthians.[190] The stated goal of avenging Crassus' death and vanquishing Rome's long-time enemy should have been a good thing for any patriotic Roman, but the problem was an oracle had claimed only a king could lead such an expedition. This hastened Caesar's demise, as his enemies in the Senate realised they would need to kill the dictator before he departed Rome on what was expected to be a lengthy campaign.

Cleopatra was in Rome on 15 March 44 BC when Caesar was assassinated by a group of conspirators during a meeting of the Senate. Without her main Roman ally and protector it was no longer safe for the Egyptian queen in the city. Nevertheless, she remained there until mid-April in the hope of securing recognition for Caesarion as Caesar's heir.

The wait ended in disappointment for Cleopatra when the contents of Caesar's will were revealed. Caesarion was not even mentioned in the will, which named Caesar's grandnephew Octavian as his primary heir.

Now it was clear that her son would not be inheriting anything, Cleopatra wisely opted to return to Egypt. Every moment she lingered in Rome, she was in danger: from her lover's assassins, who were on the prowl in the city; and from Octavian, who was on

---

[190] The title of dictator had been used in previous times of crisis, but only for a strictly limited period of time.

his way back to Italy to claim his inheritance and would undoubtedly regard Caesarion's mere existence as a threat to his status as Caesar's heir.

Not long after her arrival in Egypt, Cleopatra ordered the murder of her younger brother and co-regent Ptolemy XIV (presumably by poisoning) and named her three-year-old son Ptolemy XV (Caesarion) as co-regent in his place. The last surviving record that refers to Ptolemy XIV as being alive is an inscription dated 26 July 44 BC, so his death presumably took place later that summer. His assassination was essentially a pre-emptive strike, aimed at preventing ambitious courtiers from using him as a figurehead to oppose her rule or Ptolemy XIV himself challenging her dominance over the Egyptian government once he came of age. As Caesarion was her son and only three years old at the time, it would be far easier for Cleopatra to keep him under her control than her teenage brother. He became pharaoh in name only and all real authority remained in Cleopatra's hands.[191]

*

The murder of Caesar gave a whole new dimension to Cleopatra and Caesarion's association with Isis and Horus. In Egyptian mythology Isis' husband, Osiris, had been murdered (like Caesar). Osiris' son and heir, Horus (Caesarion), then avenged his father's death and became the ruler of the living. The Egyptian pharaohs consequently claimed they were descended from the god Horus. In Caesarion's case, however, the story highlighted that he was destined to succeed not just his mother in Egypt, but his father in Rome as well.

The most famous surviving depiction of Cleopatra and Caesarion together can be found on the rear wall of the Temple of Hathor at Dendera. This shows Egypt's co-regents making offerings to the gods, but clearly does not reflect their actual appearances as Caesarion is portrayed as a grown adult rather than a young child. Cleopatra fulfilled her traditional pharaonic duties by sponsoring various religious establishments. This included the usual suspects – numerous temples dedicated to Greek and Egyptian gods – as well as a synagogue for Alexandria's Jewish population and the impressive Caesareum of Alexandria (which was dedicated to the worship of her deceased lover, Julius Caesar).

---

[191] When Caesarion became his mother's co-regent he was added to the Ptolemaic cult as *Theos Philopator Philometor* ('the Father-loving Mother-loving God'). A massive relief was also added on the back of the temple of Hathor at Dendera, showing Caesarion, closely followed by Cleopatra, making offerings to the gods.

There is no doubt that the death of Julius Caesar left both Cleopatra and Egypt in a very dangerous situation. Now without her main Roman protector, she could only guess what approach his heirs on the one hand and his assassins on the other would take towards her kingdom. Worse still, her younger sister, Arsinoe IV, was still alive and well in Ephesus, and remained a potential figurehead for opponents of Cleopatra's regime.

In the immediate aftermath of Caesar's assassination an uneasy truce had been established between the Caesarians (led by Mark Antony) and the assassins (led by Brutus and Cassius). However, this soon broke down and resulted in yet another civil war.

In 43 BC the three most prominent Caesarians – Mark Antony, Octavian and Marcus Aemilius Lepidus – put their differences aside and formed an alliance against the common and growing threat posed by Caesar's assassins. Despite being known to historians as the Second Triumvirate, it was very different to its namesake, which had been established in 60 BC between Pompey, Crassus and Caesar. While the First Triumvirate had been an informal alliance between three powerful Romans (which allowed them to use their collective influence to dominate Roman political life), the Second Triumvirate received legal recognition. Its three members were elected to jointly rule the Republic for the next five years, and had a mandate to restore order to the Roman world and bring Caesar's assassins to justice.

The formation of the Second Triumvirate led to the outbreak of the Liberators' civil war between the Second Triumvirate and Caesar's assassins (led by Brutus and Cassius). As had been the case during previous Roman civil wars, this put Egypt in an incredibly difficult position. As the ruler of the wealthiest kingdom in the Mediterranean, Cleopatra was bound to receive requests for financial and military support off both sides, and if she failed to back the winning horse it could have fatal consequences for both her and her kingdom.

Little to Cleopatra's surprise, it was not long before she received requests for military aid off both sides – first from Gaius Cassius Longinus (one of the assassins) and soon after from Publius Cornelius Dolabella (who Mark Antony had recently appointed governor of Syria).

Cleopatra was understandably more inclined to support the Caesarians than the murderers of her lover and protector, but remained wary of Octavian (who she resented for robbing her son of his inheritance) and had little desire to get dragged into a costly and dangerous civil war. As a result of these considerations, she proceeded carefully. First she sent an excuse to Cassius, claiming she was dealing with too many domestic problems to be able to offer him any support. This was a legitimate excuse, because Egypt suffered from further food shortages between 43 BC and 41 BC, when the Nile inundated at unusually low levels once again. Nevertheless, she clearly had some resources to spare, judging from her decision to offer Dolabella limited support by sending him the four legions Caesar had left behind in Egypt, in exchange for him officially recognising Caesarion as the legitimate king of Egypt. This decision backfired when Cassius convinced these troops to defect to him in Palestine and Dolabella was killed by his own men. To make matters worse, Cleopatra's governor of Cyprus, Serapion, defied her orders by providing Cassius with a fleet of ships.

Cassius was angered by Cleopatra's refusal to assist him, but also emboldened by her excuse that her kingdom had been too severely afflicted by plague and famine to send help. Taking this as a sign that Egypt was in a weakened state (and therefore easy pickings), he started planning an invasion of that rich and bountiful country.

When these developments were brought to Cleopatra's attention, she realised Egypt would not be safe unless the assassins were defeated and became more open in her support for the Caesarians. She attempted to sail to Greece with her fleet in order to offer her personal assistance to Mark Antony and Octavian, but her ships were heavily damaged in a storm during the crossing, forcing her to return to Alexandria.

Despite Cleopatra's failure to provide any effective assistance to the Second Triumvirate, the Liberators' civil war was brought to a decisive conclusion in the autumn of 42 BC. In two separate military engagements in Greece, known collectively as the Battle of Philippi, Mark Antony and Octavian defeated Cassius and Brutus, leading to both of the assassins committing suicide.

Antony's heroics at Philippi (in comparison to Octavian's cowardice) made him the most powerful member of the Triumvirate (and therefore the Roman world). To reflect this, Antony and Octavian agreed to a redistribution of power in the aftermath of the battle. In the terms of this agreement, Antony received the eastern portion of the empire to govern (which was incredibly wealthy and had been largely subdued by Cassius); Octavian received most of the western part of the empire (along with the headache of disbanding the army and providing them with the money they were owed and lands on which to settle); and Lepidus (who had been left in charge of Rome while Antony and Octavian had embarked on their campaign against the assassins) was largely marginalised.

Soon after this had been decided, Octavian headed back to Italy, while Antony headed in the opposite direction to assert his authority over Rome's eastern territories. By the summer of 41 BC Antony had set up his headquarters at Tarsus (in southern Anatolia), from where he ruled over the eastern half of the Roman Empire, and it was at this time that his attention turned towards Egypt.

At some point after his arrival at Tarsus, Antony sent a series of written correspondences to Cleopatra, summoning her to meet him there to provide an explanation for why she had failed to give the Triumvirate any effective assistance during the civil war. However, the Egyptian queen played hard to get. As a queen, she was the one who summoned people, not the other way around, and was only persuaded to make the journey after Antony dispatched a diplomat (Quintus Dellius) to Alexandria.

Given the circumstances in which she was summoned to Tarsus, the visit could hardly have gone any better. Aiming to wow her Roman host into submission with an extravagant display of wealth and reagility, she arrived in Tarsus on a luxurious barge: adorned with purple sails and rowed by silver oars, and accompanied by the sound of music and the scent of incense. On board, the Egyptian queen was attended by beautiful boys dressed like cupids (who fanned their queen while she sat beneath a gilded canopy) and equally beautiful maids made to look like Nereids and Graces (who were steering at the rudders or working at the ropes). Meanwhile, Cleopatra herself was dressed as the goddess Aphrodite (or Isis, from the Egyptian perspective). Since taking control of the Roman east Antony had been worshipped there (particularly at Ephesus) as the Greek god Dionysus born anew. He must have been flattered by Cleopatra presenting this as a meeting between two gods, and captivated by the Egyptian queen's youth, wealth and charm.

On the day of her arrival Cleopatra invited Antony and his officers to a luxurious banquet on board her barge that evening, before hosting a second – even more extravagant – banquet on a subsequent evening. Antony tried to outdo her by hosting one of his own, but failed. Rather than being angered by this, he jokingly accepted that he had been bested, and Cleopatra soon managed to convince him that she had not supported Cassius during the civil war by arguing the Roman troops she had dispatched had been sent to assist Dolabella.

Once Cleopatra had successfully quashed the accusations against her, she formed a mutually beneficial political alliance with Antony, as well as starting an affair with him. Cleopatra was in need of a new Roman protector now Caesar was dead, and Antony – who had emerged from the Battle of Philippi as the most powerful man in Rome and the ruler of the eastern half of the empire (in Egypt's backyard) – was the obvious choice.

At the time Antony was planning a military campaign against Parthia to avenge Crassus' death, follow through with the expedition Caesar had been planning, and – most importantly – secure his place as the preeminent member of the Second Triumvirate by gloriously defeating Rome's most dangerous enemy. In order to fund this he was in desperate need of Cleopatra's wealth. He also required a forward base in the eastern Mediterranean to launch such a large campaign, and Egypt was an ideal place to have this. As Cleopatra was eager to gain Antony's favour, she agreed to assist him in his war against Parthia. In return, she persuaded Antony (who was now in control of Ephesus) to have her sister, Arsinoe IV, put to death. Given that Arsinoe was living under the protection of the Temple of Artemis at the time, her murder caused a major scandal, but was well worth the fallout for Cleopatra, who had now removed the last major rival claimant to her throne. As an added sweetener, Antony also gave Cleopatra the opportunity to get revenge on her rebellious ex-governor of Cyprus, Serapion, by having him apprehended in Tyre, where he had been seeking refuge since the defeat of Brutus and Cassius. Serapion was then handed over to the Egyptian queen, who presumably had him executed.

While gaining Antony's favour strengthened Cleopatra's hold on power by keeping her kingdom on Rome's good side and eliminating a dangerous rival, it also suited her long-term ambition to rebuild her ancestors' lost empire. As the triumvir in charge of the eastern half of Rome's empire, Antony was the only person with the authority to restore former Ptolemaic territories that had since fallen into Roman hands to Cleopatra – and in the not too distant future he would start doing precisely that.

*

Before Cleopatra returned home from Tarsus, she continued to build on her relationship with Mark Antony by inviting him to visit Alexandria. The triumvir accepted the invitation and had arrived in the Egyptian capital by November 41 BC.

Unlike Caesar, Antony received a warm welcome from the populace – for a number of reasons. The people of Alexandria had not forgotten his heroic actions during Ptolemy XII's invasion of Egypt, when he had distinguished himself by persuading the vengeful king to show mercy to the inhabitants of Pelusium and arranged an honourable burial for Berenice IV's slain husband. He maintained this favourable image by travelling to Egypt without a large military force and making an effort to assimilate with the local culture.

Throughout the winter of 41/40 BC Cleopatra treated her Roman guest to the same lavish hospitality he had received during the banquets on her barge at Tarsus. Contrary to the popular perception that he was neglectful of his duties at this time, the Egyptian alliance was well worth his time, and he delegated the responsibility of keeping the empire's eastern frontiers secure.

Nevertheless, despite the political component to their relationship, Antony and Cleopatra do seem to have genuinely enjoyed each other's company. They are reported to have spent the winter of 41/40 BC indulging in a life of leisure and luxury. Clearly they were engaged in a love affair by this point and it was during this time that they formed a society called the 'Inimitable Livers' with some of their close friends. Its members engaged in all sorts of extravagant behaviour – feasting, heavy drinking and debauchery – and sometimes played pranks or took part in games and contests. Most famously, Antony, Cleopatra and their fellow society members allegedly enjoyed wandering around Alexandria incognito and carrying out all sorts of pranks on the city's residents.

Alas, the fun and games soon came to an end.

By the spring of 40 BC Antony was compelled to leave Egypt to deal with the growing threat posed by the Parthians. Earlier that year the Parthian king Orodes II had ordered an invasion of Rome's eastern provinces. The invasion was led by his son Pacorus I and the Pompeian general Quintus Labienus, and their forces had made rapid progress: overrunning the Levant and a large portion of Asia Minor. Even more worryingly, they defeated and killed the Roman governor of Syria, Lucius Decidius Saxa, who had been appointed to the positon by Antony just a year before.

Now the governor of Syria was dead, the situation required Antony's direct attention. Antony and Cleopatra would not see each other for another three years, although they kept in touch through written correspondences and Cleopatra may have had a spy in

Antony's camp to keep her informed on any developments. Most significantly of all though, Cleopatra was pregnant by the time her lover departed and gave birth to twins in late 40 BC. Unlike Caesar with Caesarion, Antony immediately recognised them as his children and their names – Alexander Helios ('Sun') and Cleopatra Selene ('Moon') – symbolised both societal rejuvenation and Cleopatra's hope that Antony would follow in Alexander the Great's footsteps by conquering the Parthians.

Shortly after Antony set off to counter the Parthian threat, he found himself being diverted westwards in response to a failed rebellion in Italy. Known as the Perusine War (41-40 BC), it had started when his wife (Fulvia) and brother (Lucius Antonius) undermined Octavian's attempts to settle the veterans from the Battle of Philippi upon his return to Italy and stirred up unrest against him in the hope of making Antony the undisputed master of Rome. Fulvia was an ambitious individual and therefore may have acted alone (without Antony's say-so), but it is also true that Antony did not tell her to stop what she was doing and it is highly unlikely that Fulvia would have gone through with the rebellion if Antony had sent her an explicit order not to undermine Octavian.

In any event, the conflict came to an end when Octavian besieged Fulvia and Lucius Antonius at Perusia (present-day Perugia, Italy), which resulted in Fulvia fleeing to Greece and Lucius Antonius surrendering.

Antony met his wife in Greece sometime after she went into exile, but it was not a happy reunion. By then Fulvia was poorly, and her condition can hardly have been helped by the fury of her husband, who scolded her for her actions and then swiftly resumed his journey to Italy.

Not long after this Fulvia conveniently died in Sicyon (in Greece), which allowed Antony and Octavian to pin the blame for the war on Fulvia and paved the way for the two pre-eminent triumvirs to be reconciled through the Treaty of Brundisium (in September 40 BC). In recognition of Octavian's growing power since the Battle of Philippi, the agreement consolidated Antony's hold on Rome's territories east of the Ionian Sea, but compelled him to surrender his authority over Italia, Hispania and Gaul in the west of the empire. This was aimed at reducing the risk of conflict between Antony and Octavian by giving them two clearly-defined spheres of influence (with Antony in control of the East and Octavian in control of the West). In a further attempt to ensure the peace endured, Antony agreed to marry Octavian's sister Octavia.

After Antony and Octavia's wedding, the newlyweds departed for Athens, which served as Antony's headquarters for much of the next two years.[192] This must have come as a bitter blow to Cleopatra. She quite naturally regarded Octavia as a rival for Antony's affections from this point onwards and relations seem to have soured between Antony and the Egyptian queen. Nevertheless, Cleopatra remained the richest ruler in the Mediterranean, and she would not have to wait long before he came crawling back to her.

*

The three years that followed Antony's departure from Alexandria were unusually peaceful by the standards of Egypt's recent turbulent history. It was noticeably lacking in war and intrigue, and nature also took a turn for the better. The inundation of the Nile returned to normal levels, which brought the recent famine to an end and allowed agricultural production to increase.

The sudden restoration of peace, stability and productivity might have allowed the Egyptian economy to boom once more, was it not for the vast sums of money the kingdom still owed Rome from Ptolemy XII's reign, which had stripped the royal treasury bare. In an attempt at alleviating the economic crisis, Cleopatra debased silver coinage from 90 percent precious metal to 30 percent precious metal. Eventually, most silver coins were removed from circulation, and moving forward the vast majority of coinage was minted in bronze.

In addition to the economy, Cleopatra also had religious affairs to attend to. In July 41 BC, while she had been meeting with Mark Antony at Tarsus, the High Priest of Ptah, Pasherienptah III, had died. It was not until 39 BC that she got around to appointing his successor. Predictably, the position was given to Pasherienptah III's son, Imhotep-Pedubast, even though he was only seven years old at the time.

Shortly before this, in December 40 BC, the future king of Judea, Herod, had sought asylum at Cleopatra's court in Alexandria. Herod was a son of Antipater the Idumaean (who had come to Caesar and Cleopatra's aid during the siege of Alexandria) and had been appointed tetrarch of Judea (along with his brother Phasael) by Mark Antony in 41 BC. Just a year later, Antigonus II Mattathias (a nephew of the reigning High Priest of Judea, Hyrcanus II) had allied himself with the Parthians, who helped him to usurp

---

[192] Mark Antony and Octavia had two daughters together – Antonia the Elder (in 39 BC) and Antonia Minor (in 36 BC).

his uncle's throne and install an anti-Roman government. Both Hyrcanus and Phasael were captured, leading to the former being mutilated and the latter committing suicide, but Herod managed to escape Jerusalem with his life.

During Herod's brief stay in Alexandria, Cleopatra offered him a military position, but he requested to be provided with a passage to Rome instead and the Egyptian queen consented to his request.

Upon arriving in Rome, Herod appealed to Octavian and Mark Antony for assistance so he could attempt to retake Judea. As Judea was now in the hands of a Parthian ally, the two triumvirs arranged for Herod to be appointed king of the Jews by the Senate and gladly provided him with the necessary military support to gain control of his kingdom, which led to Antigonus II's defeat and execution in 37 BC.

By installing Herod as a client ruler in Judea, the Romans hoped to use him as a counterbalance to Cleopatra's influence in the East. Given that Herod's newly established kingdom contained former Ptolemaic territories, his appointment as king of Judea conflicted with Cleopatra's desire to rebuild the Ptolemaic empire and would bring the two monarchs into conflict with each other in the years that followed.

*

Despite being disappointed by Antony's long absence and his marriage to Octavian's sister, Cleopatra must surely have predicted that Antony would eventually find himself in need of her money again and come back to her. That time finally came in 37 BC, when Antony prepared to embark on his long-awaited Parthian campaign.

Before Antony was able to dedicate his attention to the Parthians he had to secure an extension to the Second Triumvirate's authority, which had officially expired on 1 January 37 BC. Later that year, Octavia acted as a mediator between her brother and husband in a meeting at Tarentum that resulted in Octavian and Mark Antony agreeing to extend the triumvirate for a further five years. As part of these negotiations, Octavian promised to provide Antony with two legions for his planned campaign against the Parthians, and Octavia provided him with a further thousand troops. However, Octavian never honoured this pledge and Antony received virtually no support off his brother-in-law for his military expedition.

Once the Treaty of Tarentum had been sealed (in the summer or early autumn of 37 BC), Antony headed east to Antioch, where he prepared to invade the Parthian

Empire. By now it was clear that he would not be receiving any effective support off Octavian, but he was reluctant to delay his campaign any longer, so he summoned Cleopatra to meet him at the city in the autumn of 37 BC.

Cleopatra travelled to Antioch with her three-year-old twins Alexander Helios and Cleopatra Selene, giving Antony the chance to meet his children for the first time. It was probably at this time that the twins received the bynames 'Helios' and 'Selene', which reflected their parents' grand plans for the future.

Antony knew he would need Egypt's resources to fight such an expensive campaign and tried to butter up the Egyptian queen by granting her a number of Roman territories in the eastern Mediterranean. In the west Cleopatra received Cyrene and the Cretan cities of Itanos and Olous. In the east these acquisitions included most of Phoenicia (excluding the coastal cities of Tyre and Sidon), part of Coele-Syria along the upper Orontes River, the area around the Palestinian city of Jericho (which the Egyptian queen leased back to Herod), and some territory around the Gulf of Aqaba on the Red sea that belonged to the Nabataean Kingdom and included Ailana (present-day Aqaba, Jordan).[193] In addition to these territorial gains, Cleopatra was also allegedly gifted the contents of the Library of Pergamon, which contained approximately 200,000 volumes and was second only to the Library of Alexandria. If this is true, it may have been more compensation than a gift, as part of the Library of Alexandria's collection was reportedly destroyed by a fire set by Caesar during the siege of Alexandria (in 47 BC).

The concessions Cleopatra received off Antony in return for financial and military support in his Parthian expedition enabled her to give the impression to her subjects that she was rebuilding the Ptolemaic Kingdom's lost empire. To mark the beginning of this new age, she started double dating her coinage in 36 BC – with the sixteenth year of her reign also being numbered the first. However, these grants were far less significant than Cleopatra wanted them to appear. The territorial 'gifts' were part of a broader attempt by Antony to stabilise the Roman east by installing new client rulers who would be loyal to him, and the lands Cleopatra received continued to be administered by Roman officials.

Nevertheless, Octavian did not hesitate to attempt to turn public opinion against Antony in Rome by presenting his actions as empowering a foreign queen at the

---

[193] The land Cleopatra received around Jericho was home to lucrative balsam and date groves and caused a great deal of friction with King Herod.

expense of the Republic. In 35 BC, he stepped up his attacks on Cleopatra by ordering statues to be erected of his wife (Livia) and sister (Octavia) to rival the one Caesar had dedicated to Cleopatra.[194] This great honour was accompanied by both women being granted the unprecedented privilege of *sacrosanctitas* (sacrosanctity), which was used to declare a temple, sacred object or person inviolable.[195] If someone harmed them, they would be considered to have acted against the gods, and anyone who killed the offender would be exempt from punishment and praised for performing a sacred duty. As an added bonus, Octavia and Livia were also made immune from *tutela*, which referred to the requirement for all Roman women (with the notable exception of the Vestal Virgins) to have a male guardian to manage their affairs on their behalf. This exemption meant Octavia and Livia were able to manage their own finances, giving them an unusual amount of independence.

*

When Antony finally departed on his Parthian campaign, Cleopatra accompanied him as far as the Euphrates. They had clearly resumed their love affair during their reunion at Antioch, because Cleopatra was pregnant with another of Antony's children by the time she returned to Alexandria. She gave birth to this child in the late summer or early autumn of 36 BC and named him Ptolemy Philadelphus, after one of the dynasty's most successful rulers (Ptolemy II).

*

Antony managed to assemble a vast army for his Parthian campaign, but it didn't prevent the whole enterprise from being a complete disaster. He was treacherously abandoned by his 'ally', the Armenian king Artavasdes II, and made things worse for himself by making a series of strategic errors. As events turned out, his army didn't even make it into Parthian territory and the expedition only lasted a few months. The furthest his invasion force got was the city of Phraaspa in Media Atropatene, which was an ally of Parthia. He spent the summer and autumn of 36 BC engaging in a siege of the city, but failed to make any headway and was compelled to withdraw before the arrival of winter.

---

[194] The first Roman woman to have a statue dedicated to them while they were alive was Cornelia (a daughter of the renowned general Scipio Africanus).
[195] The privilege of sacrosanctity had previously only been granted to tribunes.

During his retreat back to friendly territory Antony lost approximately a third of his army to disease, the bitter winter weather, and enemy attacks. This amounted to approximately 30,000 troops – ironically even higher losses than Crassus had sustained at the Battle of Carrhae (which Antony's campaign was supposed to have avenged).

Antony's depleted and dispirited army finally staggered into the coastal settlement of Leukokome (near present-day Beirut, Lebanon) in December 36 BC. He set up a camp here, where he licked his wounds and drowned his sorrows while he eagerly awaited the money, clothing and supplies he had requested off Cleopatra.

When Cleopatra arrived, the provisions she brought with her provided some much-needed relief to Antony's demoralised troops. However, the Egyptian queen had always been sceptical about the Parthian campaign and showed her disapproval by failing to bring enough money to pay the soldiers' wages.

Instead of resuming his war against Parthia straight away, Antony allowed himself be persuaded by Cleopatra to return to Alexandria. This was the logical thing to do, as it would give him time to regroup his forces and the opportunity to meet his newborn son, Ptolemy Philadelphus. It certainly made more sense than risking a second defeat by attacking the Parthians before he was ready or going to Rome (where his botched campaign would surely expose him to ridicule at best and danger at worst).

Cleopatra was not the only person who answered Antony's appeals for help in the aftermath of his failed campaign. Back in Rome, Octavian gave Octavia permission to take a force of 2,000 soldiers to her husband. These reinforcements were long overdue and significantly less than the number of troops Octavian had promised to provide Antony with under the terms of the Treaty of Tarentum. Therefore, Octavian's actions should not be interpreted as an act of charity or a gesture of goodwill. On the contrary, he was trying to put his brother-in-law in a difficult position, and essentially left Antony with two choices (both of which would work in Octavian's favour). The first option was to accept the reinforcements, thereby acknowledging he was incapable of fighting the Parthians without his fellow triumvir's support and writing off the troops Octavian had failed to provide. Alternatively, Antony could cut off his nose to spite his face and reject the offer, but by doing this Octavian would be able to turn public opinion against Antony by portraying him as wronging his wife and being scornful of his brother-in-law's generosity.

When Antony received word off his wife that she was in Athens with these reinforcements, he ordered her to send the troops and supplies to him but to not venture any further east herself. Various ancient sources report Cleopatra had a key role to play in Antony's rejection of Octavia, as the Egyptian queen feared if Antony met his wife in person she might succeed in winning back his affections and rekindling their relationship.

In any event, Octavia obeyed her husband's command and returned to Rome, where her overjoyed brother told her to leave Antony's household and move in with him. Octavia rejected her brother's orders and continued to reside in Antony's residence as a dutiful wife and mother, which was fine by him as it showed Antony up as a neglectful husband.

To make matters worse for Antony, while his military fortunes sagged and his public image plummeted, Octavian was emboldened by a series of victories that enabled him to eliminate his rivals in the West. Still sickly, but no longer so young and inexperienced, Octavian succeeded in removing the third member of the triumvirate, Lepidus, who he stripped of his offices and sent into exile in 36 BC. He also put an end to the rebellious activities of Pompey's last surviving son, Sextus Pompey, who his close friend – the talented general Agrippa – defeated at the naval Battle of Naulochus on 3 September 36 BC.[196]

Unfortunately for Antony, this shift in the balance of power was not temporary. His fortunes continued to decline for the rest of his life while Octavian's steadily rose – with fatal consequences.

*

In 35 BC Antony decided to launch a punitive attack against Armenia (whose king had betrayed him during the Parthian expedition) rather than immediately embarking on a second campaign against Parthia.

Before this took place, Antony sent Quintus Dellius to the Armenian court to propose an alliance that would be sealed by a marriage between Antony and Cleopatra's son, Alexander Helios, and a daughter of the Armenian king Artavasdes II. When Artavasdes rejected the proposal, Antony needed no further encouragement to invade

---

[196] Sextus Pompey managed to escape the Battle of Naulochus, but was captured and executed in 35 BC.

Armenia (in the spring of 34 BC). Armenia was a strategically important kingdom that could be used as a secure Roman base in a future Parthian campaign, but was by no means a great power and was quickly overwhelmed by Antony's forces, which seized control of the capital city and took the king and most of his family prisoner.

Even though the Armenian campaign was only a minor victory, Antony tried to play up its importance (and downplay the significance of his defeat against Parthia) by organising a spectacular festival that resembled a Roman triumph.[197] When he arrived back in Alexandria (in the autumn of 34 BC), he entered the city in style. Riding on a chariot and in the guise of Dionysus, he was accompanied by an extravagant military parade that included his victorious troops, the spoils of war, and his royal prisoners bound in golden chains. Eventually the procession reached Cleopatra, who was sitting on a golden throne at the temple of Serapis. When the Armenian king and his family were presented to the Egyptian queen, they refused an order to prostrate themselves before her. They earned her wrath for this act of defiance, but the festivities continued as if nothing had happened, and the Armenian royal family were imprisoned.

The festival's grand finale is known to posterity as the 'Donations of Alexandria' and took place in Alexandria's gymnasium, where the city's residents were summoned to observe a monumental ceremony presided over by Antony. While crowds of people squeezed their way inside, Antony and Cleopatra were sitting on golden thrones on a silver platform. They were dressed as Dionysus-Osiris and Isis-Aphrodite respectively, and were accompanied by their children – Caesarion, Alexander Helios, Cleopatra Selene and Ptolemy Philadelphus – who sat on slightly smaller thrones beside them.

When Antony spoke to the assembled crowd, he started by bestowing the title 'Queen of Kings' on Cleopatra and 'King of Kings' on Caesarion, before progressing to confirm them as co-regents of the traditional Ptolemaic domains of Egypt, Cyprus and Cyrenaica, as well as Coele-Syria.[198] This was fairly uncontroversial, but he then proceeded to dramatically increase the Ptolemaic Kingdom's sphere of influence by

---

[197] When news of this spectacle reached Rome, it was heavily criticised, as triumphs for successful military campaigns were supposed to be held in Rome.
[198] The title King of Kings was most commonly associated with the monarchs of the Achaemenid Empire (550-330 BC). By uniting Achaemenid and ancient pharaonic traditions, Cleopatra was asserting her sovereignty over the lands in Asia that were granted to her children during this ceremony, as well as lands in the region that she and Antony hoped to acquire in the future.

granting extensive territories to each of his children with Cleopatra in turn. His eldest son by the Egyptian queen, Alexander Helios, who was about six years old and dressed in Persian attire for the occasion, was declared king of Armenia, Media and Parthia (even though the latter two remained unconquered).[199] The couple's second son, Ptolemy Philadelphus – who was just two years old and dressed like a Macedonian – was then named king of Syria and Cilicia, and both boys were hailed as 'Kings of Kings'. Lastly, their daughter Cleopatra Selene was given Crete and Cyrene to rule over.

Despite the large swathes of territory that were granted during this ceremony, the 'Donations of Alexandria' were far less significant than they initially appear. Some of the territories it concerned weren't even under Roman control and those that were would continue to be administered by their respective client rulers. From this point onwards, the client rulers would merely have to owe allegiance to whichever of Antony and Cleopatra's children had been assigned their lands, and Alexander Helios, Cleopatra Selene and Ptolemy Philadelphus in turn owed Cleopatra and Caesarion allegiance for their possessions. Of course, Antony was the one who was in charge overall, as it was his military muscle that was propping up their empire, so Rome had not lost any power or influence as a result of this arrangement. Nevertheless, many Romans were horrified by the prospect of Roman lands being given to a foreign queen, and it was clear to Antony's enemies that he desired to establish a royal dynasty and rule over the civilised world through his extended family. For this reason, when Antony made the imprudent decision to send news of the Donations to Rome and requested that the territorial grants be ratified by the Senate, his allies in the city suppressed the information, knowing Octavian would use it against him if it fell into his hands.

Although it is unclear if Antony and Cleopatra ever got married, they may have gone through some form of marriage ceremony at the same time as the Donations. Because Antony was still married to Octavia, the union would not have been recognised under Roman law, but it would have been acceptable in Egypt due to there being a precedent for bigamy amongst Hellenistic rulers.

Even if this never happened, he caused plenty of damage to his already shaky relationship with Octavian by declaring Caesarion to be Caesar's true heir. Given that

---

[199] In 33 BC Alexander Helios was betrothed to Iotapa (the daughter of the king of Media Atropatene, Artavasdes I).

Octavian's claim to authority was based on his status as Caesar's adopted son, Antony's decision caused a fatal breach in relations with his brother-in-law that would never be healed.

*

Relations between Mark Antony and Octavian rapidly deteriorated after the Donations of Alexandria. On 1 January 33 BC Octavian began his term as consul by delivering a speech to the Senate in which he claimed Antony had been enslaved by his passion for Cleopatra and was undermining Rome's freedoms and territorial integrity by ceding vast swathes of land to a foreign monarch.[200] This marked the beginning of a prolonged propaganda war between Octavian and Antony, during which they traded insults and accusations, and spread gossip and misinformation. While Antony accused Octavian of acting unlawfully (by preventing him from exercising his right to raise troops in Italy and removing Lepidus from the triumvirate without his consent), Octavian returned fire with his own list of accusations. This included the fact that Antony had waged war on Armenia without permission and failed to share the spoils of the campaign, declared Caesarion to be Caesar's rightful heir (even though the boy had no inheritance rights under Roman law), and neglected his lawful wife – Octavia – in favour of his liaisons with the Egyptian queen.

Soon their attacks on each other ventured beyond politics and became personal, causing the private correspondences between the two triumvirs to rapidly degenerate into the sort of language that could be expected on a school playground. Antony mocked Octavian for his humble origins and cowardice in war, saying he had only been successful because he had his friend Marcus Agrippa do the fighting on his behalf. Meanwhile, Octavian reminded Antony that he was past his best and no longer capable of winning athletic competitions, unless exotic dancing and the erotic arts counted. These were just a few of the many insults that were hurled on both sides, in a feud where there was no such thing as stooping too low. This is highlighted by the Roman historian Suetonius, who quoted from a letter supposedly written by Antony and addressed to Octavian: 'What has come over you? Do you object to my sleeping with Cleopatra? But we are married; and it is not even as though this were anything

---

[200] While it was customary for both consuls to serve a full year term, Octavian only served as consul for one day – 1 January 33 BC. For the rest of 33 BC he arranged for a number of his supporters to serve as consul for short stints. He knew he would need as much proconsular support as possible in the looming conflict with Antony and by doing this he was able to elevate the status of a large number of allies in a short space of time.

new – the affair started nine years ago. And what about you? Are you faithful to Livia Drusilla? My congratulations if, when this letter arrives, you have not been in bed with Tertullia, or Terentilla, or Rufilla, or Salvia Titisenia – or all of them. Does it really matter so much where, or with whom, you perform the sexual act?'

Back in Egypt, Cleopatra was busy ensuring Antony's Roman allies remained loyal by offering them hefty bribes. The most notable of these was a royal decree (dated 23 February 33 BC) in which Cleopatra granted extensive tax privileges to a Roman general named Publius Canidius, who was Antony's right-hand man and would later serve as the commander of his land forces at the Battle of Actium. The edict allowed Canidius to export 10,000 sacks of wheat from Egypt and import 5,000 amphorae of wine into the country duty free each year. Additionally, both Canidius and his tenants were exempt from paying any taxes on his Egyptian lands.

This document was written on papyrus and addressed to a senior government official, who would have been responsible for notifying other public servants of the exemptions. It was signed off with the word *ginesthoi* ('make it so'), which was in different handwriting to the rest of the text and therefore may have been written by the Egyptian queen herself. If this is true, then it is the only extant document containing something written by Cleopatra's hand. However, it is more likely that it was written by an official who was authorised to sign on her behalf.

*

The authority Antony and Octavian had exercised under the Second Triumvirate officially ended on 31 December 33 BC. Fortunately for Antony, both of the incoming consuls for 32 BC – Gaius Sosius and Gnaeus Domitius Ahenobarbus – were loyal to him. Upon assuming office, Sosius delivered an impassioned speech before the Senate, denouncing Octavian and introducing legislation against him. Technically, Octavian was now a private citizen, as he no longer held a public office, but that did not deter him from attending the next meeting of the Senate accompanied by armed guards. Hoping to intimidate his opponents into submission, Octavian returned fire by making some accusations of his own against the consuls.

Antony's supporters in Rome got the message that they were no longer safe in the city. Consequently, both consuls and over 200 senators (approximately one third of the Senate) fled to Ephesus, where they joined forces with Antony.

As the Roman world teetered on the edge of civil war, Antony and Cleopatra departed Alexandria and began assembling a large naval force at Ephesus (at the beginning of 32 BC). Antony called on all of Rome's client rulers in the East to contribute ships and troops, and they duly responded with offers of assistance. Given that Cleopatra was the wealthiest of these rulers and had the most at stake in the struggle against Octavian, she was predictably the biggest donor – providing Antony with 200 out of the 800 naval ships he managed to obtain, as well as 20,000 talents for the war chest.

Despite the massive financial and military contributions the Egyptian queen was making, many of the senators who had fled Rome to join forces with Antony were wary of the damage her presence would inflict on the war effort. These concerns were voiced by the exiled consul Ahenobarbus, who warned Antony that allowing Cleopatra to take part in the campaign would confirm Octavian's propaganda – that Cleopatra, a foreign female monarch, was using Antony as a tool to dominate Rome – in the eyes of the Roman public. However, Cleopatra had no intention of going anywhere. Octavian's destruction was too important to her personal interests not to oversee the campaign directly and she stubbornly rejected Antony's requests that she return to Egypt. Given that her coffers were bankrolling the war effort, she had too much leverage for Antony to force her to return home, and at least one Roman – Publius Canidius Crassus – spoke up on her behalf too.

At some point in April 32 BC, Antony and Cleopatra moved their headquarters from Ephesus to Samos, where they continued their recruitment efforts, and from there they travelled west to Athens in May or June. It was during their stay in Athens that Antony finally decided to sever his remaining ties with Octavian by sending an official declaration of divorce to Octavia and ordering her to leave his home in Rome. Even though he saw little advantage in maintaining his links with Octavian any longer, by shunning his wife he certainly didn't do himself any favours in the ongoing battle to win over public opinion. After being turfed out of Antony's home, Octavia not only continued to carry out her duties by looking after her children with Antony, but also continued to take care of Antony's children from his first marriage (to Fulvia). This enabled Octavian to present his sister as a virtuous Roman wife who had been wronged by her husband. At the same time, he was able to turn Antony's close association with Cleopatra against him by presenting him to the Roman people as someone who had been put under a spell by the Egyptian queen, abandoned his Roman heritage, and adopted a dissolute Hellenistic lifestyle. By contrast, Octavian branded himself as an upstanding Roman and a defender of the Republic.

Antony's association with Cleopatra was not just losing him support in Rome. His decision to allow the Egyptian queen to be directly involved in the looming war caused many prominent Romans who had joined his army to defect. Two of the most high profile deserters in the summer of 32 BC were Lucius Munatius Plancus and Marcus Titius, which cost Antony a lot more than just their military services.

When Plancus and Titius arrived in Rome, they advised Octavian that Antony's will – which had been left with the Vestal Virgins for safekeeping – would cause a scandal if its contents became public knowledge. Eager to inflict further damage on his rival's reputation, Octavian did not hesitate to seize the will from the Temple of Vesta by force. Even though such behaviour was a flagrant breach of both sacred and legal rights, Octavian judged – correctly – that it would inflict far greater damage on Antony once his will was revealed to the people of Rome.

As soon as Octavian had the will in his possession, he highlighted its most incriminating parts, which he read out before the Senate. While the Roman public were already aware of most of these things – such as Antony recognising Caesarion as Caesar's heir and seeking to gain legal recognition for the Donations of Alexandria – the new and dramatic revelation was that Antony wanted to be buried in Alexandria and planned to make the city the new capital of the Roman world. These clauses may have been added by Octavian to incriminate his former brother-in-law and convince the public that Antony's allegiance was now to the depraved and effeminate east, not Rome. Nevertheless, no matter what Antony's wishes really were, the revelation had the desired effect of enraging the people of Rome. To remove any doubt as to where his own loyalties lay, Octavian decided to start building his own mausoleum at the Campus Martius in Rome, and he strengthened his legal position by getting himself elected consul for 31 BC.

Even though Antony's will had sparked outrage, Octavian was well aware that Antony still had many Roman supporters and that the Roman people were wary with the seemingly endless succession of civil wars. Therefore, he pushed for a declaration of war against Cleopatra rather than Antony, which would allow him to present it as a struggle against a foreign queen who had aspirations to take over the Roman world.

When the Senate finally declared war on Cleopatra (in October 32 BC) it was on tenuous grounds, given that the Egyptian queen had proven herself to be a competent, loyal and useful client ruler. The official justification was that she was providing military aid to Antony, who was a private citizen now he was no longer a triumvir. In reality though, the declaration of war had been made at Octavian's insistence. This masterstroke left Antony with two options, both of which would spell the end of his political career and maybe his life: turn his back on Cleopatra and abandon everything he had built (which would allow Octavian to become the dominant figure in the Roman world), or support her and be declared a traitor.

As far as Antony was concerned the first choice wasn't even an option. He would not face the dishonour of surrendering to his bitter rival or of abandoning his closest ally. Confident in his abilities as the greatest general of his generation, Antony would let his – and the entire Roman world's – fate to be decided in battle.

*

War finally broke out between Antony and Octavian at the beginning of 31 BC and was centred on the western coast of Greece.

In the early autumn of 32 BC, Antony and his grand armada had sailed around the coast of the Peloponnese to the Ionian Sea, bringing him within range of the Italian port cities of Tarentum and Brundisium. Unfortunately for Antony, his camp continued to suffer from internal divisions and there was disagreement over what approach to take in the war. Initially, Antony favoured attacking Italy itself. However, Cleopatra wanted to fight a defensive war in Greece where it would be easier to defend Egypt, and in the end her strategy was adopted.

While the Egyptian queen's forceful personality might have been a contributing factor to Antony's U-turn, it was mainly due to practical considerations. Now Cleopatra was going to be accompanying her lover on the campaign, it would be a tall task to invade Italy until Octavian's forces had been defeated as the presence of the Egyptian queen would be sure to unite all the inhabitants of Italy against Antony.

When it became clear that Octavian was not willing to risk intervening with his fleet just yet, Antony and Cleopatra sailed their fleet into the Ambracian Gulf, where it would be shielded from the weather and enemy attacks. The two lovers then headed north to spend the winter of 32/31 BC in Patrai, but left most of their forces behind in the gulf and spread the rest across the west coast of the Peloponnese.

By the time they returned to their fleet in the Ambracian Gulf, many of their men had perished from the inhospitable conditions there, reducing the strength and morale of their forces for the struggle that lay ahead. To make matters worse, Octavian's army had crossed over from Italy in the early stages of 31 BC and settled on the northern side of the gulf, opposite Antony and Cleopatra's forces, which were based in Actium on the southern side.

Until now, Antony and Cleopatra had benefitted from the support of various allied client rulers, who had probably calculated they would come out on the winning side. However, as Antony engaged in a series of futile skirmishes with Octavian in the vicinity of Actium throughout the summer of 31 BC it became apparent that his chances of emerging victorious were dwindling and he suffered from numerous defections. King Herod of Judea (who had been on bad terms with Cleopatra for a number of years over competing territorial claims) used an earthquake in Judea as an excuse not to show up. The Nabataean ruler Malichus I (who was still bitter about Antony ceding his territories in the Gulf of Aqaba along the Red Sea to Cleopatra, and angry with the Egyptian queen for instigating a war between Herod and his kingdom) also failed to turn up. Amyntas of Galatia and Deiotaros of Paphlagonia were present, but defected to Octavian before the Battle of Actium. And Antony was even abandoned by some of his closest Roman companions. This included Quintus Dellius, who had been busy recruiting reinforcements for Antony in Macedonia and Thrace and justified his defection by claiming Cleopatra was planning to have him murdered, and the former consul Gnaeus Domitius Ahenobarbus, who sailed across to Octavian in a small boat shortly before the Battle of Actium.

Antony was particularly upset by Ahenobarbus' decision to defect, but made the chivalrous decision to send to him all his attendants and baggage. Ahenobarbus apparently dwelled on his actions and did not take part in the battle as he died a few days after joining Octavian. The Greco-Roman historian Plutarch suggests his death was caused by 'the shame of his disloyalty and treachery being exposed'.

*

By September 31 BC Antony and Cleopatra's forces were desperately short of supplies, as a result of their fleet spending many months blockaded inside the Ambracian Gulf by Octavian and his talented admiral Agrippa. This brought the lovers under growing pressure to take decisive action before the arrival of winter.

In the weeks leading up to the most famous military confrontation of the age – the Battle of Actium – there was yet more division in Antony's camp over what strategy to adopt. The commander of Antony's land forces, Publius Canidius, suggested retreating inland, because Romans were most comfortable fighting on land. Seeing as this would have involved abandoning their navy (a large portion of which had been provided by Cleopatra) and it would be difficult to transport the Egyptian queen's treasure over the rugged terrain, Cleopatra strongly opposed this plan. Instead, Cleopatra insisted on fighting a naval battle, which would prevent Octavian's fleet from invading Egypt and give her the opportunity to escape with her war chest and as many of her ships as possible. This difference of opinion caused her previously amicable relationship with Canidius to break down, but as far as Cleopatra was concerned it was an acceptable price to pay for getting her own way.

Antony was eventually won over by Cleopatra's plan. Accepting that Octavian would have the upper hand as long as they remained where they were, he realised their best option was to try to break through the blockade and escape with their war chest and as many ships as possible, so they could regroup and live to fight another day.

Due to the amount of men Antony and Cleopatra had lost to disease, they no longer had sufficient crews for all their ships. Therefore, Antony ordered their excess ships to be burned and forcibly conscripted the local Greek population to serve as rowers or to carry supplies over the rugged mountainous terrain to his camp. As a consequence of this, Antony and Cleopatra's fleet was smaller than their enemy's. Nor were all of their crews fully trained, whereas Octavian had a fully professional force at his disposal. But these things were not too much of an issue, given that fighting a decisive battle was no longer their primary objective.

On 2 September 31 BC the long-anticipated Battle of Actium took place when Antony and Cleopatra's combined fleet sailed out of the Ambracian Gulf to confront Octavian's navy (which was being commanded by Agrippa). Cleopatra was put in command of 60 ships at the rear of the fleet and sailed aboard her flagship, the *Antonias* (easily identifiable by its distinctive purple sails). Some have argued she was put in this position to appease Antony's officers, who wanted the Egyptian queen to play a minimal role in the battle. This is probably true, but it also formed part of Antony and Cleopatra's prearranged strategy. Treasure had been loaded on board Cleopatra's ships on the night before the battle, as well as sails so they could make a quick getaway when the opportune moment arrived, and by remaining at the rear they would be able to use the rest of the fleet to shield them while they made their escape.

At some point in the afternoon, Cleopatra took advantage of a favourable change in wind to sail her portion of the fleet through an opening and retreat into the open sea.

Antony then abandoned his own ship in favour of a smaller, faster one and set sail after his lover, abandoning the bulk of his fleet to continue the battle without him.

The accounts of many Roman writers accuse Cleopatra of panicking in the battle and cowardly abandoning Antony. However, as previously mentioned, it is far more likely that this was part of a prearranged strategy to break the blockade Octavian had imposed and escape with their treasure and at least a portion of their fleet so they could continue the war in a more favourable location.

While this might have made sound strategic sense, Antony and Cleopatra's decision to abandon their navy in the middle of the battle had a devastating effect on morale. Although the battle continued for many hours after their departure, their navy surrendered the following morning, and within a few days their land forces had defected to Octavian too.[201]

*

As soon as Antony had caught up with Cleopatra, he boarded her flagship, but remained at the prow of the ship and didn't say a word to anyone. While the works of Roman propagandists claim he did this because he was angry about Cleopatra's cowardly actions, it is far more likely that he was depressed by the knowledge that he had abandoned his men in battle.

In any event, when the remnants of their fleet landed at Taenarum (on the southernmost point of the Peloponnese) two of Cleopatra's attendants – Iras and Charmian – helped reconcile her and Antony. They then continued their journey to Egypt, but parted ways when they landed at Paraitónion (present-day Mersa Matruh). From here Antony sailed on to Cyrene in order to seek the support of the Roman legions based there, while Cleopatra returned to Alexandria, hoping to reach the city before news of the disaster at Actium.

In a bold attempt at glossing over her defeat, when Cleopatra sailed into Alexandria she ensured her ships were richly decorated to give the impression she had won a stunning victory. If the truth of what had happened at Actium became public knowledge, Cleopatra feared her political opponents at home would use it to

---

[201] The commander of Antony's land forces, Publius Canidius, managed to escape to Egypt when his troops defected. However, he was only delaying the inevitable and was executed the following year (30 BC) when Octavian conquered the Ptolemaic Kingdom.

orchestrate a rebellion against her. Therefore, she did everything in her power to give an impression of business as usual. On the surface life went on as normal in the Egyptian capital and everyday government continued to function: with decrees being issued and taxes collected.

However, behind the scenes Cleopatra was making frantic preparations to escape Octavian's inevitable pursuit. The situation was so serious that she gave orders for what remained of her navy to be transported overland from the River Nile to the Red Sea, which would enable her to flee to India with her treasure. Unfortunately, she was forgetting that she had incurred the hostility of the region's Arab inhabitants (the Nabataeans) by persuading Antony to give her some of their territory in 37 BC and – more recently – instigating a war between their kingdom and Judea. Eager to get his revenge (and with the encouragement of Octavian's governor of Syria, Quintus Didius), the Nabataean king Malichus I gave orders for the ships to be burned before they could be launched, which thwarted Cleopatra's escape plan and left her trapped in Alexandria.

Now she had no way of escaping to India with her treasure, Cleopatra had little choice but to stay put and attempt to negotiate with Octavian. She tried to strengthen her hand by seeking the support of fellow eastern rulers, such as Artavasdes I of Media Atropatene, who she tried to ingratiate herself with by ordering the execution of his captive rival – the Armenian king Artavasdes II – and sending him his head. However, such gestures achieved little, as most rulers in the region realised it was only a matter of time before Octavian finished off the Egyptian queen and his former brother-in-law. This included Herod, who severed ties with Antony and Cleopatra when he travelled to Rhodes to meet Octavian. In a carefully stage-managed performance, the Judean ruler offered to resign his kingship. He stressed his loyalty to Antony and claimed the only reason why he had turned his back on his long-time ally was because of the malign influence of Cleopatra. The performance worked. Octavian was eager to isolate Antony and Cleopatra and deprive them of allies, so he allowed Herod to remain king of Judea in return for his submission.

With people deserting her left, right and centre and her options becoming increasingly limited, Cleopatra reportedly prepared herself for the worst case scenario by testing various poisons on prisoners to discover which would often the swiftest and most painless death while retaining a serene outward appearance.

Meanwhile, Antony's venture to Cyrene had yielded nothing but disappointment. The news of Octavian's victory at Actium had reached the governor of Cyrenaica, Lucius Pinarius, faster than Mark Antony, and even though Pinarius had been appointed to his position by Antony, he sensed his former ally's cause was doomed. Therefore, when Antony's messengers arrived at his court to seek the services of the four legions he had under his command, he ordered their execution and promptly defected to Octavian. He then gave the four legions to Octavian's ally, Gaius Cornelius Gallus, who used them to march on Alexandria from the west while Octavian approached from the east.

When Antony learned of Pinarius' defection he was so distraught that he contemplated committing suicide. Although his officers managed to talk him out of it and he returned safely to Alexandria, he was so depressed that he decided to live a hermit-like existence in an isolated shack on the island of Pharos rather than returning to Cleopatra. The hut Antony erected was appropriately nicknamed the *Timoneion*, after the Athenian philosopher Timon of Athens, who was renowned for his misanthropy.

Nevertheless, as a lover of luxury he was eventually persuaded to return to the comfort of Cleopatra's palace, where the defeated lovers endeavoured to spend what little time they had left living life to the full. Cleopatra made sure they celebrated Antony's fifty-third birthday in style, and they also organised a lavish festival to celebrate the coming-of-age of Cleopatra's eldest son, 16-year-old Caesarion, and Mark Antony's eldest son by Fulvia, Marcus Antonius Antyllus (who was a similar age).[202] Both boys were formally initiated into the ranks of the *ephebi* during this ceremony, which meant they were considered old enough for military service. Cleopatra hoped to use such royal spectacles to distract her subjects from their queen's dwindling fortunes, and it may also be an indication that she was preparing Caesarion to become Egypt's sole ruler in the event that she was forced to abdicate.

Meanwhile, Octavian was in no rush to finish off his opponents. In the aftermath of the Battle of Actium he focused on discharging the many thousands of surplus troops he had at his disposal now the bulk of Antony's army had defected to him. He also set about removing or securing the loyalty of the various client rulers in the East who had been appointed to their positions by Antony, although he had to make a brief return journey to Italy to suppress a mutiny amongst some of his soldiers at Brundisium.

---

[202] Marcus Antonius Antyllus was nicknamed 'Antyllus' by his father, which means 'the Archer'. However, some historians have argued that the name might actually be a corruption of 'Antonillus', which means 'little Antonius'.

After spending no longer than a month appeasing the mutinous soldiers in Italy, Octavian headed east again, where he spent some time on Rhodes.[203] During his time here, Antony and Cleopatra sent separate envoys to negotiate with him. Antony requested that he be allowed to retire from public life and live out the rest of his life in exile (preferably in Alexandria, or if that was not possible, in Athens), but was ignored by his former brother-in-law.[204] However, Octavian did reply to Cleopatra, who offered to abdicate in favour of her children and sent lavish gifts to Octavian, along with the promise of more money in the future. Unlike Antony (who had nothing left to offer), Cleopatra still possessed the largest stockpile of treasure outside Roman control, which explains why Octavian was more responsive to her. He said he would be happy with this arrangement as long as she arranged Antony's death, but Cleopatra did not agree to these terms, either because she was still loyal to Antony or did not trust Octavian to keep his word.

When Cleopatra's final envoy returned to Alexandria, Octavian dispatched a diplomat of his own to the Egyptian capital. This was a freedman named Thyrsus, who was tasked with persuading Cleopatra to kill Antony so her life and kingdom would be spared. The mission came to nothing when Antony suspected Thyrsus' foul intentions and had a violent reaction: giving orders for the diplomat to be flogged and sent back to his master empty-handed.

Now it had become clear that he wasn't going to achieve much by diplomatic means, Octavian finally moved to invade Egypt in the spring of 30 BC. On the way, he stopped at the port city of Ptolemais in Phoenicia, where King Herod offered him generous hospitality and provided his army with some much-needed supplies for their march through the desert. Octavian then closed in on Egypt from the east (Syria) at the same time as the four legions that Lucius Pinarius had surrendered to Cornelius Gallus attacked from the west (Cyrenaica). While Octavian secured the swift submission of the border city of Pelusium on Egypt's eastern frontier, in the west Gallus' army defeated Antony's forces near Paraitónion.

---

[203] It was during this stay on Rhodes that Octavian also received a visit off Herod, mentioned earlier in the chapter.
[204] Mark Antony's eldest son, Marcus Antonius Antyllus, was part of one of the three unsuccessful embassies sent to Octavian. Antyllus' father sent him with a large sum of money, hoping to secure peace, but Octavian knew he held all the cards and responded accordingly – sending the boy back to his father, but keeping the money.

On 29 July 30 BC the High Priest of Ptah, Imhotep, died at 16 years of age. While it is possible that his death was merely the result of illness or a weak constitution, it is far more likely that he was murdered by the Roman invaders. Octavian was determined to stamp out all traces of Ptolemaic rule in Egypt and the High Priests of Ptah had been a key ally of the Ptolemaic monarchy since the dynasty had been founded and exerted great influence over the country.

Once Octavian was in control of Pelusium, his forces made a rapid advance on Alexandria. Antony secured a minor victory on 31 July 30 BC when he managed to repel Octavian's vanguard near the city's hippodrome (the Lageion), but this turned out to be little more than the last gasp of his once glorious military career.

At this point Antony challenged Octavian to single combat on the pretext of preventing the needless bloodshed that would follow if their armies clashed. Predictably, Octavian declined the offer and sent the ominous reply that he could think of other ways for his rival to die.

Rather than being deterred by the initial setback his forces had faced, Octavian was determined to launch a second assault on the city, by both land and sea. This took place the following day (on 1 August) and had disastrous consequences for Antony. When he prepared to make his last stand his fleet surrendered, followed by his cavalry soon after, and his infantry was swiftly routed. By the time Antony arrived back at the royal palace, Cleopatra had retreated to her fortified mausoleum (where her treasure had been stockpiled) and locked herself inside with two close attendants – Iras and Charmian. Convinced that her lover was irreversibly ruined, she dispatched a messenger to Antony bearing the fake news that she had committed suicide, which seems to suggest that the Egyptian queen had finally decided to sacrifice Antony in the hope that Octavian would allow her to keep her kingdom. This makes sense given that the defeat and surrender of Antony's forces meant Octavian was now free to enter the Egyptian capital, leaving Cleopatra at his mercy.

When Antony was told that his lover was dead, he realised all hope was lost and was unwilling to be outdone by a woman, so ordered his slave Eros to kill him. Eros responded to the command by killing himself with his sword, which forced Antony to attempt to take his own life by stabbing himself in the stomach with his sword. Unfortunately for him the attempt was botched, and instead of securing a swift death he was left in absolute agony.

Accounts differ as to what happened after Antony had inflicted this mortal wound on himself. While some sources claim Antony learned Cleopatra was still alive and ordered his servants to carry him to her, others assert that Cleopatra arranged for her lover to be brought to her when she found out what he had done.

In any case, when Antony arrived outside the mausoleum Cleopatra was already barricaded inside, so she improvised by having his weak and nearly lifeless body lifted through a window on the first floor. Before Antony died, he offered her the only thing he had left to give – his advice. After being lain down on a couch and drinking a little wine, he encouraged Cleopatra to save herself, as long as it could be done honourably, and told her the one person she could trust in Octavian's camp was Gaius Proculeius. He also urged her not to feel pity for him, because he had been blessed with a wonderful life – in which he had risen to be the most powerful man in the world – and an honourable death.

As soon as this had been said, the 53-year-old succumbed to his wounds, bringing the life of one of Rome's greatest generals to an end.

*

While Antony breathed his last breaths, Octavian's forces were overrunning Alexandria. They marched into the city and took control of the royal palace, where Cleopatra's three youngest children – Alexander Helios, Cleopatra Selene and Ptolemy Philadelphus – were taken into their custody, although her eldest son and co-regent, Caesarion, had fled the city by this time. At 17 years of age, Caesarion was on the cusp of manhood and therefore a potential figurehead for Egyptian resistance against Octavian's invasion. Even more concerning, as an alleged son of Julius Caesar, he was a rival to Octavian's inheritance. Because of these factors, Cleopatra feared for his life, and had sent him south with a large sum of money, perhaps with instructions to go to India via the Red Sea port of Berenice.

For the time being though Octavian's attention was focused on the Egyptian queen in her mausoleum. Initially, his men negotiated with Cleopatra through a grate in the ground floor door, but she refused to surrender herself into their custody. This left them in a tricky position, because Octavian did not want Cleopatra to have the opportunity to kill herself or set her treasure on fire. Their leader needed Cleopatra alive to feature as the starring act in his Egyptian triumph back in Rome and her treasure to pay his troops, so they returned to the mausoleum sometime later with a plan. While one of Octavian's men – Gaius Cornelius Gallus – distracted Cleopatra by speaking to her by the door, another – Gaius Proculeius – fixed a ladder to the side of the building and climbed through the same first-floor window Antony had been lifted through, followed by two servants. Ironically, this was the same Gaius Proculeius that Antony had used his dying words to tell Cleopatra she could trust, but that couldn't have been further from the truth, as his actions here revealed.

Once the three men were inside the mausoleum, they crept down to the ground floor where Cleopatra was still talking by the door. As planned, they took the Egyptian queen and her two maids – Iras and Charmian – by surprise and apprehended them before Cleopatra was able to kill herself or destroy her treasure.

Before Cleopatra was escorted to the palace and placed under house arrest, Octavian permitted her to arrange Antony's funeral. By doing this he was able to present himself as behaving honourably in victory, as well as lending weight to the scandalous accusation he had made that Antony wished to be buried in Alexandria.[205]

When Octavian visited the captive queen in the palace, he tried to deter her from making any further attempts to take her own life by reassuring her that he intended to treat her more generously than she deserved. At the same time, he hinted that the safety of her children depended on her good behaviour, and remained ominously silent on his plans for her kingdom.

Soon after this meeting Cleopatra received a tipoff from a spy in Octavian's camp, who informed her that Octavian intended to send her and her children to Rome, where they would serve as the starring attraction in his Egyptian triumph. Cleopatra had feared this all along, but had no intention of suffering the same humiliating fate as her younger sister, Arsinoe IV, who had been paraded through the streets of Rome by Caesar. Instead, she immediately started planning her own suicide, which she now considered to be the least worst option available to her. At least that way she would die honourably – as a queen – and maintain control over her own fate, rather than being executed or spending the rest of her life as a prisoner.

Cleopatra died on 10 or 12 August 30 BC at 39 years of age.[206] It is unclear whether this took place in the royal palace or her mausoleum and the whole event is blurred by

---

[205] The location of Cleopatra and Mark Antony's tomb is unknown in the present day.
[206] Cleopatra probably died on 10 August if using the Roman calendar or on 12 August if following our own calendar.

speculation and legend. Apparently Octavian had charged a man named Epaphroditus with guarding the Egyptian queen and preventing her from attempting to commit suicide, but was distracted by his prisoner, who asked him to deliver a letter to his master. While Epaphroditus went to convey this message to Octavian, Cleopatra and her two attendants – Iras and Charmian – sealed themselves inside the chamber. Cleopatra enjoyed a bath, a luxurious meal and a makeover, and the three women then took their own lives.

Meanwhile, Octavian had received the note off Cleopatra, which asked him to bury her next to Mark Antony when she died. Reading between the lines, he ordered the guards to hurry back and check on their prisoner, but it was too late. When they forced their way into the chamber, the Egyptian queen and one of her handmaidens – Iras – were already dead. The second attendant, Charmian, was on the verge of death, and expired after dutifully adjusting the diadem on Cleopatra's head.

According to popular legend, Cleopatra killed herself by having a peasant deliver a basket of figs to her chamber with an asp hidden inside it and then let it bite her. However, this theory makes more symbolic than practical sense. The asp was a symbol of divine royalty, but it would have been difficult to smuggle a snake into her closely guarded quarters and no snake was found at the scene when she was discovered dead. Furthermore, it is unlikely she would have chosen to commit suicide by snake bite given her desire to have the quickest and most painless death possible while maintaining a serene external appearance. The more likely theory is that she used a poisoned hairpin to do the deed, although this is still merely speculation and no one can say for certain by what means the last queen of Egypt took her own life.

When Octavian learned he had been deceived by Cleopatra, he hastily dispatched physicians to resuscitate her, but their efforts were in vain.[207] He is reported to have been angered by this act of defiance, which had thwarted his plans. Nevertheless, he was unwilling to provoke the already hostile local population, so respected Cleopatra's wishes by arranging for her to be buried in royal style next to Antony in her mausoleum, and also ensured her loyal servants – Iras and Charmian – were given honourable burials within their queen's tomb.

---

[207] According to Cassius Dio, Octavian called on the services of a Berber tribe called the Psylli to cure Cleopatra. They allegedly had the ability to draw out snake venom, but clearly failed on this occasion.

This was a landmark moment in history. The life of Egypt's last queen had come to an end, leaving over three millennia of pharaonic rule in jeopardy. But for the time being it still had a king.

Before Octavian had taken control of Alexandria, Cleopatra had attempted to save the life of her son and heir, Caesarion, by sending him to Upper Egypt with ample funds, probably with the intention of him seeking asylum in Ethiopia, Nubia or India. However, the boy was betrayed by his tutor, Rhodon, who may have persuaded him to return to Alexandria by convincing him that Octavian would make him pharaoh.

Of course, Octavian had no intention of doing anything of the sort, and Rhodon was well aware of that. Instead of being confirmed as his mother's successor when he fell into the clutches of Octavian (in late August 30 BC), Caesarion was apprehended and put to death, perhaps by strangulation. When deciding the Egyptian king's fate, Octavian received some sound advice off the Alexandrian philosopher Arius Didymus, who counselled that there could only be one heir to Julius Caesar and as long as Caesarion was alive he would always pose a threat to his authority.[208] The argument was compelling and brought the life of Egypt's last pharaoh to a sudden, premature and bloody end at just 17 years of age.

Caesarion's step-brother Marcus Antonius Antyllus met a similar fate at around the same time.[209] Not long after the suicides of his father and step-mother, he was betrayed to Octavian by his tutor Theodorus, who had his eyes set on a priceless gem his student was wearing on a chain around his neck. Antyllus had been seeking refuge in a shrine (probably inside the Caesareum) but that did nothing to prevent Octavian's men from seizing the boy and dragging him outside. Although he begged for his life to be spared, his pleas were in vain. Given that he was Mark Antony's rightful heir and had recently been declared an adult, he posed too much of a threat to be kept alive and Octavian had him beheaded. As soon as this grisly deed had been carried out, Theodorus stole the jewel from his student's corpse and sewed it into his belt, but he got his comeuppance when Octavian had him crucified for the theft.

---

[208] Octavian held Arius Didymus in high esteem, even though he was a citizen of Alexandria.
[209] Marcus Antonius Antyllus was either 16 or 17 years old at the time of his death.

Epilogue

While most of the Ptolemies faded into obscurity after the demise of their dynasty, Cleopatra's cult endured for four centuries after her death, and today she is a household name. It was the discovery of a Ptolemaic artefact – the Rosetta Stone – which gave birth to the academic discipline of Egyptology and Cleopatra became a major icon in the sudden craze for ancient Egyptian history and culture (Egyptomania) that followed.

Ironically, it is the works of Roman historians that she has to thank for her fame, given that these accounts have inspired countless sculptures, paintings, poems, plays, operas, and – most recently – Hollywood blockbusters down through the ages. Therefore, it is the Romans more than anyone else who have influenced our image of Cleopatra, although their accounts of Egypt's last queen are unsurprisingly full of propaganda and are a classic example of history being written by the victors.

Octavian was eager for the victories that had made him the dominant figure in the Roman world to be remembered as being against foreign enemies rather than against fellow Romans, and therefore the Egyptian queen was regarded as a key component in the story of his rise to power. To fit the narrative he desired to promote, Cleopatra's life as a politician was largely ignored. Instead, she was presented as an immoral foreign woman who desired to dominate the Roman world by seducing its leading figures – first Julius Caesar, then Mark Antony. By conquering Egypt, Octavian was regarded as having saved Rome from this threat and upheld its superior culture, which was defined by virtuousness, patriarchy and masculinity.

*

The defeat and death of Cleopatra brought about the very situation she had spent her life trying to avoid. Egypt lost its independence and became a province of Rome, bringing three centuries of Ptolemaic rule and three millennia of pharaonic tradition to an end.

Once Egypt was under Octavian's control, he gave orders for all public statues of Mark Antony to be torn down. Cleopatra's monuments were spared this fate, reportedly because a friend of the late Egyptian queen named Archibius paid Octavian a bribe of 2,000 talents to preserve them. However, his desire to avoid antagonising the native population probably contributed to the decision as well.

Due to the tender age of Cleopatra's three youngest children (Alexander Helios, Cleopatra Selene and Ptolemy Philadelphus), they were spared the grisly fate suffered by their elder half-brothers, Caesarion and Marcus Antonius Antyllus. Rather than being killed, all three children were brought back to Rome where they featured in Octavian's triumph in the summer of 29 BC. The death of their mother meant she couldn't take part in this triumphal procession in person, but Octavian compensated for this by having her depicted on an effigy with an asp clinging to her, which is the first known reference to Cleopatra's alleged suicide by snake bite.

At the end of these festivities, Cleopatra's three surviving children and Mark Antony's younger son by Fulvia (Iullus Antonius) were taken into the household of Octavia, who became their guardian. However, it is disconcerting that both Alexander Helios and Ptolemy Philadelphus disappeared from historical records at this point, which has led many historians to assume that they died soon thereafter.

Fortunately, much more is known about the fate of Cleopatra Selene, who Octavian married off to one of his allies – Juba II – a few years later.

Juba II's father, Juba I of Numidia, had been defeated by Julius Caesar after supporting the Pompeians during Caesar's civil war. Consequently, Juba II had been raised in Rome, where he had become a man of culture and developed a particular passion for history. He most likely married Cleopatra Selene in 25 BC and the newlyweds would have been able to bond through their shared experience of being humiliated and orphaned as a result of Roman civil wars.

Later that year (25 BC), Juba II became the Roman client king of Mauretania. The royal couple turned the former Carthaginian city of Iol (present-day Cherchell, Algeria) into their kingdom's capital and renamed it Caesarea Mauretania in honour of Augustus (Octavian). Following in the footsteps of her Ptolemaic ancestors, Cleopatra Selene turned the city into a centre of Hellenistic culture and learning, and encouraged many of the scholars, artists and advisers who had served at her mother's court in Alexandria to settle there.

Cleopatra Selene died in about 5 BC. Her husband continued to rule for nearly three decades, until his death in 23 or 24 AD. He was succeeded by their son, Ptolemy of Mauretania, who had been named in honour of his mother's Ptolemaic heritage.

Ptolemy's reign came to a bloody end in 40 AD when he was executed on the orders of the emperor Caligula during a visit to Rome. There are various theories why

Caligula decided to do this. Ptolemy may have been suspected of being involved in a plot against the emperor (orchestrated by the senator and general Gaetulicus) or angered Caligula by unlawfully minting his own royal coinage and wearing regalia reserved for the emperor during his stay in Rome. Alternatively, Caligula might have simply envied Ptolemy's wealth and sought to strengthen his control over his client kingdom by turning it into a province.

In any case, the death of Ptolemy of Mauretania brought the Ptolemaic line to an end, although a cult dedicated to Cleopatra endured until the fourth century AD and a queen of the short-lived Palmyrene Empire named Zenobia (r. 267-272 AD) tried to legitimise her brief annexation of Egypt by claiming descent from Cleopatra.[210]

*

In January 27 BC, Octavian adopted the name Augustus ('the revered') and was granted sweeping constitutional powers that enabled him to establish himself as Rome's first emperor – bringing the Roman Republic to an end and ushering in the Principate era. Therefore, while Cleopatra's death brought one of the most famous periods in human history to an end (the age of the Egyptian pharaohs), it paved the way for the beginning of another (the age of the Roman emperors).

In the four centuries that followed Cleopatra's death, the emperor Augustus and his successors treated Egypt as their personal property and ruthlessly exploited the country's fabled wealth. They plundered its agricultural and mineral resources, such as its grain to feed Rome's teeming masses, its gold (from the Eastern Desert) to keep the imperial coffers full, and its supply of the 'imperial purple' variety of porphyry (from a group of quarries in the Red Sea Hills known collectively as Mons Porphyrites) to keep the empire's sculptors busy. They also used its advantageous geographical position (situated at the crossroads between Africa, Europe and Asia, and with access to both the Mediterranean and Red Seas) to promote Roman commercial interests. This particularly concerned trade with India, where oriental luxuries were acquired for consumption by Rome's aristocracy.

---

[210] The Palmyrene Empire (named after its capital city, Palmyra, in present-day Syria) was a short-lived breakaway state from the Roman Empire resulting from the Crisis of the Third Century. At its height it included a large portion of Asia Minor, as well as the Roman provinces of Syria Palaestina, Arabia Petraea, and Egypt.

In recognition of its importance, Egypt was governed by a prefect, who was selected by the emperor from the Equestrian class. This contrasted with other Roman provinces, which were administered by governors from the highest and most influential class in Roman society – the Senatorial order.

By leaving Egypt in the hands of someone from a relatively modest background, the emperor knew the prefect would owe their political fortunes to them, and therefore be directly answerable to them. At the same time, it would prevent Egypt from ending up in the hands of someone who had the necessary contacts and influence to use Egypt's resources in a bid for power.

The first person to be appointed Prefect of Egypt was a friend of Octavian named Gaius Cornelius Gallus. However, he soon overstepped the mark, which showed Octavian had been wise not to entrust its governance to a member of the powerful and ambitious Senatorial class. After leading a successful campaign to suppress a revolt in Thebes in 29 BC, Gallus had a monument erected at the Philae temple complex to glorify his accomplishments. Such behaviour brought him into disgrace with Octavian. As a warning to all future prefects, he was stripped of his position and recalled to Rome, where he committed suicide.

*

As things turned out, Egypt would not regain its independence for another 2,000 years. It was subjugated and exploited by a series of empires after the fall of Rome and its strategic position and continued wealth resulted in it being fought over by successive civilisations – between the Romans and Arabs, Christians and Muslims, the British and French, and most recently the Allied powers and Nazi Germany in World War Two.

Today, Egypt's days as a major power in its own right are long over, and the legacy of its pharaohs has been reduced to the romantic ruins of their tombs, temples and monuments. Nevertheless, the allure of pharaonic civilisation is as alive as ever, and draws both tourists and academics to Egypt from all over the world.

As for the subject of this book – the Ptolemies – this much can be said. Despite their flaws (of which there were many) they could hardly have been more successful at fostering a flourishing centre of learning and scholarship in their capital. Alexandria was home to the greatest library and research facility in the ancient world, which attracted the best and brightest minds throughout the Mediterranean. Thanks to these efforts, some of the most monumental developments in the history of medicine, mathematics and science were made, and much of our knowledge of ancient Greek literature derives from the work of Alexandrian scholars. For a family with a tendency for inbreeding, infighting and bloodletting, they couldn't have hoped for a better legacy.

Also by B.R. Egginton

Non-fiction

Cleopatra: Queen of Egypt

Edward VI: England's Boy King

Edward VI's Chronicle (Edward VI)

Richard II: The Tyranny of the White Hart

The Princes in the Tower: An Enigma… 500 Years in the making

Nicholas II: The Fall of the Romanovs

Henry Hotze: The Master of Confederate Diplomacy

Historiography for Beginners

Archaeology for Beginners

Twelve Olympians: The Greek Pantheon Made Easy

Shorthand SOS: Learn Teeline Shorthand FAST

Public Affairs for Journalists: Concise Edition

Ice Hockey Rulebook

Fiction

The Sixth Number

A Kingdom of Our Own

The Chronicles of Ascension

History Quest: The Plot

The Prince and the Pauper: Annotated Edition (Mark Twain)

Trivia

The Ultimate History Quiz

The Ultimate Mythology Quiz

The Ultimate US Presidents Quiz

The Ultimate British Prime Ministers Quiz

The Ultimate British Royal Navy Quiz

The Ultimate English Monarchs Quiz

The Ultimate French Monarchs Quiz

Printed in Great Britain
by Amazon